Mark Janzen has brought toge … ars representing the major views of … will become the starting point for all t … ice and arguments, especially for the … as the view that a historical exodus cannot be proven. The "five views" format is ideally suited for engaging criticism and responses to this basic historical question for the Hebrew Scriptures. Students and scholars will benefit from this frank assessment of the major views in the field.

—***Richard S. Hess,*** professor of Old Testament and Semitic languages, Denver Seminary

A pioneering achievement! All too often, biblical scholars attend only to the voices that harmonize with their own. Here we take front row seats as five leading experts present their views of the exodus in learned, lucid, and accessible prose, and then respond to and critique one another. The format is a welcome innovation in the publication of biblical scholarship for a broad audience.

—***Joshua Berman,*** professor of Hebrew Bible, Bar-Ilan University

Featuring five current scholarly views, this book is a reader's feast on the biblical exodus. Ranging across gaps, problems, and interpretations of the textual, archaeological, and scientific data, the work reveals the complex nature of the issues in a robust and forensic manner. The book is an essential text for study of the historical exodus.

—***Dr. Karin Sowada,*** Department of Ancient History, Macquarie University

This stimulating volume brings together experts from evangelical and nonevangelical scholarship to debate the date of Israel's exodus from Egypt—one of the most important and controversial issues in biblical archaeology. No other work offers the latest interaction on the exodus in such an accessible format. An ideal textbook for courses on the book of Exodus.

—***Jerry Hwang,*** associate professor of Old Testament, Singapore Bible College

Five Views on the Exodus offers a thorough investigation of the historical details of the exodus that helpfully identifies and demonstrates the methodological, theological, and disciplinary commitments that fuel an ongoing debate about a formative biblical event. Written by experts who offer a mass of evidence for consideration, this book is an essential resource for anyone entering the discussion.

—***Michelle Knight***, assistant professor of Old Testament and Semitic languages, Trinity Evangelical Divinity School

It is always a treat when experts in various disciplines engage each other in respectful dialogue, and especially so when the topic is this fascinating and when their conclusions are this divergent. The editor and contributors are to be commended for having this conversation, even if at times it is uncomfortable, and for inviting the rest of us to listen in.

—***Bill T. Arnold***, Paul S. Amos Professor of Old Testament Interpretation, Asbury Theological Seminary

FIVE VIEWS ON THE EXODUS

Books in the Counterpoints Series

Church Life

Evaluating the Church Growth Movement
Exploring the Worship Spectrum
Remarriage after Divorce in Today's Church
Understanding Four Views on Baptism
Understanding Four Views on the Lord's Supper
Who Runs the Church?

Bible and Theology

Are Miraculous Gifts for Today?
Do Christians, Muslims, and Jews Worship the Same God? Four Views
Five Views on Apologetics
Five Views on Biblical Inerrancy
Five Views on Law and Gospel
Five Views on Sanctification
Five Views on the Church and Politics
Five Views on the Extent of the Atonement
Four Views on Christian Spirituality
Four Views on Christianity and Philosophy
Four Views on Creation, Evolution, and Intelligent Design
Four Views on Divine Providence
Four Views on Eternal Security
Four Views on Hell
Four Views on Moving beyond the Bible to Theology
Four Views on Salvation in a Pluralistic World
Four Views on the Apostle Paul
Four Views on the Book of Revelation
Four Views on the Church's Mission
Four Views on the Historical Adam
Four Views on the Role of Works at the Final Judgment
Four Views on the Spectrum of Evangelicalism
Genesis: History, Fiction, or Neither?
How Jewish Is Christianity?
Show Them No Mercy
Three Views on Christianity and Science
Three Views on Creation and Evolution
Three Views on Eastern Orthodoxy and Evangelicalism
Three Views on the Millennium and Beyond
Three Views on the New Testament Use of the Old Testament
Three Views on the Rapture
Two Views on Homosexuality, the Bible, and the Church
Two Views on the Doctrine of the Trinity
Two Views on Women in Ministry

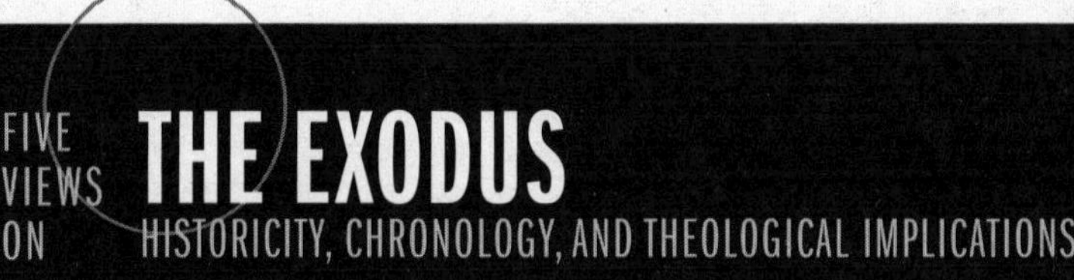

Scott Stripling

James K. Hoffmeier

Peter Feinman

Gary A. Rendsburg

Ronald Hendel

Mark D. Janzen, general editor
Stanley N. Gundry, series editor

ZONDERVAN ACADEMIC

Five Views on the Exodus

Requests for information should be addressed to:
Zondervan, *3900 Sparks Dr. SE, Grand Rapids, Michigan 49546*

Zondervan titles may be purchased in bulk for educational, business, fundraising, or sales promotional use. For information, please email SpecialMarkets@Zondervan.com.

ISBN 978-0-310-12039-1 (audio)

Library of Congress Cataloging-in-Publication Data

Names: Stripling, Scott, author. | Hoffmeier, James Karl, 1951- author. | Feinman, Peter Douglas, author. | Rendsburg, Gary, author. | Hendel, Ronald S., author. | Janzen, Mark, 1980- editor. | Gundry, Stanley N., editor.
Title: Five views on the Exodus : historicity, chronology, and theological implications / Scott Stripling, James K Hoffmeier, Peter Feinman, Gary A Rendsburg, Ronald Hendel ; Mark D Janzen, general editor ; Stanley N. Gundry, series editor.
Description: Grand Rapids : Zondervan, 2021. | Series: Counterpoints | Includes index.
Identifiers: LCCN 2020048340 (print) | LCCN 2020048341 (ebook) | ISBN 9780310108740 (paperback) | ISBN 9780310108757 (ebook)
Subjects: LCSH: Exodus, The--History of doctrines. | Bible. Exodus--Criticism, interpretation, etc. | Jews--History--To 1200 B.C.
Classification: LCC BS680.E9 F58 2021 (print) | LCC BS680.E9 (ebook) | DDC 222/.1206--dc23
LC record available at https://lccn.loc.gov/2020048340
LC ebook record available at https://lccn.loc.gov/2020048341

Cover design: Tammy Johnson
Cover photo: © Bumihills / Shutterstock
Interior design: Kait Lamphere

Printed in the United States of America

---

21 22 23 24 25 26 27 28 29 30 31 /LSC/ 15 14 13 12 11 10 9 8 7 6 5 4 3 2 1

CONTENTS

ABOUT THE EDITOR AND CONTRIBUTORS

Mark D. Janzen (PhD, University of Memphis, ancient Egyptian history) is assistant professor of history at Louisiana College. He also holds a master's degree in biblical and Near Eastern archaeology from Trinity Evangelical Divinity School. Mark is the deputy director of the Karnak Great Hypostyle Hall Project, an epigraphy project focusing on the Karnak Temple in Luxor, Egypt. He has written on the historicity of Moses, New Kingdom history, the Amarna period, epigraphy, and various archaeological topics.

Scott Stripling serves as provost at the Bible Seminary in Katy, Texas, and is director of excavations for the Associates for Biblical Research at Khirbet el-Maqatir and Shiloh. He has excavated in Jordan and Jerusalem as well and is the author of *The Trowel and the Truth.*

James K. Hoffmeier is Emeritus Professor of Old Testament and Ancient Near Eastern History and Archaeology at Trinity Evangelical Divinity School. He is an Egyptologist and archaeologist who has written numerous articles and books supporting the historicity of the exodus, including *Israel in Egypt.* He was also the director of excavations at Tell el-Borg in northern Sinai.

Peter Feinman is the founder and president of the Institute of History, Archaeology, and Education. He received his BA in history from the University of Pennsylvania, a MEd from New York University, an MBA from New York University, and an EdD from Columbia University. He is the author of *Jerusalem Throne Games*, an analysis of the writing of the Hebrew Bible, source criticism, and biblical history.

Gary A. Rendsburg holds the Blanche and Irving Laurie Chair in Jewish History at Rutgers University and has written numerous books and articles on Hebrew language and the Bible. His most recent book is

How the Bible Is Written; he coedited *Did I Not Bring Israel out of Egypt?*; and he has pioneered the view that the exodus should be dated to the reign of Ramesses III (ca. 1186–1155 BCE), roughly a century after the more traditional late date.

Ronald Hendel is Norma and Sam Dabby Professor of Hebrew Bible and Jewish Studies at the University of California, Berkeley. He is the author or editor of numerous books and articles on the Hebrew Bible, including *The Hebrew Bible: A Critical Edition*, *The Book of Genesis: A Biography*, and *Steps to a New Edition of the Hebrew Bible*. He is a well-regarded expert on memory and its impact on culture, history, and the Hebrew Bible.

ABBREVIATIONS

ABD	*Anchor Bible Dictionary.* Edited by D. N. Freedman. 6 vols. New York, 1992
ABRL	Anchor Bible Reference Library
AeL	Ägypten und Levante
AIL	Ancient Israel and Its Literature
AJA	*American Journal of Archaeology*
ANET	*Ancient Near Eastern Texts Relating to the Old Testament.* Edited by J. B. Pritchard. 3rd ed. Princeton, 1969
ARM	Archives royales de Mari
BAR	*Biblical Archaeology Review*
BASOR	*Bulletin of the American Schools of Oriental Research*
BBR	*Bulletin for Biblical Research*
BBRSup	Bulletin for Biblical Research Supplement
Bib	*Biblica*
BibOr	Biblica et Orientalia
BN	*Biblische Notizen*
BRev	*Bible Review*
BurH	*Buried History : Quarterly Journal of the Australian Institute of Archaeology*
CHANE	Culture and History of the Ancient Near East
CBQMS	Catholic Biblical Quarterly Monograph Series
COS	*The Context of Scripture.* Edited by W. W. Hallo and K. L. Younger. 3 vols. Leiden, 1997–2002
ChrEg	*Chronique d'Egypte*
DCH	*Dictionary of Classical Hebrew.* Edited by D. J. A. Clines. Sheffield, 1993–2011
EA	El-Amarna tablets. According to the edition of J. A. Knudtzon. *Die el-Amarna-Tafeln.* Leipzig, 1908–1915. Continued in A. F. Rainey, *El-Amarna Tablets, 359–379.* 2nd rev. ed. Kevelaer, 1978
ErIsr	*Eretz-Israel*

HALOT	L. Koehler, W. Baumgartner, and J. J. Stamm, *The Hebrew and Aramaic Lexicon of the Old Testament.* Translated and edited under the supervision of M. E. J. Richardson. 4 vols. Leiden, 1994–1999
HBAI	*Hebrew Bible and Ancient Israel*
HTR	*Harvard Theological Review*
HTS	Harvard Theological Studies
IEJ	*Israel Exploration Journal*
JANESCU	*Journal of the Ancient Near Eastern Society of Columbia University*
JAOS	*Journal of the American Oriental Society*
JBL	*Journal of Biblical Literature*
JCS	*Journal of Cuneiform Studies*
JEA	*Journal of Egyptian Archaeology*
JETS	*Journal of the Evangelical Theological Society*
JNES	*Journal of Near Eastern Studies*
JSSEA	*Journal of the Society for the Study of Egyptian Antiquities*
LCL	Loeb Classical Library
MSJ	*The Master's Seminary Journal*
NEAHL	*The New Encyclopedia of Archaeological Excavations in the Holy Land.* Edited by E. Stern. 4 vols. Jerusalem, 1993
OBO	Orbis Biblicus et Orientalis
OHAE	*Oxford History of Ancient Egypt.* Edited by Ian Shaw. Oxford: Oxford Univ. Press, 2000.
OLA	Orientalia Lovaniensia Analecta
OLZ	*Orientalistische Literaturzeitung*
PEQ	*Palestine Exploration Quarterly*
RBL	*Review of Biblical Literature*
RdÉ	*Revue d'égyptologie*
SAAB	*State Archives of Assyria Bulletin*
SAOC	Studies in Ancient Oriental Civilization
SBLDS	Society of Biblical Literature Dissertation Series
TA	*Tel Aviv*
VT	*Vetus Testamentum*
VTSup	Supplements to Vetus Testamentum
WBC	Word Biblical Commentary
WTJ	*Westminster Theological Journal*

BIBLE VERSIONS

Unless otherwise indicated, Scripture quotations in chapters 1, 3, and 5 are from the NIV, Scripture quotations in chapter 2 are from the ESV, and Scripture quotations in chapter 4 are the author's translations.

INTRODUCTION

THE EXODUS: SOURCES, METHODOLOGY, AND SCHOLARSHIP

MARK D. JANZEN

It is a story we return to time and time again. With outstretched arms, beard and cloak blowing in the wind, Moses, famously portrayed by Charlton Heston, proclaims triumphantly, "The Lord of Moses will do battle for us!" The camera pans out, revealing a sea amid a storm. The heavens roar, the winds howl, and the waves part. Dry land appears, and the Hebrews cross the sea. Miraculously, God safely delivers his people from bondage in Egypt. For many, this iconic moment from the classic 1956 film *The Ten Commandments* (Paramount Pictures) is synonymous with the exodus. For a younger generation, perhaps mention of the exodus conjures up memories of DreamWorks' 1998 animated film *The Prince of Egypt* or Twentieth Century Fox's 2014 epic *Exodus: Gods and Kings*. Clearly, Hollywood finds the themes of oppression and redemption inherent in the exodus event to be fitting grist for the filmmaker's mill. While Hollywood producers notoriously take liberties with historical accuracy, they are right about at least one thing when it comes to the exodus: those timeless themes remain as relevant now as ever.

For this reason, among others, the exodus event has importance far beyond our mere entertainment. It is a foundational event for the three largest monotheistic faiths in the world, making it significant to billions of Jews, Christians, and Muslims. Ancient Hebrews valued it as *the* uniquely transformative event from their past. It is the only explicit explanation the Bible gives for ancient Israel's origin. No event in the Old Testament or Hebrew Bible looms larger than the Hebrews' exodus from Egypt; it is referenced by biblical writers in nearly every time period, and mentions of either the exodus or Moses fill the pages of every major genre, from narrative to poetry to prophecy. Yair Hoffman estimates that the exodus is mentioned more than 120 times in the Old Testament, and that does not include the exodus account itself (Exod 1–15).[1]

Despite its ubiquitous presence in Scripture and its centrality to three major religions, questions abound. Did it really happen as recorded in the Pentateuch? Did it happen at all? If it happened, then when? Who was the pharaoh? Is it just a great story that was embellished in its retellings down through the ages? Is it just a metaphor for redemption? If so, does it even matter if it's historical or if Moses actually existed? What does the exodus mean for us today?

Answers to those questions are not easy, and readers should be wary of books, films, documentaries, or blogs that claim to have all the answers regarding the exodus. Scholars debate the historicity of the exodus, its relationship to archaeology and Egyptology, and the composition of the text as we have it. These are vital issues, many of which remain difficult to resolve. Those who hold to a historical exodus disagree about when it took place. Nevertheless, there is a host of ancient data that I believe readers will find revelatory and engaging. The issues and the potential evidence are complex, but they are not insurmountable.

All too often, scholarly treatments of these issues take place in a vacuum, with little cross-disciplinary discussion. Collaborative books are few and far between, though there are some excellent ones.[2] However, authors generally write these for their fellow experts. We hope this book

---

1. Yair Hoffman, "A North Israelite Typological Myth and a Judean Historical Tradition: The Exodus in Hosea and Amos," *VT* 39 (1989): 170.

2. Such is the case with the two recent impressive and comprehensive works: Thomas E. Levy, Thomas Schneider, and William H. C. Propp, eds., *Israel's Exodus in Transdisciplinary Perspective: Text, Archaeology, Culture, and Geoscience*, Quantitative Methods in the Humanities and Social Sciences (New York: Springer, 2015) and James K. Hoffmeier, Alan R. Millard, and Gary A. Rendsburg, eds., *"Did I Not Bring Israel out of Egypt?" Biblical, Archaeological, and Egyptological Perspectives on the Exodus Narratives*, BBRSup 13 (Winona Lake, IN: Eisenbrauns, 2016). The latter was written largely as a response to the former.

contributes uniquely to the overall conversation by being academically rigorous yet approachable and relevant. I hope the dialogue throughout this book demonstrates the value of collaboration, even when it involves substantial disagreements. After all, scholarship is a back-and-forth conversation built on evidence, analysis, argument, and counterargument.

In the subsequent chapters, five experts in the fields of archaeology, Egyptology, and biblical studies will explain their views of the exodus and the evidences supporting those views, as well as their methodologies and philosophical underpinnings. Each chapter of the book centers on one particular view. The author shares his view, and then the other contributors respond to him, before the chapter's author is given final say in a rejoinder.

Safe to say, if you love a good debate, you've come to the right place! The structure of a book like this welcomes debate, and our authors will disagree about fundamental and vital issues. They come from diverse backgrounds and hold various, or even contradictory, views on doctrines like inerrancy and the divine inspiration of Scripture. Readers will have to decide for themselves whose case is most compelling.

Shifting Sands: Potential Pitfalls and the Evidence

Perhaps the most vexing issue about the exodus narrative is the simple fact that there is no direct, physical evidence of the event, nor of Moses, from ancient Egypt. If such direct evidence did exist, perhaps there would be less need for a book like this! But this is not to say ipso facto that the event is fictitious.[3] While I will leave that debate for my colleagues in the chapters to follow, it is worth setting the stage here. As readers will soon find out, there is a mountain of circumstantial evidence that requires interpretation, hence the debate about questions like

3. For positive assessments of the historicity of the exodus tradition, see James K. Hoffmeier, *Israel in Egypt: The Evidence for the Authenticity of the Exodus Tradition* (Oxford: Oxford Univ. Press, 1996) and Kenneth A. Kitchen, *On the Reliability of the Old Testament* (Grand Rapids: Eerdmans, 2003), 241–313. Others find the event to be fictitious or have no bearing on Israelite origins; for examples see Robert B. Coote, *Early Israel: A New Horizon* (Minneapolis: Fortress, 1990) and Donald B. Redford, "The Great Going Forth: The Expulsion of West Semitic Speakers from Egypt," in *Israel's Exodus in Transdisciplinary Perspective: Text, Archaeology, Culture, and Geoscience*, ed. Thomas E. Levy, Thomas Schneider, and William H. C. Propp, Quantitative Methods in the Humanities and Social Sciences (New York: Springer, 2015), 437–48.

whether the exodus took place, how many people it involved, and when it occurred if it did so.

That said, despite the wonderful data archaeology has provided (and you'll soon see plenty of it!), estimates concerning our coverage of ancient sites, particularly in the Egyptian delta and Sinai Peninsula, are incredibly low. Satellite imagery shows that less than 1 percent of Egypt has been excavated,[4] meaning that much material in the delta awaits discovery or is simply gone. As for Sinai, Richard Elliott Friedman notes that skeptics "assert we've combed the Sinai and not found any evidence. . . . That assertion is just not true. There have not been any major excavations in the Sinai."[5] An indeterminate amount of data either is forever lost or remains to be discovered.

Still, there is no shortage of issues to discuss. Data from a wide variety of sources and fields of study is germane to the exodus. Studying its particulars requires more than just interpreting the Pentateuch or marshaling comparative evidence from Egypt. Certainly, those are important, but scholars also must use information derived from archaeology, history, anthropology, and a host of other fields of study. Several languages are involved: ancient Egyptian, Biblical Hebrew, and potentially Koine Greek, depending on one's view of the value of the Septuagint. It truly takes years of study to properly engage with so many disciplines.

All of this is why it is important to maintain a healthy skepticism regarding books, movies, documentaries, or blogs that do not seek the opinions of learned experts. Another purpose for this book is to equip readers with enough information to recognize when such "studies" are deceiving them. It is entirely too easy to spread misinformation in the information age. I fervently hope this book proves to be a useful resource for fact-checking such sources.

---

4. Abigail Tucker, "Space Archaeologist Sarah Parcak Uses Satellites to Uncover Ancient Egyptian Ruins," Smithsonian 47, no. 8 (December 2016): 38–40, https://www.smithsonianmag.com/innovation/space-archaeologist-sarah-parcak-winner-smithsonians-history-ingenuity-award-180961120/.

5. "The Exodus Is Not Fiction: An Interview with Richard Elliott Friedman," *Reform Judaism* (Spring 2014), 6–8, https://reformjudaism.org/exodus-not-fiction. See also Mark D. Janzen, "Making a Case for the Historicity of Moses," *Christian Research Journal* 42, no. 1 (2019): 34–41, www.equip.org/article/making-a-case-for-the-historicity-of-moses/.

Everyone's Favorite Topic: Chronology

Before diving into the subsequent chapters, it is helpful to note a few things about archaeology, Egyptology, and chronology. Ask any historian, archaeologist, or Biblicist what the most complex topic they study is, and they will likely say chronology. Absolute dates are few and far between, so nearly all ancient chronology is relative, with only a few lynchpin dates available. One is the eclipse recorded by the Assyrian Eponym Chronicle in 763 BC. Astronomers are able to pinpoint this to June 15, 763.[6] The Assyrians recorded additional eclipses during the seventh century, as did the Babylonians. These references are the bedrock of ancient chronology, and dates for earlier events and individuals are computed relative to them, hence the term "relative chronology."

Archaeologists divide excavated material into large periods according to the predominant material used for tools and weapons at that time, such as bronze and iron. These can be further divided into subperiods to facilitate discussion and add nuance. The periods more relevant to this book are the Late Bronze and Iron I Ages (see table 1).

Table 1: Archaeological Periodization in the Ancient Near East*

Neolithic period	8500–4300
Chalcolithic period	4300–3300
Early Bronze Age	3300–2300
Early Bronze Age IV / Middle Bronze Age I	2300–2000
Middle Bronze Age II	2000–1550
Late Bronze Age	1550–1200
Iron Age I	1200–1000
Iron Age II	1000–586

*After the standard work by Amihai Mazar, *Archaeology of the Land of the Bible: 10,000–586 BCE* (New York: Doubleday, 1990).

6. Alan R. Millard, *The Eponyms of the Assyrian Empire 910–612 BC*, SSA 2 (Helsinki: Neo-Assyrian Text Corpus Project, 1994), 2; Kenneth A. Kitchen, "Establishing Chronology in Pharaonic Egypt and the Ancient Near East: Interlocking Textual Sources Relating to c. 1600–664 BC," in *Radiocarbon and the Chronologies of Ancient Egypt*, ed. A. J. Shortland and C. Bronk Ramsey (London: Oxbow, 2013), 1–18.

Egyptian Chronology

Egyptian chronology is based on the interpretation of ancient texts as well as radiocarbon dates derived from appropriate excavated material and even volcanic explosions, in addition to the aforementioned lynchpin dates. In particular, dates for the Pharaonic period (ca. 3000–664 BC) derive from a complex combination of ancient king lists, inscriptions which give us the year date of a king's reign for a particular event, lists of officials or religious events, and astronomical observations. The margin for error for the New Kingdom is about a decade.[7] As one moves farther back in time, the margin expands.

Egyptologists use two overarching schemas to manage the staggering longevity of ancient Egypt. Ever since the Egyptian priest Manetho (third century BC) wrote a history of Egypt in Greek, scholars have used his thirty dynasties as a basic chronological framework.[8] These dynasties are then placed into groups according to whether Egypt was united and generally powerful (Kingdom phases) or fragmented into smaller polities (Intermediate periods). While this system is not perfect, there is nearly unanimous agreement that it admirably organizes a long period of time.

Conversely, there is much debate regarding the reigns of many notable pharaohs, and scholars continue to debate the chronological particulars. Specifically, the Eighteenth Dynasty (early-date exodus) contains a discrepancy of roughly twenty years, but as Bietak and Höflmayer note, "the two systems—the radiocarbon and the historical chronology—have periods of agreement such as the Thirteenth and 14th centuries."[9] It is not my intention to weigh in on that debate

---

7. Ian Shaw, "Chronology," in *OHAE*, 480–81.

8. For more see A. J. Shortland, "An Introduction to Egyptian Historical Chronology," in Shortland and Ramsey, *Radiocarbon and the Chronologies of Ancient Egypt*, 19–28.

9. Manfred Bietak and Felix Höflmayer, "Introduction: High and Low Chronology," in *The Synchronisation of Civilisations in the Eastern Mediterranean in the Second Millennium B.C. III: Proceedings of the SCIEM 2000–2nd EuroConference, Vienna, 28th of May–1st of June, 2003*, ed. Manfred Bietak and Ernst Czerny, Contributions to the Chronology of the Eastern Mediterranean 9 (Vienna: Österreichischen Akademie der Wissenschaften, 2007), 13–23. This is a very useful introduction. More recently see also Kenneth A. Kitchen, "Establishing Chronology in Pharaonic Egypt and the Ancient Near East: Interlocking Textual Sources Relating to c. 1600–664 BC," in Shortland and Ramsey, *Radiocarbon and the Chronologies of Ancient Egypt*, 1–18.

here, but readers should note that the debate about chronology is why they will see different dates for a couple of pharaohs throughout this book. Please consult table 2, which follows the most widely accepted historical chronologies of Egypt for the dates of the rulers of the New Kingdom.[10]

To my knowledge, every scholar engaging in serious scholarship who holds to a historical exodus places it during New Kingdom Egypt (1550–1069 BC), with the Hebrew sojourn in Egypt taking place either in the late Middle Kingdom (2055–1650 BC) or Second Intermediate period (1650–1550 BC).[11]

On This We Agree: Semites in Egypt

Prior to the New Kingdom, northern Egypt (Lower Egypt) was ruled by a group of Semites known as the Hyksos, "the rulers of foreign lands," during the Second Intermediate period.[12] Egyptologists agree that excavations in the delta reveal a strong Semitic presence during the Hyksos era (ca. 1650–1540 BC), continuing into the New Kingdom. The most significant site excavated in the delta is Tell el-Dab'a, ancient Avaris, the Hyksos capital. Manfred Bietak and his team have extensively excavated Avaris since 1966, unearthing a plethora of material culture demonstrating strong affinities to the Levant. Among their finds are religious and domestic architecture, evidence of burial customs, ceramics, and bronze tools and weapons.[13] There is no debate whatsoever that a significant number of Semites settled in the Nile delta during these time periods.

---

10. Readers should note that these chronological matters are far too complex for an introduction of a book like this to cover in full, and such chronological minutiae move far beyond the scope and intent of this book. Curious readers can find ample coverage of chronology in the sources cited in this section.

11. For the beginning of the New Kingdom, see Betsy M. Bryan, "The 18th Dynasty before the Amarna Period (c. 1550–1352 BC)," in *OHAE*, 207–64. For the later Eighteenth Dynasty and the Ramesside era, see Jacobus Van Dijk, "The Amarna Period and the Later New Kingdom," in *OHAE*, 265–307. For details see Hoffmeier, *Israel in Egypt*, 62–68.

12. For more on the Hyksos and the Second Intermediate period, see Janine Bourriau, "The Second Intermediate Period (c. 1650–1550 BC)," in *OHAE*, 172–206.

13. For much more see Manfred Bietak, *Avaris and Piramesse: Archaeological Exploration in the Eastern Nile Delta* (London: Oxford Univ., 1986).

Eventually, rulers from Thebes in southern Egypt (Upper Egypt) defeated the Hyksos and drove them out of Egypt, uniting Egypt once more.[14] Determined to create a buffer zone in western Asia to keep a Hyksos-type of situation from occurring again, New Kingdom pharaohs aggressively campaigned in Syria-Palestine, carving out a substantial empire. Pharaohs brought back thousands of prisoners of war and other captives to work on agricultural estates and building projects. Typically, Egyptian texts refer to them with the catchall term "Asiatic." Overall, this was a time of unprecedented prosperity in Egypt, and Semites continued to live in the delta in large numbers.[15]

Biblical Data and the Views in This Book

If one holds to a historical exodus, there are three possible dates, each of which is based on a combination of biblical and archaeological data. While I will leave a full articulation of these views to their respective authors, what follows is a brief introduction to each view.

Scholars who hold to the so-called early-date exodus place the event during the first half of the New Kingdom, the Eighteenth Dynasty (see table 2). Specifically, our first contributor, Scott Stripling, argues for a fifteenth-century exodus (1446 BC). For those holding to this early date, the exodus occurred during the reign of one of Egypt's greatest warrior-pharaohs, Thutmose III, or his son and successor, Amenhotep II, depending on whether one follows High or Low chronology (cf. table 2).[16] This view is based on a literal reading of the dates given in the Bible, such as 1 Kgs 6:1, which tells us that Solomon began to build the temple in the 480th year after the Israelites left Egypt. Stripling also draws on his knowledge of archaeological data to argue for this date.

14. Bryan, "The 18th Dynasty before the Amarna Period," 207–64.

15. Archaeologists have found Canaanite goods in several burials in the delta region. More details can be found in Hoffmeier, *Israel in Egypt*, 62–68.

16. Stripling follows the High chronology, while this introduction and the rest of our contributors follow the Low chronology with potentially minor variations. Table 2 follows the standard Low chronology.

Table 2: Historical Chronology of the New Kingdom*

Eighteenth Dynasty	
Ahmose	1550–1525
Amenhotep I	1525–1504
Thutmose I	1504–1492
Thutmose II	1492–1479
Thutmose III	*1479–1425 (possible pharaoh of the exodus for 15th-century date)*
Queen Hatshepsut	1473–1458 (reigned while Thutmose III was young)
Amenhotep II	*1427–1400 (possible pharaoh of the exodus for 15th-century date)*†
Thutmose IV	1400–1390
Amenhotep III	1390–1352
Akhenaten	1352–1336
Neferneferuaten	1338–1336 (possible coregency with Akhenaten)
Tutankhamun	1336–1327
Ay	1327–1323
Horemheb	1323–1295 (exact length of his reign is still debated)
Nineteenth Dynasty	
Ramesses I	1295–1294
Seti I	1294–1279
Ramesses II	*1279–1213 (pharaoh of the exodus for 13th-century date)*
Merenptah	1213–1203
Amenmesse	1203–1200? (usurper who ruled Upper Egypt briefly)
Seti II	1200–1194 (possibly ruled Lower Egypt from 1203 on)
Siptah	1194–1188
Queen Tausret	1188–1186

(cont.)

Twentieth Dynasty	
Sethnakht	1186–1184
Ramesses III	*1184–1153 (pharaoh of the exodus for 12th-century date)*‡
Ramesses IV	1153–1147
Ramesses V	1147–1143
Ramesses VI	1143–1136
Ramesses VII	1136–1129
Ramesses VIII	1129–1126
Ramesses IX	1126–1108
Ramesses X	1108–1099
Ramesses XI	1099–1069

*These dates are the widely accepted historical chronology based on Shaw, "Chronology," 484–85.

† Scott Stripling follows a slightly different chronology, which pushes Amenhotep II's reign back farther, making him the pharaoh of an exodus in 1446 BC.

‡ There is considerable debate about when his reign began. Many scholars place Ramesses III's first regnal year in 1186 or 1187, as Gary A. Rendsburg does in his chapter, for example.

Conversely, James Hoffmeier and Peter Feinman date the exodus to the reign of Ramesses II (1279–1213 BC), another of Egypt's most powerful pharaohs. This is usually called the late-date exodus, but we choose to call it more precisely the thirteenth-century exodus. Exodus 1:11 mentions Pi-Ramesses/Ramses as one of the store cities built by the Hebrews during their time in Egypt. Because this city was used for a brief window of time (ca. 1275–1130 BC), many regard it as a key chronological datum, and its dates of use suggest a thirteenth-century exodus.[17] Critically, this contradicts a literal reading of 1 Kgs 6:1, so scholars like Hoffmeier, Feinman, and Kitchen treat the 480-years reference as symbolic.[18] Hoffmeier and Feinman agree on the date but take very different approaches. Hoffmeier uses a host of Egyptian data

17. For more on this important delta city, see Mark D. Janzen, "(Pi-)Rameses—The Delta Capital of Ramesside Egypt," in *Lexham Geographic Commentary on the Pentateuch*, ed. Barry Beitzel (Bellingham, WA: Lexham, forthcoming 2020–2021).

18. For Kitchen, see *On the Reliability of the Old Testament*, 255–56.

to make a case for the historicity of the exodus narrative, as he's done throughout his academic career. Feinman seeks to find the human element in the story by comparing it with Egyptian texts and finds similarities between the Hyksos and the Levites.

Like Hoffmeier and Feinman, Gary A. Rendsburg does not read the reference to 480 years in 1 Kgs 6:1 as a literal number. Unlike his colleagues, he opts for a twelfth-century exodus, during the reign of Ramesses III (1184–1156 BC), Egypt's last truly powerful pharaoh. Rendsburg's view is based on the increase in settlements in the Levant during the Iron I period, which he believes is because of former pastoralists transitioning to more permanent dwellings. Additionally, Rendsburg sees evidence of a declining empire during the reign of Ramesses III, making the departure of an indeterminate number of slaves more likely during his reign than during periods of great Egyptian strength.

In our final chapter, Ronald Hendel explains that the exodus is too steeped in layers of cultural memory for scholars to determine its historicity. He opines that while a smaller exodus is not out of the question, determining its precise details and historicity is nearly impossible. A cultural memory portrays the past with particular emphasis on present relevance. Thus the author(s) of the exodus account authoritatively told the version he wanted his audience to hear. As a result, "cultural memory distorts, omits, and fictionalizes aspects of the past," Hendel writes. This means the event is "not plain history, nor is it pure fiction."

With(out) Further Ado

My primary goal for this book is to provide readers with a nuanced treatment of the exodus that highlights and discusses the diverse data pertaining to ancient Israel's most formative event. I hope readers will appreciate the complexity of the topic but also emerge from their time with the book with a fuller understanding of the exodus, the texts that comprise the account as we have it in Scripture, its potential historicity, and its chronology. As the editor of this volume, I have endeavored to represent each view equitably and charitably while allowing our authors to speak for themselves, even if that makes the discussion a bit more heated at times.

Because the debate touches on important matters of faith, at times the debate is rather personal. Generally, scholarship seeks to steer clear of such things, but no one is totally objective. In places where the debate is more heated, I hope readers will find it stimulating and recognize the professionalism of our authors. Additionally, I believe that one's faith need not impinge upon scholarship, and it should be noted that this is a book written by scholars of both Jewish and Christian background. Out of respect for this, we have allowed our authors to use either BC/AD or BCE/CE dating schemes.

Finally, in the interest of full disclosure, my own view is that a historical exodus took place, largely as recorded in the Pentateuch. I place it during the thirteenth century but acknowledge that no view is free from important lingering questions. I'm pleased to report that in compiling this book, I have learned a great deal from each of the authors. I have had ample opportunity to reexamine my own view, which is what a scholarly endeavor should achieve! I hope the book does the same for you, dear reader.

CHAPTER ONE

THE FIFTEENTH-CENTURY (EARLY-DATE) EXODUS VIEW

SCOTT STRIPLING

The biblical authors inexorably link the identity of the ancient Israelites with a miraculous deliverance from Egyptian slavery, but many scholars, such as Bernard F. Batto, challenge the historicity of the exodus: "The biblical narrative in the books of Genesis through Joshua owes more to the folkloric tradition of the ancient Near East than to the historical genre and cannot be used to reconstruct an authentic history of ancient Israel."[1] However, four of the five authors of this book believe that an exodus of Hebrews from Egypt to Canaan actually occurred, albeit at different times. Clearly, intelligent and sincere people can arrive at different conclusions after evaluating the same data. Discussions concerning when this watershed event happened evoke great passion, and at times conflict, even among those who believe that Scripture is historically reliable.

If we consider the biblical text in isolation, most biblical scholars agree the internal biblical chronology points us to a fifteenth-century BC exodus. Though the biblical evidence seems clear, it must also be considered in light of the archaeological evidence. Historical matters are seldom simple. Having directed excavations at two important sites in

1. Bernard F. Batto, *Slaying the Dragon: Mythmaking in the Biblical Tradition* (Louisville: Westminster John Knox, 1992), 102.

the highlands of Israel—Khirbet el-Maqatir (Ai?) and Shiloh—I am grateful for archaeology. However, while the material culture at these and other sites illuminates the biblical text, it often raises more questions than it settles. Despite the good work of scores of archaeologists in Egypt and the territories to its north, a staggering amount of ancient ruins remain unexcavated. Vandalism, urban sprawl, war, natural disasters, politics, and lack of funding limit what the trowel can reveal. The unexcavated remnants of antiquity may contain critical evidence that could clarify the timing of the exodus and conquest. As of this writing, there is no consensus among scholars who hold to a historical exodus event concerning its timing.

Methodological Approach to the Exodus Dilemma

The ancient Egyptians almost never recorded events which portrayed them unfavorably, so it would be surprising to find a record of the exodus. Regardless of their impulse to omit these events, there are written sources and archaeological remnants that can establish the historicity of the exodus, but it is critical that we assign proper weight to these written sources and the material remains. Proper epistemology enables reliable historiography. In this essay I argue that the written text is less subjective than human interpretations of the material culture, and therefore it ought to receive primacy in our considerations. Hill juxtaposes the differences in methodology between early-date versus late-date advocates when he writes, “At issue in the controversy over the date of the Exodus is the interpretation of the biblical and extrabiblical data. Proponents of the early-date position *emphasize the literal interpretation of the biblical numbers* . . . and selectively appeal to archaeology for support (e.g., *both camps cite archaeological evidence* from Jericho and Hazor in support of their positions). Those holding to the late-date view understand the biblical numbers symbolically and *place priority on the extrabiblical historical information and archaeological evidence*.”[2]

Hill correctly summarizes the methodological divide among scholars. Early-date adherents give greater weight to the Bible, whereas late-date purveyors tend to elevate archaeology in their historiography.

2. Andrew E. Hill, “Exodus,” in *A Survey of the Old Testament*, ed. Andrew E. Hill and John H. Walton, 3rd ed. (Grand Rapids: Zondervan, 2009), 106, 108, emphases mine.

In this essay I will argue that strong archaeological evidence supports the early date as well, but the case for an early date begins with the text of Scripture. Archaeological excavation, properly conducted, illuminates the written word of God, and vice versa, but if the two appear to conflict, early-date advocates will defer to the biblical text.

In the case of the exodus, the Bible serves as the most complete ancient written source, and it should be read as a historically reliable account. Any proposed discrepancy must be evidence-based, not an argument from silence. Consider the minimalist argument about the existence of King David. The argument that King David may not have existed evaporated in 1993 when Avraham Biran's team at Tel Dan recovered the "House of David" inscription.[3] Whenever legitimate textual discrepancies occur, the historian may rightly seek extrabiblical clarification. However, I am unaware of any instances in which extrabiblical texts contradict biblical texts, although they do at times provide a different perspective. Such is the case with Sennacherib's account of his Jerusalem siege versus the Chronicler's account (2 Chr 32).[4] The New Testament evangelists certainly differ in details, yet the diversity enhances the authenticity. Eyewitnesses rarely report identical details of an event.

The Pentateuch is clearly of ancient origin. The late seventh-century BC Silver Scrolls/Amulets from Tomb 25 at Ketef Hinnom preserve small portions of Exodus and Numbers. Undoubtedly, Ketef Hinnom II quotes the Priestly Blessing (Num 6:24–26). At Kuntillet Ajrud, Pithos B, which dates one century earlier, echoes or paraphrases the same passage.[5] Moreover, Ketef Hinnom I (lines 3–6) likely quotes or alludes to Exod 20:6. Similarly, the Deir 'Alla Plaster Inscriptions (also known as the Balaam Inscription) date at least to the eighth century BC and synchronize with the Num 22–24 narrative. The dates of these sources testify to the antiquity of the pentateuchal narratives. The fragments that I have mentioned did not just appear out of thin air in the

3. Avraham Biran and Joseph Naveh, "The Tel Dan Inscription: A New Fragment," *IEJ* 45 (1995): 1–18.

4. For Sennacherib's account see "Sennacherib's Siege of Jerusalem," trans. Mordechai Cogan (*COS* 2.119B:302–4).

5. Nadav Na'aman, "A New Outlook at Kuntillet 'Ajrud and Its Inscriptions," *Maarav* 20, no. 1 (2013): 39–51.

eighth century, suggesting that the exodus account existed in the First Temple period (1200–586 BC), and likely much earlier. But the Bible is not our only written source for the exodus.

Before the twenty-first century AD, epigraphers had failed to identify a single extrabiblical literary source besides the Deir 'Alla Plaster Inscriptions relating to the biblical account of the exodus and sojourn. That changed at the turn of the new millennium with the publication of the Berlin Pedestal.[6] Then, in 2016, Douglas Petrovich presented sixteen inscriptions from the Sinai, three of which purport to document the exodus and associated people and events.[7] The Amarna tablets and Merenptah Stela also provide germane inscriptional evidence that deserves consideration.[8]

Archaeological evidence also supports a date for the exodus sometime in the Eighteenth Dynasty (1550–1292 BC). I see sites like Tell el-Dab'a in the Egyptian delta as a possible synchronism between the archaeological data and the exodus account (Exod 2–12). I also see evidence at Mount Ebal in Israel's highlands. As we will discover, Tell el-Dab'a, Mount Ebal, and other pertinent sites such as Jericho, Ai, and Hazor offer vital data.

Pseudoarchaeology complicates the issue and confuses the general public. Since about 1990, a cadre of self-proclaimed researchers have made sensational claims about the exodus and other biblical events. They claim to have found proof of the exodus. Refuting the unfounded claims of chariot wheels at the bottom of what might be the biblical *yam sûp* lies outside the purview of this chapter. Yet while nonsensical claims like these distract us from serious academic debate, fortunately there is real archaeology that can illuminate the exodus and its associated events for us.

As I present in the following section, reasonable evidence places Jacob's descendants (the Israelites) in Egypt some time during the five-hundred-year period from the Twelfth to the Eighteenth Dynasties—

6. Manfred Görg, "Israel in Hieroglyphen," *BN* 106 (2001): 21–27.

7. Douglas Petrovich, *The World's Oldest Alphabet: Hebrew as the Language of the Proto-Consonantal Script* (Jerusalem: Carta, 2016).

8. William L. Moran, ed. and trans., *The Amarna Letters* (Baltimore: Johns Hopkins Univ. Press, 1992); Michael Hasel, "Merneptah's Reference to Israel: Critical Issues for the Origin of Israel," in *Critical Issues in Early Israelite History*, ed. Richard S. Hess, Gerald A. Klingbeil, and Paul J. Ray Jr., BBRSup 3 (Winona Lake, IN: Eisenbrauns, 2008), 47–60.

from the nineteenth to the fifteenth centuries BC (1900–1400 BC). Similarly, a scholarly consensus among evangelicals, with rare exceptions, situates the Israelites in Canaan no later than the Late Bronze Age II (ca. 1400–1200 BC). Advocates for the early date favor their arrival at the end of the fifteenth century, or the Late Bronze Age IB in archaeological parlance. If the evidence I present proves accurate—that both the Bible and archaeology place the Israelites in Egypt for hundreds of years and then locate them in Canaan for more than one millennium—then it appears obvious that they left Egypt at some point on this timeline. In the Bible the exodus account precedes and follows historically verifiable accounts; therefore, no reason exists to view the account itself as etiological. The biblical and extrabiblical evidence both attest to the historicity and chronology of the early Israelites and their fifteenth-century exodus from Egypt.

Biblical Evidence for an Early Exodus

The ancestral narrative in Genesis reveals that Joseph became the second most powerful person in Egypt, the world's ancient superpower. Joseph likely served as Egypt's vizier (chief administrator). He settled his family in the choice land of Goshen, in the Egyptian delta. However, a shift in the political climate plunged Jacob's descendants into slavery. Several biblical passages verify that the Israelite deliverance from slavery occurred in the fifteenth century. These excerpts include 1 Kgs 6:1, Judg 11:26, 1 Chr 6:33–37, Ezek 40:1, and Acts 7:29–30. Taken together, their weight tips the exegetical scale decisively toward the early date.

Evidence from 1 Kings 6:1

Solomon began to build the First Temple in the 480th year after the exodus (1 Kgs 6:1). Synchronization with Assyrian records places this construction in 967 BC. A primary principle of archaeology is to move from the known to the unknown. This principle works for chronology as well. To the known date of 967 BC, we add 479 years to arrive at the biblical date of 1446 BC.

Unlike the Hebrew text, which places the exodus in the 480th year before the building of Solomon's Temple, the Septuagint states that the exodus occurred in the 440th year. For this reason, some archaeologists, such as Steven Collins, favor 1406 BC as an exodus date.[9] Regardless, both chronologies see a mass migration occurring in the fifteenth century BC. Others, such as David Rohl, embrace the 1446 BC date but argue that Egyptian history must be downdated several centuries and that the exodus occurred late in the Middle Bronze Age.[10] When I refer to the early date of the exodus, I am referring to 1446 BC, in the middle of the Late Bronze I period.

Agreeing with W. F. Albright, late-date adherents see little or no evidence in the archaeological record of a conquest at the end of the fifteenth century, so they violate Occam's razor and form a metaphorical equation in which 480 really means 300.[11] They postulate that the writer of 1 Kings was referring to twelve idealized generations of forty years when he arrived at the number 480, but because a generation is really twenty-five years, the number should be 300 instead (12 generations × 25 years = 300 years).[12] Scholars like Kenneth Kitchen use this formula to place the exodus in the thirteenth century, where they see stronger evidence for the exodus and conquest.[13] With this approach to dating, late-date advocates would have us believe that the biblical writer was either confused or practicing hyperbole. I find both of these unlikely.

Evidence from Judges 11:26

According to Judg 11:26, Jephthah declares to the Ammonite king, "For three hundred years Israel occupied Heshbon, Aroer, the surrounding settlements and all the towns along the Arnon. Why didn't you retake them during that time?" Once again, we are fortunate to start with an agreed-upon date, approximately 1100 BC, for Jephthah. From here, the math is simple: 1100 + 300 = 1400 BC. This date closely harmonizes with the 1 Kgs 6:1 date because the Israelites did not conquer the region

---

9. Steven Collins, *Let My People Go! Using Historical Synchronisms to Identify the Pharaoh of the Exodus* (Albuquerque: Trinity Southwest Univ. Press, 2012), 104–32.

10. David Rohl, *Exodus: Myth or History?* (St. Louis Park, MN: Thinking Man Media, 2015), 71–85. Rohl's views have failed to gain traction among scholars.

11. Albright originally embraced 1446 BC as the exodus date, but he could not find archaeological evidence for it, so he switched to the late date.

12. Kenneth A. Kitchen, *On the Reliability of the Old Testament* (Grand Rapids: Eerdmans, 2003), 308–10.

13. Kitchen, *On the Reliability of the Old Testament*, 308–10.

of Ammon until the end of the forty-year wilderness sojourn. Do we have another confused biblical writer or speaker? If so, the Chronicler suffered from a similar disorientation.

Evidence from 1 Chronicles 6:33–37

First Chronicles 6:33–37 presents a genealogy of the temple musicians from Heman in David's time to Korah in Moses' time, eighteen generations altogether. Adding a nineteenth generation brings us back to Solomon. Wide agreement exists among scholars today that a generation averages twenty-five years, so an approximate equation for estimating this time looks like this: 19 generations × 25 years = 475 years.[14] When 475 is added to 967 BC (Solomon's fourth regnal year), we land in the mid-fifteenth century (1442 BC). If the exodus occurred in the mid-thirteenth century, the average length of the nineteen generations from Korah to Solomon would be approximately 15.2 years. This is highly improbable, especially since not all the ancestors of Heman would have been firstborn.

Evidence from Ezekiel 40:1

The Hebrew text of Ezek 40:1 indicates that it was Rosh Hashanah (New Year's Day) and also the tenth of the month when Ezekiel saw his vision in 574 BC. Rosh Hashanah was on the tenth of the month only at the start of a Jubilee Year (Lev 25:9–10). Ezekiel, as a priest, would have known when Sabbatical and Jubilee Years were due. The *Seder Olam*, ch. 11, and the Babylonian Talmud record that Ezekiel's vision was at the end of the seventeenth Jubilee cycle and that another Jubilee was due in the eighteenth year of Josiah (623/22 BC by modern scholarship). Both figures place the start of counting for the Sabbatical and Jubilee Years in 1406 BC, in agreement with the 1446 date for the exodus calculated from 1 Kgs 6:1 and the subsequent forty years in the wilderness.[15]

---

14. While I object to late-date advocates' conversion of forty to twenty-five based on an assumption that the biblical writer intended the reader to understand 300 even though he wrote 480, I agree that the average biblical generation was twenty-five years.

15. Andrew E. Steinmann, *From Abraham to Paul: A Biblical Chronology* (St. Louis: Concordia, 2011), 51.

Evidence from Acts 7:29–30

In Stephen's speech in Acts 7, he proclaims that the pharaoh from whom Moses fled died after a "long period" (Exod 2:23) while Moses was spending forty years in the Midian desert. Exodus 2:23 and 4:19 disclose that the oppression pharaoh died before Moses' return. In the Eighteenth Dynasty (ca. 1570–1320 BC), only Thutmose III (1504–1450 BC) reigned more than forty years.[16] If he is the oppression pharaoh, then Amenhotep II would be the exodus pharaoh. This synchronizes with the early date. Stephen was a brilliant apologist, and it would be a mistake to dismiss his chronological insights.

Based on the witness of these five biblical passages, the data clearly points us to the fifteenth century. I am not convinced by the shaky exegesis of late-date advocates who compress the 480 (actually 479) years of 1 Kgs 6:1 to 300 years. If they are correct, why does the "incorrect" date harmonize with so many scriptural passages? Surely, late-date advocates have vast archaeological evidence to override the overwhelming textual strength of the early date. We shall see.

Extrabiblical Evidence for an Early Exodus

Before we turn to the archaeological evidence, let's first consider the extrabiblical evidence for the early date of the exodus. Much like the biblical evidence, the extrabiblical evidence suggests not only *that* the exodus occurred (historicity) but *when* it occurred (chronology). A variety of ancient sources and sites attest to the reality and timing of the exodus.

Evidence from Josephus and Manetho

Two historians from the classical world discuss the reality and timing of the exodus: Josephus and Manetho.[17] Josephus, a first-century AD Jewish historian, cited Manetho, an Egyptian priest from the Ptolemaic era (ca. 270 BC), who identified the exodus pharaoh as "Amenophis"

---

16. These dates derive from standard High chronology.

17. Manetho, *History of Egypt and Other Works*, trans. W. G. Waddell, LCL 350 (Cambridge: Harvard Univ. Press, 1940).

(*Ag. Ap.* 1.2.227–53).[18] The only pharaohs named Amenophis reigned in the Eighteenth Dynasty, and the dates of their reigns synchronize with an early exodus. Of the four pharaohs named Amenophis (or Amenhotep), only Amenhotep II resembles Josephus's citations of Manetho.

Unfortunately, Josephus's knowledge of the Eighteenth Dynasty is imperfect, as he understands Amenophis to be a fictitious king's name. Josephus confuses the Hyksos departure described in Manetho with the exodus of the Israelites centuries later. Despite Josephus's ignorance of what his source was saying, his citations of that source are enough to reconstruct and preserve Manetho's perspective, which separated the Hyksos expulsion and the Israelite exodus by a long period of time. If Amenhotep II was indeed the exodus pharaoh, the oppression pharaoh who immediately preceded him would have been Thutmose III, and as previously mentioned, Exod 2:23 specifies that the pharaoh from whom Moses fled prior to his forty years in Midian had a long reign, which matches Thutmose III. Supporters of a thirteenth-century exodus who generally name Ramesses II as the exodus pharaoh are confronted with an additional problem here. The two pharaohs who preceded Ramesses II reigned only one year and eleven years (Ramesses I and Seti I).

Evidence from Tell el-Dab'a

In 1990 Manfred Bietak's Austrian team began excavations in the Nile delta at Tell el-Dab'a, almost certainly the site of ancient Avaris, which later was incorporated into the city of Rameses that is mentioned in the book of Exodus.[19] Bietak's stratigraphic analysis reveals a clear abandonment in the mid-Eighteenth Dynasty, during or after the reign of Amenhotep II.[20] An abandonment during his reign comports with

18. Editor's note: Pharaohs with this name are now generally known by the name Amenhotep. In this book, where "Amenophis" appears instead it is because of Josephus's use of that name.

19. I provide fuller explanation of the identification of Rameses in the logistics section.

20. See Douglas Petrovich, "Toward Pinpointing the Timing of the Egyptian Abandonment of Avaris during the Middle of the 18th Dynasty," *Journal of Ancient Egyptian Interconnections* 5, no. 2 (2013): 9–28.

the evidence. The animal burials that were dug into the abandonment phase lack any pottery from the Amarna or Ramesside periods, and the latest identifiable pottery dates to the reign of Amenhotep II, who was probably the pharaoh of the exodus.[21] If this identification is correct, the Avaris abandonment serves as potential evidence of the exodus, and the strata below the abandonment stratum may reflect Israelites in Egypt when the Bible places them there. Much of Avaris Stratum d/1 (in Area F/I) to Stratum c (Area H/I–VI) points to the presence of a Semitic population until the mysterious abandonment. There is no evidence of a Semitic population at Avaris in the Nineteenth Dynasty when Ramesses II ruled Egypt (the timing of the late-date theory).

The possible evidence for Israelites at Avaris in the nineteenth century BC includes the potential identification of Di-Sobekemḥat—the first attested Asiatic to bear the title ruler of Retjenu—as Joseph's second son, Ephraim.[22] Di-Sobekemḥat was buried in Area F/I at Avaris (Stratum d/1) in an elaborate tomb (F/I–m/18–Gr. 3) with numerous extravagant grave goods.[23] His name means "He who was appointed by Sobekemḥat," a vizier, arguably Joseph, who served during the reigns of Sesostris II (the abundance pharaoh) and Sesostris III (the famine pharaoh).

The Austrian excavations at Tell el-Dab'a have produced two results that contribute to the credibility of the fifteenth-century exodus. The first is the discovery of an extensive palatial district at the site, thereby proving that Memphis was not the only city with an Eighteenth Dynasty palace. Had that been the case, it would make incredible the exodus account of pharaoh summoning Moses and Aaron from their homes in adjoining Goshen to the palace in one night (Exod 12:31).

21. Douglas Petrovich, "Amenhotep II and the Historicity of the Exodus-Pharaoh," *MSJ* 17 (Spring 2006): 81–110.

22. Douglas Petrovich, *New Evidence of Israelites in Egypt from Joseph to the Exodus* (Carta: Jerusalem, forthcoming). The toponym Retjenu signifies that this official had his origins in the Levant. Manfred Bietak, *Avaris: The Capital of the Hyksos: Recent Excavations at Tell el-Dab'a* (London: British Museum Press, 1996), 26.

23. Robert Schiestl, *Tell el–Dab'a XVIII: Die Palastnekropole von Tell el-Daba', Die Gräber des Areals F/I der Straten d/2 und d/1* (Vienna: Österreichischen Akademia der Wissenschaften, 2009), 363–86.

The second result pertains to anomalies in radiocarbon dating. Bietak has demonstrated an offset in the carbon 14 dates in Egypt beginning in the fifteenth century. From the fourteenth century BC to modern times, carbon 14 matches other dating metrics, plus or minus fifty years. But carbon 14 dates diverge from the other metrics beginning in the fifteenth century BC. The offset generally increases as we move farther back in time. This is important because the biblical date for the exodus is 1446 BC. The offset being proposed neutralizes any carbon 14–based arguments against the biblical date of the exodus and conquest. Unfortunately, the majority of the academic community has ignored Bietak's rigorous carbon 14 research, done in partnership with the VERA radiation laboratory of the University of Vienna. As we will discuss regarding Jericho, the carbon 14 stakes are high and the ramifications profound.

Evidence from Serabit el-Khadim and Wadi Nasb

Epigraphic evidence for the early exodus comes from sites in the southwestern Sinai: Serabit el-Khadim and the Wadi Nasb. We will consider two inscriptions from Serabit el-Khadim (Sinai 375a and Sinai 361) and one from the Wadi Nasb (Sinai 376).

In 1905 Flinders Petrie recovered and recorded several inscriptions from Serabit el-Khadim, a mining site exploited heavily in the New Kingdom (Eighteenth–Twentieth Dynasties). Petrie's most significant find, Sinai 375a, reveals the proto-Sinaitic script (also known as the proto-consonantal script), an antecedent of the Hebrew block script.[24] Proto-consonantal Hebrew letters and Middle Egyptian hieroglyphs, quite distinct from one another, appear side by side in Sinai 375a. Part of the text reads vertically, and part reads horizontally. In 2016 Douglas Petrovich translated the inscription as follows:

> Vertical script: "The overseer of minerals, Ahisamach."
>
> Horizontal script: "The one having been elevated is weary to forget."[25]

---

24. W. M. Flinders Petrie, *Researches in Sinai* (New York: Dutton, 1906).
25. Petrovich, *World's Oldest Alphabet*, 175.

Sinai 375a in high contrast

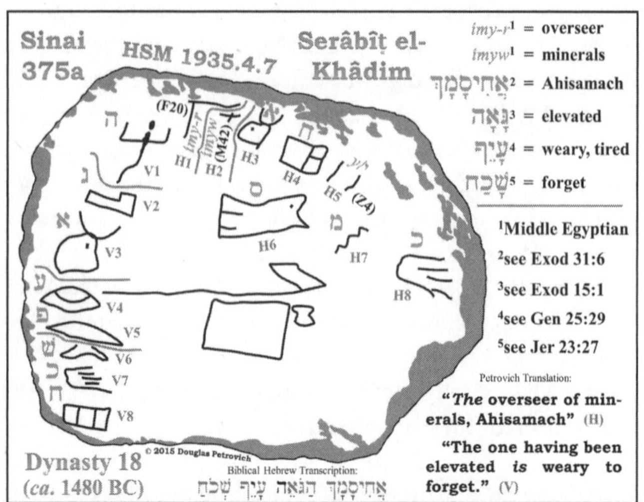

Douglas Petrovich translation of Sinai 375a

Sinai 375a dates to about 1480 BC, just a few decades before the Bible indicates that the Israelites experienced a miraculous deliverance from Egypt. Shortly after their departure in 1446 BC, Moses recorded God's instructions regarding the tabernacle.

> I have chosen Bezalel . . . to make artistic designs for work in gold, silver and bronze . . . and to engage in all kinds of crafts. Moreover, I have appointed Oholiab son of [Ahisamach], of the tribe of Dan. . . . I have given ability . . . to make everything I have commanded you: the tent of meeting, the ark of the covenant law. (Exod 31:2–7; cf. 38:21–23)

The Semitic name Ahisamach appears only in the book of Exodus (twice) and on Sinai 375a. Oholiab plausibly apprenticed under his father, Ahisamach, in the years leading up to the exodus. He used the skills developed in slavery before the exodus to build the tabernacle. If Petrovich is correct, Sinai 375a testifies to the presence of an Israelite in Egypt, in the first half of the fifteenth century BC, whose son or close relative took part in the exodus.

Sinai 361 represents a second important inscription from Serabit el-Khadim. Discovered by Romain Butin in his 1932 expedition, it consists of a large upper fragment and a small lower fragment. Bedouin workers discovered the large fragment in situ. Petrovich dates Sinai 361 to the mid-fifteenth century BC and translates the proto-Sinaitic text as follows:

> Our bound servitude had lingered. Moses then provoked astonishment. It is a year of astonishment because of the lady.[26]

Whoever wrote the inscription suffered a prolonged period of slavery by the mid-fifteenth century BC. This could refer to the Israelites. The second sentence removes all doubt by mentioning Moses, the Israelite deliverer. To date this is the only contemporary extrabiblical reference to the historical Moses. If Petrovich's reading stands, a case can be made that the astonishment refers to the miracles associated with the exodus.

As with Sinai 375a, Petrie discovered the Sinai 376 inscription in 1905. The discovery occurred at the Wadi Nasb. In 1961 Georg Gerster rediscovered and published the inscription.[27] The archaic elements of the

---

26. Petrovich, *World's Oldest Alphabet*, 160.

27. While Gerster recorded the inscription, Albright translated it: "O father E[l], gra[nt] to (my) companion [re]st beside him." Georg Gerster, *Sinai: Land der Offenbarung* (Frankfurt: Büchergilde Gutenberg, 1961), 62; William F. Albright, *The Proto-Sinaitic Inscriptions and Their Decipherment*, HTS 22 (Cambridge: Harvard Univ. Press, 1969), 28–29, fig. 11.

script point to the Thirteenth Dynasty (eighteenth century). The text mentions Sekhemre Khutawy Khabaw, a Thirteenth Dynasty pharaoh who reigned for only three years (ca. 1775 BC). Petrovich translates the inscription this way:

> The house of the vineyard of Asenath and its innermost room were engraved. They have come to life.[28]

Who is Asenath? Can she be linked to an Israelite from the period of the Egyptian sojourn? Genesis 41:45 and 46:20 mention Asenath as the wife of Joseph, the daughter of Potiphera, a priest from the city of On (Heliopolis). As Pharaoh's gift to Joseph, she bore for him Ephraim and Manasseh. If Asenath of Genesis is the Asenath of Sinai 376, another example can be added to the growing number of Israelites in Egypt during the period that the early date places them there.

Evidence from the Amarna Tablets

A coincidental find at Tell el-Amarna, Egypt, in 1887 yielded 382 clay tablets mostly written in Akkadian cuneiform script and dating to about 1370 BC. These tablets contained the pleas to Pharaohs Amenhotep III and Akhenaten (Amenhotep IV) from the rulers of the Canaanite city-states under their hegemony. Cities like Shechem (EA 244 and EA 246), Jerusalem (EA 286 and EA 287), and Megiddo (EA 243 and EA 244) complained of being overrun by the marauding Habiru. Eilat Mazar, in her 2009–2010 Ophel excavation, recovered a cuneiform fragment which may be an archival copy of Abdi-Heba's appeal to Pharaoh Akhenaten.[29] Abdi-Heba ruled Jerusalem in the fourteenth century. Jerusalem was indeed occupied at the time of the early date.

Taken together, the biblical books of Joshua and Judges portray an initial surge into Canaan followed by a slower and more methodical supplanting of the Canaanite city-states in the following generations. In the fourteenth century these cities were besieged, as the Bible indicates. The Amarna term *ḫābiru* (Habiru) linguistically points to the

28. Petrovich, *World's Oldest Alphabet*, 65.

29. Eilat Mazar et al., "A Cuneiform Tablet from the Ophel in Jerusalem," *IEJ* 60 (2010): 4–21.

biblical Hebrews, although the term had wider connotations, just as the biblical term Hebrew referred to more than the descendants of Jacob (cf. Gen 39:14).[30]

The designation Habiru generally describes nomadic marauders in the Late Bronze Age. The Habiru who embraced Yahwistic monotheism became known as the biblical Hebrews. According to Exod 12:38, "many other people" (NIV) or "a mixed multitude" (KJV) participated in the exodus. Some of the Egyptian officials even "feared the word of the Lord" (Exod 9:20). About forty-one years later, at the great covenant ceremony, we learn that "both the foreigners living among them and the native-born were there" (Josh 8:33).

Evidence from the Soleb Hieroglyph

Amenhotep III ruled Egypt in the early fourteenth century. At his Soleb Temple in upper Nubia, a hieroglyph refers to "the land of the Shasu, [those of] Yhw." Shasu is a general term for Levantine nomads. Yhw is broadly understood to refer to Yahweh, the God of the Israelites. The Bible refers to the nomads or seminomads in fourteenth-century Palestine who worship Yahweh as Hebrews or Israelites. The term Shasu likely includes multiple nomadic groups, such as the Habiru. The scribes of Amenhotep III differentiated the particular Shasu to whom they referred by noting that they worshiped Yahweh. It appears likely that the group to which this inscription refers are the Israelites who are in Canaan just one generation after the early date places them there.[31] The late date does not comport with the Soleb Hieroglyph.

Evidence from the Berlin Pedestal

Another important evidence of Israel in Canaan shortly after the fifteenth-century exodus resides in the Egyptian Museum in Berlin. Three name rings appear on Statue Pedestal Relief 21687. From left to right (in English), they read as follows: Ashkelon, Canaan, and Israel. Unfortunately, because the granite slab broke, the final third of the Israel

---

30. Nadav Na'aman, "Habiru and Hebrews: The Transfer of a Social Term to the Literary Sphere," *JNES* 45 (October 1986): 271–88.

31. Charles Aling and Clyde Billington, "The Name Yahweh in Egyptian Hieroglyphic Texts," *Artifax* 24, no. 4 (Autumn 2009): 15–18.

name ring is missing on the right edge of the relief.[32] In 2001 Manfred Görg published the cartouches and deciphered the damaged toponym as Israel.[33] Wolfgang Zwickel and Pieter van der Veen corroborate Görg's identification, while James Hoffmeier rejects it.[34] The orthography points to an Eighteenth Dynasty date; however, a Nineteenth Dynasty scribe likely copied 21687 from the original version. The names and their proximity to one another is significant because of a similar arrangement on the Merenptah Stela, which also mentions Israel. If Görg's reading withstands scrutiny, then the Berlin Pedestal provides strong evidence for Israel in Canaan in the Eighteenth Dynasty, likely in the fourteenth century. This too substantiates the case for the early date.

Evidence from the Merenptah Stela

Another inscription that documents Israel in Canaan after the exodus is the Merenptah Stela, also known as the Israel Stela. Flinders Petrie discovered the stela in western Thebes in 1896.[35] In the final three lines of the twenty-eight-line stela, Merenptah, the son of Ramesses II, documents his campaign in Canaan and the existence of Israel as an established nation in the late thirteenth century. Like all royal propaganda, it employs hyperbole: "Israel is laid waste, his seed is no longer; Khurru [Syria] is become a widow because of Egypt."[36] The dating of this to the late thirteenth century is significant because an exodus in the mid-thirteenth century followed by a forty-year wilderness sojourn and an initial conquest of six years does not allow adequate time for the development and recognition of national Israel at the end of the same century.

---

32. David E. Graves, *Famous Discoveries That Support the Reliability of the Bible*, vol. 2 of *Biblical Archaeology*, 2nd ed. (Toronto: Electronic Christian Media, 2018), 153–55.

33. Görg, "Israel in Hieroglyphen," 21–27.

34. Wolfgang Zwickel and Pieter van der Veen, "The Earliest Reference to Israel and Its Possible Archaeological and Historical Background," *VT* 67 (2017): 129–40; James K. Hoffmeier, "What Is the Biblical Date for the Exodus? A Response to Bryant Wood," *JETS* 50 (2007): 225–47. Hoffmeier presents six alternative ways of reading the hieroglyph in question. None of them represent a known toponym (place-name). The only rendering that satisfies this is "Israel."

35. W. M. Flinders Petrie, *Six Temples at Thebes, 1896* (London: Quaritch, 1897), 13.

36. "The Israel Stela," trans. Edward F. Wente Jr., in *The Literature of Ancient Egypt: An Anthology of Stories, Instructions, Stelae, Autobiographies, and Poetry*, ed. William Kelly Simpson, 3rd ed. (New Haven: Yale Univ. Press, 2003), 360.

Evidence from Jericho

All Levantine archaeologists agree that City IV at Jericho suffered a massive destruction that closely matches the Josh 6 account. The massive mudbrick superstructure collapsed outward, the interior stone walls fell, and a conflagration consumed the city after the collapse of the walls. All of this comports with Josh 6:24. Kathleen Kenyon, one of Jericho's primary excavators, recognized that the walls collapsed prior to the fire.[37]

Excavated storage jars full of wheat indicate that the fall of Jericho occurred in the early spring (cp. Josh 5:10 with ch. 6). Although strongly fortified, Jericho did not endure a long siege, as evidenced by the full jars (Josh 6:15–20). After that, Jericho had no major settlement until Iron Age IB, in agreement with Josh 6:26 and 1 Kgs 16:34.

There is strong consensus regarding these facts. However, the dating of the destruction deeply divides archaeologists. Four teams have excavated Tell es-Sultân, the site of ancient Jericho. The two of them most germane to dating the destruction are the expeditions of Garstang (1930–1936) and Kenyon (1952–1958). Garstang dated the destruction to the end of the fifteenth century, in harmony with the biblical date for the conquest of Canaan.[38] He based his conclusion on ceramic dating and several scarabs from the Eighteenth Dynasty. Kenyon, however, dated the destruction to the mid-sixteenth century BC.[39]

She argued that Garstang's ceramic dates were erroneous and that his scarabs were commemorative, having been produced hundreds of years after the reigns of the pharaohs whom they document. She further built her case on the dates of the walls. Her research prompted most scholars to abandon the early date of the conquest. But was Kenyon correct in dismissing a fifteenth-century destruction? Let's examine her three arguments.

First, Kenyon did not excavate any imported Cypriot bichrome ware—ware typical of Late Bronze I sites in the southern Levant, especially along

---

37. Kathleen M. Kenyon, *The Architecture and Stratigraphy of the Tell, Part 1: Text*, ed. Thomas A. Holland, vol. 3 of *Excavations at Jericho* (Oxford: Oxford Univ. Press, 1981), 110.

38. John Garstang and J. B. E. Garstang, *The Story of Jericho*, 2nd ed. (London: Marshall, Morgan & Scott, 1948), 133–53, 167.

39. Kathleen M. Kenyon, *Digging Up Jericho: The Results of the Jericho Excavations, 1952–1956* (London: Praeger & Benn, 1957), 261–62.

the *Via Maris*. Although Kenyon did not record Late Bronze I Cypriot bichrome pottery in her Area H, Garstang found it in abundance. Kenyon ignored the local Late Bronze I ceramics and instead posited an argument from silence. Bryant Wood, who earned a doctor of philosophy degree in Late Bronze Age pottery, showed Kenyon's ceramic analysis to be in error.[40]

Second, Kenyon dismissed the four Eighteenth Dynasty scarabs from Jericho as spurious. She thought they were commemorative, originating long after the fifteenth century. She offered no substantiating evidence for her rejection, but obviously, authentic Eighteenth Dynasty scarabs at Jericho would be problematic for her dating scheme. The scarab sequence from the Jericho tombs began in the Thirteenth Dynasty, but the scarabs in question belong to the subsequent Eighteenth Dynasty pharaohs: Hatshepsut, Thutmose III (additionally a seal), and Amenhotep III (two scarabs), in chronological order. With the inclusion of Hatshepsut, this chronological sequence supports an occupation at Jericho at the time of the early exodus date. Why? Because while those of later times may have wanted to honor the first three pharaohs, especially Thutmose III, Hatshepsut became persona non grata after her troubled administration. No one would ever want a replica of her scarab.

Third, Kenyon maintained that Jericho's outer fortification walls could not pertain to the biblical story because they were Middle Bronze walls and the biblical date was at the end of Late Bronze I. I agree with Kenyon on the age of the walls. However, the issue under dispute is the date not of the construction of the walls but of when they fell. Kenyon's arguments melt under the heat of cross-examination.

The carbon 14 data also plays an important role in the dating of Jericho's destruction. In 1995 Bruins and Plicht reported that carbon 14 tests of grain samples found at Jericho yielded extremely early dates (1601–1566 BC and 1561–1524 BC) at a confidence level of 68 percent.[41] These samples came from the same jars that demonstrated the city fell in the early spring. The radiocarbon results loosely matched Kenyon's

40. Bryant G. Wood, "Did the Israelites Conquer Jericho?" *BAR* 16, no. 2 (March/April 1990): 44–58.

41. Hendrik J. Bruins and Johannes van der Plicht, "Tell Es-Sultan (Jericho): Radiocarbon Results of Short-Lived Cereal and Multiyear Charcoal Samples from the End of the Middle Bronze Age," *Radiocarbon* 37, no. 2 (1995): 218.

destruction estimate of 1580 BC, and many scholars hold them as decisive in dating City IV's destruction. But Bietak's findings, buttressed by the recent and careful argumentation of Daphna Ben-Tor, neutralize the strength of this argument.[42] Jericho's carbon 14 dates are too early by far more than one century. Bietak, one of the most respected archaeologists of his generation, affirms that carbon 14 dates from the Eighteenth Dynasty need to be downdated by 170 years.[43] For dates earlier than the Eighteenth Dynasty, the offset is uniformly 120 years. Furthermore, carbon 14 dates always vary plus or minus fifty years, so the carbon 14 dates of Bruins and Plicht, properly calibrated, synchronize with the early date. I confidently use carbon 14 testing as a dating metric as far back as the fourteenth century. However, secure dating comes from a triangulation of metrics: ceramic analysis, glyptic material such as coins (in later periods) and scarabs, and carbon 14 testing (properly calibrated by dendrochronology and other metrics). We cannot rely on carbon 14 dating alone. Even when clean organic samples emerge from sealed loci, someone still needs to calibrate the test, so the possibility of human error or bias remains.

An analysis of Jericho's pottery, scarabs, walls, and grain together erode confidence in Kenyon's destruction date, leaving us with no good reasons to dismiss the biblical date for the destruction of Jericho.

Evidence from Ai

Widespread agreement exists that et-Tell, ten miles north of Jerusalem, contains the ruins of Abraham's Ai of Gen 12–13; however, the identity of Ai of Josh 7–8 remains hotly debated.[44]

According to one viewpoint, et-Tell represents Ai of both the Abraham and Joshua narratives. However, Callaway's excavation at et-Tell from 1964 to 1972 failed to document any evidence of occupation

---

42. Daphna Ben-Tor, "Evidence for Middle Bronze Age Chronology and Synchronisms in the Levant: A Response to Höflmayer et al. 2016," *BASOR* 379 (2018): 43–54.

43. Manfred Bietak and Felix Höflmayer, "Introduction: High and Low Chronology," in *The Synchronisation of Civilisations in the Eastern Mediterranean in the Second Millennium B.C. III: Proceedings of the SCIEM 2000–2nd EuroConference, Vienna, 28th of May–1st of June, 2003*, ed. Manfred Bietak and Ernst Czerny, Contributions to the Chronology of the Eastern Mediterranean 9 (Vienna: Österreichischen Akademie der Wissenschaften, 2007), 20.

44. Richard S. Hess, "The Jericho and Ai of the Book of Joshua," in Hess, Klingbeil, and Ray, *Critical Issues in Early Israelite History*, 33.

from the fifteenth century.[45] The site already lay in ruins long before Abraham arrived there. It remained in ruins until Iron Age I, long after Joshua. To compensate for the absence, some scholars postulate that Joshua's Ai was merely a pastoral town or forward base, in effect, a temporary city formed to resist the Israelites.[46] This can be neither proven nor disproven.

The other viewpoint is that hundreds of years after Abraham, the name Ai migrated to the nearby site of Khirbet el-Maqatir. Bryant Wood excavated Khirbet el-Maqatir from 1995 to 2000 and 2009 to 2013, and I directed the excavations there from 2014 to 2017.[47] Local tradition dating at least back to the 1800s equated Khirbet el-Maqatir with Ai.[48] Wood and I set forth eight lines of evidence that connect Josh 7–8 with Khirbet el-Maqatir.[49] Three of the criteria are archaeologically verifiable.

First, Khirbet el-Maqatir was inhabited at the time of the Israelite conquest. Abundant Late Bronze I pottery populates Khirbet el-Maqatir, and much of it is hard as concrete because of being refired in a conflagration after being initially fired in a kiln. Other evidence of occupation at the time of the early date includes an Eighteenth Dynasty scarab from a sealed locus just above bedrock, a nearby severed ram's head, and an infant burial in a Late Bronze I jar. The neonate burial confirms that there were women at the fortress (Josh 8:25).

Second, the site had a fortification system with a northern gate. Joshua 7:5 and 8:29 mention the gate of Ai, and 8:11 and 8:19 place it on the northern side. Excavations revealed six gate socket stones and one intact gate chamber on the north of the site. The presence of a

---

45. Joseph A. Callaway, "Ai (Place)," *ABD* 1:125–30.

46. Steven M. Ortiz, "The Conquest of Ai: Text and Archaeology," in *ESV Archaeology Study Bible* (Wheaton, IL: Crossway, 2018), 295.

47. The Khirbet el-Maqatir excavation was conducted on behalf of the Associates for Biblical Research (ABR).

48. Edward Robinson and Eli Smith, *Biblical Researches in Palestine and the Adjacent Regions: A Journal of Travels in the Years 1838 and 1852*, 3rd ed. (London, 1867), 1:448; Bryant G. Wood, "From Ramesses to Shiloh: Archaeological Discoveries Bearing on the Exodus–Judges Period," in *Giving the Sense: Understanding and Using Old Testament Historical Texts*, ed. David M. Howard Jr. and Michael A. Grisanti (Grand Rapids: Kregel, 2003), 266.

49. Bryant G. Wood, "The Search for Joshua's Ai," in Hess, Klingbeil, and Ray, *Critical Issues in Early Israelite History*, 237–38; Scott Stripling and Mark Hassler, "The 'Problem' of Ai: Solved After Nearly Forty Years of Excavation in the West Bank of Israel," *Bible and Spade* 31, no. 2 (Spring 2018): 40–44.

gate complex indicates the existence of a perimeter wall. Sections of the perimeter fortification wall measure thirteen feet (four meters) thick.

And third, Khirbet el-Maqatir exhibited signs of conflagration. Joshua 8:19 and 8:28 reveal that the Israelites burned the site of Ai. The Bronze Age stratum at Khirbet el-Maqatir contains pockets of ash throughout the site. This, along with the aforementioned refired Late Bronze IB pottery and calcined bedrock near the gate, document that the site experienced a conflagration as mentioned in Josh 8.

Evidence from Hazor

Joshua 11:10 describes Hazor as "the head of all these kingdoms," and judging by sheer size, that was certainly the case. It sat on a major Bronze Age highway and controlled the region north of the Sea of Galilee. The Israelites burned Hazor, just as they had Jericho and Ai. Excavations at Hazor by Yigael Yadin (1955–1958 and 1968–1969) and Amnon Ben-Tor (1990–present) uncovered evidence of a destruction layer from the time of the conquest.[50] Two important destruction layers exist at Hazor. The older one, Stratum XV in the upper city (Stratum 2 in the lower city), dates to Late Bronze I and, I believe, corresponds to Joshua's fifteenth-century conquest. The later one, Stratum XIII in the upper city (Stratum 1A in the lower city), dates to Late Bronze 2B. If Bryant Wood is correct, the later destruction corresponds to Deborah and Barak's implied thirteenth-century destruction (Judg 4:24).[51]

Another possibility exists. The Merenptah Stela describes Merenptah's campaign in Canaan at the end of the thirteenth century. Destruction strata at several Palestinian sites date to this very time, a time when Judges portrays Israel as weak and divided. Albright assigned the destructions of Tell Beit Mirsim, Beitin, and Lachish to Joshua and the Israelites.[52] I suggest that Merenptah may be responsible for wreaking havoc in Canaan, as he claims. The fact that Judges does not

---

50. Yigael Yadin, *Hazor: The Rediscovery of a Great Citadel of the Bible* (New York: Random House, 1975); Amnon Ben-Tor, "The Fall of Canaanite Hazor: The 'Who' and 'When' Questions," in *Mediterranean Peoples in Transition: Thirteenth to Early Tenth Centuries BCE; In Honor of Professor Trude Dothan*, ed. Seymour Gitin, Amihai Mazar, and Ephraim Stern (Jerusalem: Israel Exploration Society, 1998), 456–67.

51. Bryant G. Wood, "The Rise and Fall of the 13th-Century Exodus-Conquest Theory," *JETS* 48 (2005): 476–77.

52. Wood, "Rise and Fall," 475–76.

mention this campaign is irrelevant because we have inscriptional proof that it occurred, perhaps archaeological proof too. Recent excavations at Gezer (SWBTS Stratum 12B = HUC Stratum XV) concluded that its destruction in the late thirteenth century should be attributed to Egyptians.[53] This is almost certainly evidence of Merenptah's invasion.

Late-date proponents see Hazor's Stratum XIII/1A as evidence of the conquest and conflagration by Joshua. This approach leaves Hazor's implied destruction under Deborah and Barak (or Merenptah) without attestation in the archaeological record. Early-date proponents have no such problem. They assign Stratum XV/2 to Joshua in the fifteenth century and Stratum XIII/1A to Deborah and Barak (or Merenptah) in the thirteenth century. Even if Hazor's thirteenth-century destruction was not at the hands of Deborah and Barak (or Merenptah), no reason exists to prefer Stratum XIII/1A (thirteenth century) over Stratum XV/2 (fifteenth century) for Joshua's destruction. The iconoclastic desecration of Hazor's cultic area in the late thirteenth century may have been at the hands of Israelites, but the biblical text does not require or document it.

Evidence from Mount Ebal

After victory at Ai (Josh 8), the Israelites held a covenant ceremony with God at or near Shechem, with Mount Gerizim on one side and Mount Ebal on the other. Joshua built an altar on Mount Ebal (v. 30). From 1978 to 1992 Adam Zertal conducted a survey of the tribal territory of Manasseh. In 1980 he discovered a large rectangular altar on the second step on the east side of Mount Ebal at el-Burnat, which he correctly dated to the end of Late Bronze II. Excavation followed between 1982 and 1987. The altar resembled the biblical description of the altar of sacrifice. As a result of this discovery, Zertal became a believer in the historicity of the biblical narratives. Zertal excavated the altar and some of its footprint-shaped enclosure. Unfortunately, he died before completing his final publication of the altar. However, *Tel Aviv* journal devoted a complete issue to his preliminary report.[54] The preliminary report yields some fascinating observations. On the surface this altar

---

53. Personal email correspondence on January 26, 2019, with Steven Ortiz, director of Gezer's renewed excavations.

54. Adam Zertal, "An Early Iron Age Cultic Site on Mt. Ebal: Excavation Seasons 1982–1987," *TA* 14 (1987): 105–65.

seems to support the late date. However, an earlier altar lies beneath the thirteenth-century altar. Scholars have largely ignored this fact.

The earlier round altar (Installation 94), measuring two meters in diameter, could very well be Joshua's altar. In Zertal's mind, the round altar was constructed just one generation before the rectangular altar. I see it as more than one century older and believe that Zertal's Stratum II should be subdivided and that the material just above bedrock in Pit 250, Surface 61, and Installation 94 derives from the Late Bronze IB (late fifteenth century). I propose that these loci and installations pertain to a different century. I call this Stratum IIB. Zertal describes the round altar.

> Installation 94, which is an integral part of Surface 61, was unearthed in the eastern part of this surface. It is 2 m. in diameter and built of medium-size stones, some of them charred, protruding 20–25 cm. above the surface. Its southern side is covered by Wall 13 of Stratum 1B (Pl. 6:2), which effectively cancelled its use. It was found covered with stones, beneath which was a 10 cm. layer of clean ash containing many animal bones, some burnt. *The installation is located in the exact centre of the overlying building.*[55]

How can we ascertain the correct date for the older altar and why is it venerated ("in the exact centre") by enclosure within the rectangular altar? In a personal conversation on June 20, 2018, Shai Bar, professor of archaeology at Haifa University, who is preparing the final publication of Zertal's Mount Ebal excavation, told me that the carbon 14 samples from the 1980s came from unreliable contexts, so this dating metric is of no value. He also said that a fifteenth-century scarab of Thutmose III that Zertal recovered has disappeared, along with a second scarab belonging to Ramesses II and deriving from Stratum 1B, so it is impossible to reexamine them. Glyptic expert Baruch Brandl judged the Thutmose III scarab to be commemorative and belonging to the thirteenth century.[56] This is nothing new. The identification of

---

55. Zertal, "Early Iron Age Cultic Site," 110, emphasis mine.

56. Baruch Brandl, "Two Scarabs and a Trapezoidal Seal from Mount Ebal," *TA* 14 (1987): 166–72.

Eighteenth Dynasty scarabs from sites like Mount Ebal, Shiloh, and Jericho are often judged to be commemorative because they challenge the dominant late-date theory. The theory now drives interpretation. The criteria for determining which Eighteenth Dynasty scarabs derive from the time of the pharaoh they portray and the ones that do not, if any, are subjective. Joshua 8 gives no indication of the altar's repeated use, so it need not be dated by pottery. That said, Zertal does document a biconical jug, a shallow bowl, and a carinated bowl which best fit in the Late Bronze I–II transition.[57]

I recommend a reexamination of the altar and a proper restoration of it. Furthermore, excavation of another section of the enclosure would likely clarify the stratigraphy and yield clean carbon 14 dates from each stratum. All material should be wet-sifted so that no critical information eludes identification.[58] Unfortunately, Mount Ebal lies within a politically sensitive area near modern Nablus, and the chances of further excavation seem remote, at least for now.

So where does this leave us? Zertal died before final publication, the carbon 14 samples are unreliable, the scarabs are missing, and Bar's final report is still years away. As noted, there was a small amount of Late Bronze IB pottery beneath the Iron Age I pottery and bone matrix. I believe that this pottery, a Late Bronze pumice chalice from Pit 250, a small amount of animal bone from inside the round altar, and the Thutmose III scarab all point to a fifteenth-century date for the round altar. Everyone agrees with Zertal that the rectangular altar dates to the thirteenth century. The round altar likely belongs to the late fifteenth century and is plausibly the altar that Joshua built. One hundred percent of the stones of the round altar are unworked as per the requirement of Josh 8:31. The Mount Ebal evidence comports well with the early date.

Evidence from Other Ancient Sources

The archaeological evidence from other ancient sources enjoys a high degree of verisimilitude with the biblical descriptions. The material

57. Zertal, "Early Iron Age Cultic Site," 137.

58. In 2017–2019, the first three seasons of the ABR excavation which I directed at Shiloh, my team recovered ten scarabs, eight from the wet-sifting process. Even though the material had been dry-sifted, workers had been unable to detect the dirt-encrusted scarabs. Once washed, they were easily spotted. Zertal's dump piles likely contain additional scarabs.

culture in the fifteenth century BC matches what we would expect from reading the Old Testament. Several examples illustrate the point. For one, the covenant structure of Deuteronomy mirrors that of Hittite suzerain treaties at the same period. These treaties generally followed the same consistent five-point model found in the Pentateuch.[59]

Furthermore, tablets from the second millennium BC document the cost of a slave. Joseph's brothers sold him into slavery for twenty shekels (Gen 37:28). In the early second millennium, the cost of a slave averaged twenty-two shekels, according to the Code of Hammurabi, the Mari tablets, and other documents.[60] Probably because of inflation, the cost of a slave gradually increased over time. In the Third Dynasty of Ur (ca. 2112–2004 BC), the cost was only ten shekels, while after the eighteenth century it increased to thirty shekels, until in the first millennium the price rose to as much as fifty to sixty shekels.[61] During the Persian Empire prices reached 90–120 shekels.[62] The progressive price increase of a slave in the second millennium BC does not prove a fifteenth-century exodus, but it does establish verisimilitude.

Randall Price offers several additional examples of the verisimilitude presented in the exodus account: a delivery stool (cf. Exod 1:16); Egyptian loanwords (the name of Moses in Exod 2:10 is probably an Eighteenth Dynasty name); diction ("land flowing with milk and honey" [Deut 31:20] comports with the Tale of Sinuhe and the Annals of Thutmose III); uniform use of the term pharaoh which matches Eighteenth Dynasty parlance, not that of the Nineteenth Dynasty; accounts of poorly treated Semitic slaves in Egypt; and the importance

59. Kenneth A. Kitchen, "The Patriarchal Age: Myth or History?" *BAR* 21, no. 2 (March/April 1995): 48–57, 89–95.

60. "The Code of Hammurabi," trans. Theophile J. Meek, in *ANET*, 170, 175–76, §§116, 214, 252; Georges Boyer, *Textes Juridiques*, ARM 8 (Paris: Imprimerie Nationale, 1958), 23, n. 10:1–4; Adam Falkenstein, *Einleitung und systematische Darstellung*, vol. 1 of *Die neusumerische Gerichtsurkunden*, Bayerische Akademie der Wissenschaften, Philosophisch–historische Klasse, Abhandlungen, Neue Folge 39 (Munich: Beck, 1956), 88, n. 5.

61. Falkenstein, *Einleitung und systematische Darstellung*, 88–90; Isaac Mendelsohn, *Slavery in the Ancient Near East: A Comparative Study in Babylonia, Assyria, Syria, and Palestine from the Middle of the Third Millennium to the End of the First Millennium* (Oxford: Oxford Univ. Press, 1949), 117, 155, n. 164.

62. C. H. W. Johns, *Money Loans, Legal Decisions, Deeds of Sale, Slave Sales*, vol. 3 of *Assyrian Deeds and Documents: Recording the Transfer of Property, Including the So-Called Private Contracts, Legal Decisions and Proclamations Preserved in the Kouyunjik Collections of the British Museum; Chiefly of the 7th Century B.C.* (Cambridge: Bell, 1901), 542–46.

of magic in Egypt (cf. Exod 7:9–10).[63] Such specificity stems from contemporary eyewitnesses. Later writers would lack knowledge of such details.

Even the scarcity of destruction evidence in Late Bronze IB Canaan fits the timing of the Israelite conquest. Moses instructed the Israelites, "When the Lord your God brings you into the land he swore to your fathers, to Abraham, Isaac and Jacob, to give you—a land with large, flourishing *cities you did not build*, *houses* filled with all kinds of good things you did not provide, *wells* you did not dig, and *vineyards* and *olive groves* you did not plant . . ." (Deut 6:10–11, emphasis mine). This instruction may clarify why Joshua records the burning of only three strongholds (Jericho, Ai, and Hazor). The Israelites lacked motivation to destroy the cities of Canaan. After all, the Canaanite infrastructure represented generational wealth they stood to inherit.

Logistics of the Exodus

Ancient texts, including the Bible, underwent an editorial process. Moses wrote the Pentateuch, but he likely did not write about his own death. Editorial updating created some anachronisms that require explanation. Likewise, the dynamic nature of the meaning of words in ancient languages like Hebrew, at times, create surface contradictions. I explore these logistical tensions in the following sections.

The Anachronism "Rameses" in Exodus 1:11

An anachronism is something that does not belong in the time context in which it occurs. When Raphael painted Plato and Socrates carrying books in *The School of Athens*, he was unaware that books did not exist in the fourth century. His anachronism was unintentional. However, sometimes anachronisms are intentional and meant to help later readers understand where events occurred after place-names changed. This is important to the present discussion because the sole biblical passage that seems to contradict the early date contains an apparent anachronism. Exodus 1:11 indicates that the enslaved Israelites built the storage city

63. Randall Price with H. Wayne House, *Zondervan Handbook of Biblical Archaeology: A Book by Book Guide to Archaeological Discoveries Related to the Bible* (Grand Rapids: Zondervan, 2017), 84.

of Rameses, but a city by that name is unknown in the archaeological record of the Eighteenth Dynasty (1550–1292 BC).

How could the Israelites build the city of Rameses, a Nineteenth Dynasty name, in the Eighteenth Dynasty? Ancient Avaris (modern Tell el-Dab'a) had a large Asiatic (Semitic) population that abandoned the site in the mid-fifteenth century. Ramesses II rebuilt the northeastern sector of Avaris (modern Qantir) in the mid-thirteenth century and renamed it after himself. Later, scribes updated the name of the site so that readers in their times would know the location of the famed store city.

Such anachronisms occur commonly in the modern world and the ancient world. I live in Houston, Texas. The name of the city, at least part of it, was Harrisburg until 1926. A modern writer would never refer to my city as Harrisburg, lest he or she direct people to Pennsylvania instead of Texas. Similarly, Gen 14:14 mentions the city of Dan in the patriarchal era, but the city's name is not changed from Laish to Dan until the period of the Judges (Judg 18:29). This type of intentional anachronism explains the surface discrepancy of Exod 1:11. Proponents of a late date should have no problem accepting that the city named Rameses could be an intentional anachronism, since it is named in the days of Jacob and Joseph, long before the exodus (Gen 47:11).

Population Density and the Meaning of ʾElep

Regardless of the exodus date, the size of the Israelite population perplexes many scholars. A census was taken at the beginning and end of the forty-year wilderness sojourn (Num 1:45–46; 26:51). Both censuses counted more than six hundred thousand warriors, presumably men twenty to forty years old. There appears to be a translation error of the Hebrew word *ʾelep* (plural *ʾălāpîm*), which certainly meant "one thousand" later in biblical history, but if it meant the same thing in the Late Bronze Age, there would have been several million people migrating from Egypt to Canaan. Deuteronomy 7:7 states, "The Lord did not set his affection on you and choose you because you were more numerous than other peoples, for you were the fewest of all peoples." This indicates that the Israelites were smaller in population than the nations dwelling in Canaan, and no archaeologist holds that the total native population of Canaan in the Late Bronze Age exceeded three hundred thousand.

The Amarna tablets substantiate this. So how do we resolve this apparent contradiction? The resolution lies in the semantic range of *ʾelep/ʾălāpîm*. The Hebrew vocabulary was a fraction of the size of a modern vocabulary, so words often held multiple meanings. In the Late Bronze Age, *ʾelep* likely meant "platoon" or "fighting unit." If these units each contained ten men, there would have been around six thousand men in Israel's army, and the total population would have numbered around forty thousand people.

Given the size of the kingdoms and cities that the Israelites encountered, this works well. We need look no farther than Jericho to understand the problem. Within the nine walled acres of Jericho, there could not possibly have been more than four thousand people, and only about one thousand of the men would have been of traditional fighting age. If there were around six thousand men in Israel's army, the Israelite advantage would have been 6:1 instead of 600:1. Under the latter scenario, there was no need for a miracle. But at 6:1 and with a heavily fortified city, the people of Jericho stood a chance of withstanding the Israelite siege. While we cannot be certain of the exact size of Joshua's army or the total Israelite population, smaller numbers yield greater glory for God and are more consistent with Deut 7:7.

Theological Implications

The evidence I have presented indicates the exodus actually happened, and it happened when the Bible says that it happened—in the mid-fifteenth century. This reality profoundly impacts Judeo-Christian theology and related fields. The historicity of this seminal event in the middle of the Late Bronze Age suggests that other important biblical events deserve a presuppositional expectation of accuracy. Theologians should read the text critically, not skeptically. The entire biblical corpus reveals a verisimilitude with what the archaeologists' trowels have brought to light in the material culture of the southern Levant. This fact should empower those who teach or write about scriptural matters to move beyond theoretical constructs to convey a solid and authoritative message. Ultimately, if the Bible is true, then the God of the Bible holds a moral claim on all of humanity. Nothing could have more far-reaching implications.

RESPONSE TO SCOTT STRIPLING (THE THIRTEENTH-CENTURY EXODUS VIEW)

JAMES K. HOFFMEIER

Scott Stripling well represents the fifteenth-century exodus date, using the traditional arguments. My response focuses on disputing the chronological basis for the 1447/6 BC date, as most of the evidence adduced to support this date is questionable. Everything collapses if the chronological foundation is undermined.

Numbers and Chronological Issues

First, I reject Stripling's claim that "most biblical scholars agree the internal biblical chronology points us to a fifteenth-century BC exodus." Without a systematic survey of biblical scholars and a study of all written material on the subject, such sweeping assertions are meaningless. If one limits biblical chronology to 1 Kgs 6:1 (480 years from Solomon's third year [967 BC] back to the exodus) and Judg 11:26 (300 years since arrival of Israelite settlers in Transjordan),[64] then a fifteenth-century date seems obvious. Yet given the context of Jephthah's claim about the Israelites' taking control of a segment of Transjordan upon coming out of Egypt (Judg 11:13–16), the 300-occupation-year period (v. 26) could be a hyperbolic figure to strengthen Israel's claim to the land.

There are other biblical data to consider. If one works backward from Solomon's reign, tallying the figures in the book of Judges followed by the numbers in 1 and 2 Samuel regarding Samuel, Saul, and

64. The assumption is that Jephthah ruled Israel around 1100 BC. Add 300 = 1400, the beginning of the conquest/settlement after 40 years in the wilderness and an exodus from Egypt in 1447 BC.

David, a minimal range of 633–650 years results,[65] indicating the exodus occurred before 1600 BC. Giving priority to the 480-year figure of 1 Kgs 6:1 requires one to dismiss the dates in Judges, even though a straightforward reading suggests the judgeships can be simply added up. This illustrates the dangers of simply adding up the dates without considering their context or how the ancients likely understood them. The judges could overlap, or literary factors could be at work, both of which potentially impact chronology.

Stripling also accepts the 120-year life span of Moses as constituting three 40-year periods. One wonders why the same reckoning is not applied to 480 as 12 × 40-year periods. Rather he uses the 40-year blocks as chronological markers—40 years each in Egypt, Midian, and the wilderness—even though it forces one into incredible readings of some biblical texts and requires revising Egyptian chronology. Exodus 2:11–12 reports that when Moses "had grown up" *(wayyigdal)*, he went to see the conditions of the Hebrews, striking dead an Egyptian official and leading to the flight to Midian. Stripling appeals to the NT, where Stephen divides Moses' life into three 40-year periods (Acts 7:23, 30, 36), a reflection of the then-current rabbinic interpretation of the life of Moses.[66]

Factors Militating against This Interpretation

1. Life expectancy in the ancient Levant was about forty years.[67] Even the average life span of Judean kings, according to Edwin Yamauchi's calculation, was forty-four years.[68] Analysis of human remains by anthropologists agree with literary data. Myriam Seco Álvarez reports that of sixty-one burials exposed from Thebes from ca. 2100–2000 BC, most of the adults were twenty to forty years old, and only one woman was forty to sixty years old.[69] Psalm 90 refers to seventy and eighty years

---

65. See Hoffmeier, "What Is the Biblical Date for the Exodus?" 227–28.

66. I. Howard Marshall, *Acts*, TNTC (Grand Rapids: Eerdmans, 1980), 140.

67. Philip J. King and Lawrence E. Stager, *Life in Biblical Israel* (Louisville: Westminster John Knox, 2001), 8.

68. Edwin M. Yamauchi, "Age and the Aged," in *Dictionary of Daily Life in Biblical and Post-Biblical Antiquity*, ed. Edwin M. Yamauchi and Marvin R. Wilson, 4 vols. (Peabody, MA: Hendrickson, 2014–2016), 1:27.

69. Myriam Seco Álvarez, "Preliminary Study of XIth Dynasty Necropolis Located Northeast of the Temple of Millions of Years of Thutmose III," *Twelfth International Congress of Egyptologists, 3rd–8th November 2019, Cairo, Egypt: Book of Abstracts* (Cairo: MoA, 2019), 4.

as long life spans. The former is "the normal limit of human life, and only a few individuals would live to see their seventieth birthday," A. A. Anderson observes, and only in "exceptional cases a man might reach the age of eighty."[70] In Stripling's view Moses married when most men would be approaching death, and he lived approximately three times longer than the average individual of his day.

2. Because of short life expectancy, marriage occurred typically in the early to mid teens. In Egypt "girls were married at between twelve and fourteen," and boys "between fourteen and twenty."[71] The Instruction of Ankhseshonqy advises men to "take a wife when you are twenty years old, that you may have a son while you are young."[72] According to the Torah, men could be conscripted into the military from age twenty (Num 1:3), with the expectation that the soldier would already be married (Deut 20:7). Under normal circumstances, then, a man would marry and have a child by age twenty, and therefore be a grandfather around age forty. Could it be that forty years represents the approximate time from one's birth to the birth of one's grandchild? By this reckoning, at age forty when Moses fled to Midian, he already should have been a grandfather.

According to Stripling's reconstruction, forty years after Moses arrived in Midian and married Zipporah, he returned to Egypt at eighty.[73] Exodus 4:20 reports that "Moses took his wife and *sons*, put them on a donkey and started back to Egypt" (emphasis mine). It is hard to imagine Zipporah, Gershom, and Eliezer (likely aged thirty-eight and thirty-six at this time) all riding on a donkey together! The fact that Moses' boys ride demonstrates that they were young. Houtman notes the obvious: "One gets the impression that Moses' child(ren) was (were) still small at the time of his return."[74] The Beni Hasan scene of traveling Asiatics shows two toddlers riding a donkey, while all other travelers walk, including a prepubescent lad.[75] Clearly, the forty-year sojourn in Midian does not fit the details of the narrative.

---

70. A. A. Anderson, *The Book of Psalms* (London: Marshal, Morgan & Scott, 1972), 2:653.

71. Yamauchi, "Age and the Aged," 3:230.

72. "The Instruction of Ankhseshonqy," in Miriam Lichtheim, *Ancient Egyptian Literature* (Berkeley: Univ. of Californian Press, 1980), 3:168.

73. Exodus 7:7 identifies Moses as eighty years old when he confronted Pharaoh.

74. Cornelis Houtman, *Exodus*, HCOT (Kampen: Kok, 1993), 1:427.

75. Percy E. Newberry, *Beni Hasan* I (London: Egypt Exploration Fund, 1893), xxx–xxxi.

Stripling then takes this literal forty-year period a step farther. He opines, "As previously mentioned, Exod 2:23 specifies that the pharaoh from whom Moses fled prior to his forty years in Midian had a long reign, which matches Thutmose III." He consequently claims that Ramesses II can't be the exodus pharaoh, since his predecessor, Seti I, reigned only fifteen years. Exodus 2:23 does *not* specify forty years, rather "during that long period" (lit. "in those many days"), as Stripling contends.

From the standpoint of Egyptian history and chronology, this reconstruction of Moses' life is seriously flawed. The first 20/21 years of Thutmose III's 54 year reign (1479–1425), Hatshepsut (his aunt) was *de facto* ruler because at his accession Thutmose was "a very young child or even 'a nursling'."[76] Accordingly, Hatshepsut might be Moses' antagonist from whom he fled during her first 13/14 years only to return 40 years later when Thutmose III died in year 54.[77]

If the exodus occurred in 1446, forty years earlier falls around 1487 and the pharaoh was Thutmose II (1492–1479 BC, according to the Low chronology), who barely left a mark on the Egyptian landscape. Betsy Bryan observes, "The nearly ephemeral nature of Thutmose II's rule is underlined by the paucity of his monuments in general, and their absence in the north of Egypt."[78] How could Thutmose II, who is not credited with any major building projects in the delta, be the pharaoh of the oppression?

Moreover, Stripling clings to the High chronology, in which Thutmose III reigned from 1504–1450 BC, and Amenhotep II from 1452–1425 BC. During the 1980s–1990s a series of conferences on absolute chronology led most Egyptologists to favor the lower dates for New Kingdom.[79] Accordingly, Thutmose III's reign is 1479–1425 BC, and

---

76. David O'Connor, "Thutmose III: An Enigmatic Pharaoh," in *Thutmose III: A New Biography*, ed. Eric H. Cline and David O'Connor (Ann Arbor: Univ. of Michigan Press, 2006), 21.

77. If Moses fled early in Thutmose III's independent reign (ca. 1458–1425), it lasted only thirty-three years.

78. Betsy M. Bryan, "The 18th Dynasty before the Amarna Period," in *The Oxford History of Ancient Egypt*, ed. Ian Shaw (Oxford: Oxford Univ. Press, 2000), 226. Since Bryan wrote this, inscribed limestone blocks from a temple of Thutmose II have been uncovered at Tell Heboua in north Sinai (Mohamed Abd el-Maksoud and Dominique Valbelle, "Tell Hébuoua II," *RdÉ* 62 [2011]: 13–15).

79. Paul Aström, ed., *High Middle or Low: Acts of an International Colloquium on Absolute Chronology Held at the University of Gothenburg, 20th–22nd August 1987*, 3 vols. (Gothenburg: Paul Aströms, 1987–1998); Manfred Bietak, ed., *The Synchronisation of Civilisations in the Eastern Mediterranean in the Second Millennium B.C. I: Proceedings of an International*

Amenhotep II's is 1427–1400 BC. Suddenly, Stripling's dating scenario falls apart because 1446 lands in the reign of Hatshepsut/Thutmose III, and the previous ruler, Thutmose II (the pharaoh from whom Moses supposedly fled) reigned but thirteen years, not forty years.

In addition, 1446 falls on or around Thutmose III's regnal year 31. Years 29–31 saw Thutmose III and his armies advancing north to take control of the Syrian coast in order to attack inland Qadesh in year 33.[80] Nothing in these records suggests that Egypt had experienced a major military setback at home as described in the book of Exodus. It is inconceivable that the trauma of the exodus on Egypt in 1446 could be followed a year later by one of Thutmose's greatest military triumphs in north Syria!

What should we do with the 480 figure, the foundation of the early exodus date? One scenario is to reckon this as 12 × 40, twelve generations. I have argued that forty represents the time from the birth of a man to his grandson. Hence twelve generations may not be intended in 480. Alternatively, I have suggested that the 480 is what Assyriologists call a *Distanzangabe*, which Julian Reade describes as "an approximation relating to the distant past."[81] Assyrian rulers cite large numbers, like 720 years between the founding of a temple or temple renovations and some important past event. One such case is from the reign of Tukulti-Ninurta, who declared that 720 years stood between the building of the Ishtar Temple in Assur by Ilushumma and Tukulti-Ninurta's rebuild. Reade doubts that the 720 years should be taken literally, suggesting it likely represents "an approximation relating to the distant past" and that 720 derives from "12 times 60" (sixty is a special number in Sumerian).[82]

Similarly, the 400-Year Stela of Ramesses II apparently commemorated the dedication of the Temple of Baal/Seth and the restoration of the cult by Ramesses.[83] I stand by my earlier proposal: "Could it be

---

Symposium at Schloss Haindorf, 15th–17th of November 1996, and at the Austrian Academy, Vienna, 11th–12th of May 1998, Contributions to the Chronology of the Eastern Mediterranean 1 (Wien: Österreichischen Akademie der Wissenschaften, 2000).

80. Donald B. Redford, *The Wars in Syria and Palestine of Thutmose III*, CHANE 16 (Leiden: Brill, 2003), 217–28.

81. For a complete discussion of this, see Hoffmeier, "What Is the Biblical Date for the Exodus?" 237–38.

82. S. N. Kramer, *The Sumerians: Their History, Culture, and Character* (Chicago: Univ. of Chicago Press, 1963), 91–92.

83. Pierre Montet, "La stèle de l'an 400 retrouvée," *Kêmi* 4 (1933): 191–215; Labib Habachi, "The Four Hundred Year Stela Originally Standing in Khatâ'na-Qantir or

that the 480 years of 1 Kgs 6:1 is an Israelite *Distanzangabe*? If so, its purpose was not to provide a historical datum per se but rather to create a link between the building of Israel's temple and the event that led to YHWH becoming the God of Israel."[84]

A Final Chronological Note

Stripling believes that Heman's genealogy in 1 Chr 6:33–37 supports the 1446 exodus date. Since Heman was a contemporary of David, the nineteen generations back to Korah (left Egypt at the exodus) would equate to 25 × 19 = 475, and when this is added to Solomon's third year of 967 BC, you arrive at the year 1442, which is close to 1446. However, since Korah was an adult at the exodus (cf. Num 16), only eighteen generations should be counted. As I have argued earlier, fatherhood began around or before age twenty, which is 18 × 20 = 360 and places you around 1327 BC. Further, if you multiply eighteen generations at an eighteen-year average, a date of 1291 BC results. Or if a seventeen-year average is used to calculate, 1273 is the date (Ramesses II reigned 1279–1213). Obviously, one can play with the numbers and get a date to suit one's chronology.

Two Egyptological Notes

First, Stripling cites the questionable, broken hieroglyphic text from the Berlin Museum that purportedly contains the name Israel to support the early date. The text's date is in dispute, ranging from the time of Amenhotep III (1390–1353) to the time of Ramesses II (1279–1213). He naturally favors the earlier dating. I welcome any new evidence for early Israel and am willing to revise my dating of the exodus and the arrival of Israel in Canaan if the evidence is clear and compelling. In this case neither the reading and linguistic correspondence nor the dating are certain. The critical word in this inscription is only partially preserved, and the proposed reading does not correspond to the writing of "Israel" as found in the Merenptah Stela. To read "Israel" requires bending the standard rules for reading Semitic words in Egyptian, and there

---

Avaris-Piramesse," in *Actes du XXIXe Congrès international des Orientalistes, Égyptologie*, ed. Georges Posener (Paris: Asiathèque, 1975), 1:41–44.

84. Hoffmeier, "What Is the Biblical Date for the Exodus?" 239.

are a number of possible readings for the geographical term, including "Ilshalir," "Ilsharil," "Irshalir," "Irsharil," and "Irshalil," but not "Israel."[85]

I was able to study images of the inscription with Kenneth Kitchen in his home in Woolton some years ago, and he concurred that Israel was not a credible reading. Before his death in 2012, I was able to have a conversation with Manfred Görg about his reading "Israel" in this text.[86] He admitted that the reading "Israel" was a very tentative proposal. Esteemed Egyptologist Robert Ritner does not support this reading either.[87] The Berlin pedestal cannot be read as "Israel" with any certainty. Its dating remains debated and should not be used to date the exodus.

Second, Stripling claims that the occurrence of Israel in the Merenptah Stela, dating to ca. 1208 BC, is too close to the proposed thirteenth-century exodus; the forty years in the wilderness and commencing the conquest/settlement "does not allow adequate time for the development and recognition of national Israel at the end of the same century." This is a baseless assertion. An exodus during the early decades of Ramesses II's sixty-seven-year reign, 1270–1250 BC, minus forty years in the wilderness (even if a rounded off figure) places the entry into Canaan between 1230 and 1210. Even limited military action in Egypt's vassal state would have caught Pharaoh's attention and may even have contributed to the timing of Merenptah's campaign. By Stripling's reckoning, the Israelites were in Canaan for two centuries, attacking cities like Gezer, Lachish, and Hazor, but received no response from Egypt until Merenptah's day. That is hard to believe, unless the Israelites recently arrived in Canaan in the later thirteenth century.

---

85. Hoffmeier, "What Is the Biblical Date for the Exodus?" 240–42.

86. Görg, "Israel in Hieroglyphen," 21–27.

87. Robert Ritner, "The Supposed Earliest Hieroglyphic Mention of Israel (Berlin AM 21687): A Refutation," in *Semitic, Biblical, and Jewish Studies in Honor of Richard C. Steiner*, ed. Aaron J. Koller, Mordechai Z. Cohen, and Adina Moshavi (New York: Yeshiva Univ. Press, 2020). This article is in press. I am grateful to Professor Ritner for sending me the page proofs of his article in advance of its publication.

RESPONSE TO SCOTT STRIPLING (THE THIRTEENTH-CENTURY HYKSOS/ LEVITE-LED EXODUS VIEW)

PETER FEINMAN

Stripling takes the position that a historical exodus occurred in the fifteenth century BC. He is aware that his position is at variance with the views of the other contributors to this book as well as with the views of most biblical scholars, especially those who reject a historical exodus. In his contribution Stripling takes great pains to substantiate the fifteenth-century claim both archaeologically and biblically.

There is a problem in his intentions as expressed in the final paragraph, titled "Theological Implications." He claims that the archaeological truth of a historical exodus suggests that other biblical stories also should be considered historical: they "deserve a presuppositional expectation of accuracy." In other words, the Bible is true. This truth is not simply limited to the historical act of human beings leaving Egypt but true in a theological sense. His concluding sentences reveal the truth of this contribution: "Ultimately, if the Bible is true, then the God of the Bible holds a moral claim on all of humanity. Nothing could have more far-reaching implications."

That's the problem. Consider another historical conundrum involving text and archaeology: the Trojan War as told in the *Iliad*. Suppose archaeologists proved that a war between the Mycenaeans and Trojans really did occur and in the twelfth century BC. Such a claim is hardly far-fetched. It is quite reasonable now for classical scholars to accept the historicity of such a confrontation. Does that prove anything about Zeus? If one accepts the historicity of the Trojan War, is one then obligated to accept the existence of the gods of the Mycenaeans and be guided by their moral claims?

If the American Revolution really occurred in history, does that mean the United States is a city on a hill and God's New Israel?

If the Russian Revolution really occurred in history, does that mean that the Soviet Union really was the wave of the future?

Similarly, Stripling is wrong to suggest that a 1446 BC historical exodus means "the God of the Bible holds a moral claim on all of humanity."

In my own contribution to this book, I too claim there was a historical exodus. However, I make no religious or theological conclusions based on that historicity. I am quite willing to accept that Ramesses II really did pray to his father Amun-Re at the battle of Qadesh shortly before the exodus, without accepting or even commenting on the existence of that deity or any claims that deity has on all humanity. Similarly, I am quite willing to accept that Moses prayed to the God of Israel before and during the historical exodus without it meaning that such a deity exists, chose Israel, or intervened in history. So even if Stripling and I agreed on the date, our understandings of the meaning of the historicity of the exodus are substantially different.

These differences carry over into the proof itself. Suppose archaeologists could confirm not only the historicity of the *Iliad* but also the existence of individuals like Achilles, Hector, and Agamemnon. What would that prove about their dialogue, motives, and actions? Not much. Suppose one excavated Valley Forge, Saratoga, and Yorktown and proved that there really had been a war between England and the United States. What would that prove about what the human characters who participated in the war actually said and did, and their motives? Even with voluminous correspondence and documents authentically dated to specific people on specific dates about specific events, there is still much room for debate. What exactly does the Declaration of Independence mean? Now eliminate all those texts and try to write a history of the American Revolution based on the archaeology alone.

In response you may say we have the equivalent texts from the exodus; we have the biblical texts. Stripling is aware of this problem. He writes, "The Pentateuch is clearly of ancient origin." He cites some examples from the eighth century BC to suggest that a biblical account of the exodus is much older. That still leaves centuries between the fifteenth-century date and the earliest Israelite writing about the foundational event of their own history. By contrast, I subscribe to the view that the Song of the Sea, among other brief writings and names, originated as part of the thirteenth-century BC exodus. Israel did not exist in silence for centuries after its creation in the midst of a world that had writing and songs.

Turning to the biblical evidence, Stripling places great emphasis on 1 Kgs 6:1 to calculate his historical exodus in 1446 BC. Other contributors to this book have raised questions regarding this supposition in their own original contributions even before the responses. They apparently anticipated the citation of this verse and launched a preemptive strike. Therefore there is no need for me to repeat here what they already have said.

I do wish to elaborate on two points raised in Rendsburg's contribution. He notes that Babylonian king Nabonidus in the sixth century BC claimed that an Akkadian named Naram-Sin ruled 3,200 years earlier. This archaeologically authentic text from the sixth century postulates a date based on the formula of 40 years × 8 × 10 periods. The number forty will be familiar to biblical readers and from the Mesha Stela, which Rendsburg does not cite. The point here is not to attempt to understand what these and similar numbers in other texts meant to the Babylonians or Moabites or Egyptians; instead it is to recognize that numbers convey nonliteral messages. Regardless of what the precise message was, it was not a literal message. It was not a literal message in Moab. It was not a literal message in Babylon. It was not a literal message in Egypt. And it was not a literal message in Israel. The recognition that 1 Kgs 6:1 should not be taken as a literal number invalidates the basis of Stripling's approach. He starts with an inappropriate interpretation of the biblical text to determine his date of the exodus and then turns to the archaeology to prove it.

There are additional issues with the dating. How exactly did Israel maintain such a detailed and precise chronological measurement for all those years? If the Egyptian and Mesopotamian states, with their vast bureaucracies, employed round numbers that delivered messages, and little Moab did too, the likelihood is that Israel did. Furthermore, the biblical texts have an extensive chronological framework. How does this date fit within the larger scope? One might think that its placement is part of a larger message. Did a biblical writer seek to proclaim that not only was the temple in Jerusalem the cosmic geographic center but its creation also was at the cosmic chronological center? Stripling extracts a verse from the Bible without providing any context or explanation for it.

The same considerations apply to Stripling's use of Judg 11:26. I agree with him that Jephthah is a historical figure. I also agree that 1100 BC is a reasonable date for him. I disagree with the implication that the story dates to the same time. I disagree that the writer of this verse had any access to the words historical Jephthah spoke, just as Homer did not have access to the words of any of the figures in the *Iliad*. His judgment may also be questioned.

The three hundred years cited in this verse also is likely to have been a symbolic figure delivering a message, even if we can't quite decipher it. In a separate publication on time, I focused on the number forty.[88] I noted in passing the usage of numbers based on three (thirty, three hundred) without offering any explanation for it. In Rendsburg's contribution to this book, he suggests that the average generation may have been thirty years. Typically, scholars consider twenty-five years to be the biological generation and, perhaps, forty to be the symbolic duration. Rendsburg's observations raise the possibility that perhaps different writers employed different numerical schemes, one based on three and the other based on four. I don't know if this is so, but in reading these contributions, I think it is an idea worth exploring. The point here is that Stripling simply accepts numbers on face value as literally true. While that may be valid for an economic document when someone is buying sheep or goats, it does not seem to be accurate in the official narratives in the ancient Near East. And I haven't even mentioned the issue of body counts!

Another historical question concerning the fifteenth-century BC date for a historical exodus is, where's Israel? Where is Israel prior to Ramesses II and the thirteenth-century BC exodus? Stripling is aware of this issue. He attempts to fill the gap by citing the work of Douglas Petrovich on early alphabet inscriptions, including "three of which purport to document the exodus and associated people and events."

88. Peter Feinman, "The Hyksos and the Exodus: Two 400-Year Stories," in *What Difference Does Time Make?* ed. Richard Beal and JoAnn Scurlock (Oxford: Archaeopress, 2019), 136–51.

"Purport" is not the strongest of affirmations available to use. This uncertainty is reinforced farther on when Stripling writes, "If Petrovich is correct . . ." Stripling is aware that Petrovich's interpretations have not met with wide acceptance. I suspect it is limited to those who already accept a fifteenth-century BC date for the exodus and are wrestling with the challenge of filling the gap.

It isn't as if there were no Egyptian records during this period from 1446 BC to the documented appearance of Israel in the Merenptah Stela ca. 1207 BC. No pharaoh mentioned Israel during this time despite the various campaigns to Canaan with their lists? Instead Israel is mentioned precisely when one would expect it to be identified by name: after its creation in the time of Ramesses II.

As for the Habiru/Hebrew connection, the best that can be said is that it is one of the great false leads in biblical scholarship. Stripling presents the Habiru as "nomadic marauders in the Late Bronze Age." They are better described as displaced people who at times served as warriors or mercenaries. There is no archaeological connection between the biblical Hebrews and the archaeological Habiru. The basis for the purported connection is the need to find Israel in history prior to Ramesses II.

Stripling is right to mention the Shasu and their god Yhw. These intriguing people and deity are a necessary part of the attempt to reconstruct the historical context in which Israel emerged. However, one should not overstate the case. Stripling's comment that "Yhw is broadly understood to refer to Yahweh, the God of the Israelites" is slightly deceptive. Yes, Yhw is broadly understood to refer to Yahweh. The questions then to be raised are, first, how Israel, a people named after El, became connected with that word, and second, how that Shasu deity Yhw became defined as the deity who led Israel out of Egypt. Stripling states that the "Bible refers to the nomads or seminomads in fourteenth-century Palestine who worship Yahweh as Hebrews or Israelites" but provides no verses to substantiate this assertion. I lean toward the Midianite or Kenite hypotheses. In this scenario Moses allies with anti-Egyptian nomads. He then redefines the Shasu deity into an Israelite one who acts in history in what becomes the exodus. Regardless of whether one accepts my view, more is needed than Stripling provides to explain how Israel shared a deity name with the Shasu.

These ruminations lead to my last point. At some point a historical exodus in 1446 BC requires real human beings to have decided to act against Pharaoh, the mightiest human in their known world. There is no such consideration in Stripling's contribution. The implicit assumption that the biblical text provides the explanation for the human motivations should be made explicit and justified. The issue of "where is the man Moses?" arises with other contributors as well and will be elaborated on in my final comments.

RESPONSE TO SCOTT STRIPLING
(THE TWELFTH-CENTURY EXODUS VIEW)

GARY A. RENDSBURG

My preference throughout my academic career has been simply to state the facts and provide my own interpretation, without necessarily critiquing the views of other scholars. In the present instance, however, the editors of this volume have requested dialogue between and among the five contributors, and thus perforce I must depart from my normal practice and offer some criticisms.

I begin with the attempt by Scott Stripling to assign a fifteenth-century date to the exodus, which suffers in the extreme on several fronts.

1. First and foremost is the author's desire to accept the literalness of the 480-year figure which appears in 1 Kgs 6:1. Such a blithe acceptance, however, flies in the face of all that we know about biblical narrative style and parallel writings from the ancient Near East. I explain this clearly in my essay, and I repeat that information here (without the footnotes).

> The use of round numbers, especially multiples of forty, and exaggerated ones, is characteristic of the epic tradition. Examples include God's words to Abram that his ancestors would be strangers in a foreign land for four hundred years (Gen 15:13), the forty years of wandering (Deut 29:5), Moses' age of 80 at his first appearance before Pharaoh (Exod 7:7), his death at the age of 120 (Deut 34:7), the various instances of forty and eighty in the book of Judges (3:11, 30; 5:31), and the forty-year reigns of both David and Solomon (2 Sam 5:4; 1 Kgs 11:42).
>
> This same use of exaggerated numbers using multiples of forty is attested in both Egyptian and Akkadian literature.

> For the former, note the 400-Year Stela found at Tanis, dated to ca. 1300 BCE, even if we cannot be sure about the specific anniversary commemorated. For the latter, note that Nabonidus, king of Babylon (r. 556–539 BCE), asserted that Naram-Sin, king of Akkad (r. ca. 2254–ca. 2218 BCE) ruled 3,200 years earlier, when we know that the distance separating the two rulers is actually ca. 1,700 years.
>
> All of this is simply to say that no historical reconstruction should be based on the 480-year time span mentioned in 1 Kgs 6:1. Over time, and especially during the period of the kingdoms of Israel and Judah, accurate records were kept by royal chancelleries, so that the years provided in the canonical book of Kings (at least from 1 Kgs 12 onward), which in turn derive from the annals of the kings of Israel (1 Kgs 14:19) and the annals of the kings of Judah (1 Kgs 14:29), are most reliable. However, this same accuracy does not apply to the round, exaggerated numbers used in the early biblical tradition.

If Stripling wishes to accept the 480-year figure of 1 Kgs 6:1, then heuristically and methodologically, he also should be willing to accept the 3,200-year figure declaimed by Nabonidus, even though we know that such is an impossibility (see my essay for details). On this particular issue, if not more broadly, the historian should approach the biblical text and an ancient Near Eastern historiographic text in the same manner. I, for one, do so by recognizing the round and inflated numbers used in both of these passages.

2. Stripling relies on the genealogies in the book of Chronicles, for example, by noting the eighteen generations which span Heman and Korah in 1 Chr 6:33–37, thereby positing a similar distance between David and Solomon (with whom Heman is contemporary) and Moses (with whom Korah is contemporary). But why privilege this genealogy and ignore David's own genealogy? As I observe, David is only five generations removed from his ancestor Nahshon (Ruth 4:20–22), who is a member of the exodus-and-wilderness generation as the brother-in-law of Aaron (Exod 6:23). As I further observe, comparative evidence, especially in light of the worldwide study conducted by David Henige, informs us that lineage lengthening is much more common than lineage

telescoping. We have every reason to assume that David's genealogy is accurate and that Heman's has been artificially lengthened. As I demonstrate, this is certainly the case for two other individuals—Samuel and Zadok—for whom the Chronicler needed to invent Levite genealogies; one will assume the same for Heman.

3. A minor point: Stripling refers to the date indicated in Ezek 40:1 as "Rosh Hashanah (New Year's Day)," perhaps implying that the passage denotes the later Jewish holiday known by this name. It does not: note that while the Torah indicates month 7, day 1, as a festival day (Lev 23:24–25; Num 29:1), its significance is not indicated. To be sure, it does not gain the name Rosh Hashanah until the Mishnah, ca. 200 CE (m. R.H.. 1:1). More crucial, Ezek 40:1 refers to the tenth day of the new year, which would be month 1 (not month 7), day 10.[89]

4. Using *Seder Olam*, a later rabbinic text, to reconstruct the chronology of the biblical period constitutes a risky business and sends one down a very slippery slope. Most glaring is the compression of the entire Persian period in this rabbinic source to fifty-two (!) years,[90] when it is in fact approximately two hundred years (538–330 BCE).

5. There is no evidence to connect Sobekemḥat, a vizier who served Sesostris II and Sesostris III during the Twelfth Dynasty, with Joseph. Ditto for Di-Sobekemḥat, a ruler of Retjenu (~ Canaan) during this same period, with Ephraim. Full stop. The same holds for the reading of Asenath in Sinai 376 and the association with Asenath in the Bible.

6. Moreover, even if one were to accept the aforementioned identifications, Stripling trips himself up on internal grounds: how can Joseph be a vizier to Twelfth Dynasty pharaohs and Asenath be mentioned in a Thirteenth Dynasty text one century later?

7. There is no reason to assume that the people denoted by the term 'the land of the Shasu of Yhw' in the Soleb Inscription are to be located in the land of Canaan. More likely, as I have argued, they were denizens of the great Southland, stretching across Sinai, modern-day southern Israel, and modern-day southern Jordan. Note the collocation of 'the land of the Shasu of Yhw' and 'the land of the Shasu of Se'ir' in

89. See the extended discussion in Jacob Milgrom and Daniel I. Block, *Ezekiel's Hope: A Commentary on Ezekiel 38–48* (Eugene, OR: Cascade, 2012), 60–63.

90. H. L. Strack and Günter Stemberger, *Introduction to the Talmud and Midrash*, 2nd ed. (Minneapolis: Fortress, 1996), 326.

both the Soleb and Amara Inscriptions, suggesting the general area of the Southland.[91]

See my chapter herein for further elucidation.

8. It is rather staggering that Stripling could devote several pages to the Mount Ebal altar and not cite the standard work on the subject, to wit, Ralph K. Hawkins, *The Iron Age I Structure on Mt. Ebal*.[92] Hawkins strongly supports Zertal's interpretation of the data, including the founding of the site ca. 1250 BCE, based especially on the pottery analysis. Stripling would have us believe that the site was founded several centuries earlier, in order to accommodate his early-dating scheme, but his arguments require special pleading. His sole piece of evidence is the Egyptian scarab found at the site, bearing the name of Thutmose III (r. 1479–1425 BCE). But with no other evidence pointing to the fifteenth century (especially the pottery!), one will conclude (with Hawkins and others) that the scarab either was a trinket or heirloom of some sort, still in someone's possession two centuries later, or had been manufactured in the thirteenth century for its protective qualities.[93] Parallels to these phenomena are well known, including the presence of scarabs bearing the name of Thutmose III on mummies dated to the second century CE (!), sixteen centuries after this pharaoh lived.[94]

9. The most telling statement in Stripling's chapter is the following: "The theory now drives interpretation" (within the context of the Mount Ebal altar discussion). While he uses these words to counter the argument of another scholar, in truth they are much more applicable to his own attempt to argue for a fifteenth-century date for the exodus.

10. On *ʾălāpîm*, see the series of articles on the subject in *Vetus Testamentum* published during the years 1995–2001 by E. W. Davies, Jacob Milgrom, Mark McEntire, Colin Humphreys, and the present

91. See further Gary A. Rendsburg, "Israelite Origins," in *"An Excellent Fortress for His Armies, a Refuge for the People": Egyptological, Archaeological, and Biblical Studies in Honor of James K. Hoffmeier*, ed. Richard E. Averbeck and K. Lawson Younger (University Park, PA: Eisenbrauns, 2020), 327–39, esp. 328.

92. Ralph K. Hawkins, *The Iron Age I Structure on Mt. Ebal: Excavation and Interpretation*, BBRSup 6 (Winona Lake, IN: Eisenbrauns, 2012).

93. I am grateful to Ralph Hawkins (Averett University) for an email exchange (April 2020) in which we discussed these issues further.

94. Hawkins, *The Iron Age I Structure on Mt. Ebal*, 66–67 (with the specifics of the scarab discussed on pp. 68–71). For the primary work, see Baruch Brandl, "Two Scarabs and a Trapezoidal Seal from Mount Ebal," *TA* 13–14 (1986–1987): 166–72, plate 20.

writer.[95] Their omission is curious, even though in the main the consensus among said scholars (see especially Humphreys) supports Stripling's analysis of *'elep* in the census figures in Num 1 and 26 connoting "platoon, fighting unit," and not literally "thousand."

11. It is most unusual to interject one's own personal beliefs into academic writing, to wit: "Ultimately, if the Bible is true, then the God of the Bible holds a moral claim on all of humanity" (penultimate sentence of the essay). I doubt that Muslims, Hindus, Buddhists, and others would accede to this audacious privileging of one sacred text for all of humanity.

In sum, Stripling's attempt to date the exodus to the fifteenth century has nothing to commend it. The author is not au courant on the scholarly literature; he does not seem to understand the basic workings of Biblical Hebrew language and literary style; he picks and chooses data points as he likes, without a critical eye; and most crucial, the approach suffers in the extreme from special pleading.

95. My contribution is Gary A. Rendsburg, "An Additional Note to Two Recent Articles on the Number of People in the Exodus from Egypt and the Large Numbers in Numbers i and xxvi," *VT* 51 (2001): 392–96, with citations of the articles by the other authors just mentioned.

RESPONSE TO SCOTT STRIPLING
(THE EXODUS AS CULTURAL MEMORY VIEW)

RONALD HENDEL

I'm pleased to be invited to this dialogue, but I confess to being an outsider. As a scholar in a secular research university (Berkeley) and as a Jew (Reform), I'm doubly outside the world of evangelical scholarship. My remarks should be taken with some allowance for this difference of perspective. I begin not with a commitment to biblical inerrancy but with a commitment to thinking hard about complicated issues and evidence, no matter where it might lead me. I call this academic freedom, but some evangelical critics call this academic license (to do harm). Anyway, my criticisms—and there are many—are rooted in my approach to scholarly inquiry.

Scott Stripling's essay begins with a methodological commitment to biblical inerrancy. The Bible, he writes, "should be read as a historically reliable account." Then he adds, "Though the biblical evidence seems clear, it must also be considered in light of the archaeological evidence." I'm not sure why this must be so. If the Bible is historically reliable, getting into the details of the archaeological evidence might just complicate or muddy the picture. If the Bible is inerrant, I don't see why this step should be necessary. Maybe he wants to defend the Bible's reliability for the benefit of non-inerrantists, but then he shouldn't start with a commitment to inerrancy. In any case, as Striping points out, there is also the problem of sorting out false or deceptive claims regarding the archaeological evidence. He writes, "Pseudoarchaeology complicates the issue and confuses the general public." At least some of Stripling's examples are best described by his term "pseudoarchaeology." His other examples are either dubious or irrelevant to the question of the date and historicity of the exodus.

I will address some cases in his section titled "Extrabiblical Evidence for an Early Exodus," setting aside the ones having to do with dates based on pottery or carbon dating, with which I have no expertise. My conclusion is that none of these cases provide any support for a fifteenth-century date of the exodus.

Josephus and Manetho

In Josephus's excerpts from Manetho, a third-century BCE Egyptian priest, we have an account of a King Amenophis who had a namesake advisor, also Amenophis, who was a wise prophet. This prophet advised the king to enslave the lepers of Egypt, but the lepers eventually revolted and ruled Egypt for thirteen years. The ruling lepers turned the laws of Egypt upside down and abolished the worship of the gods. King Amenophis finally gathered an army and defeated the lepers and their allies, the Hyksos, and drove them out of Egypt to Syria. Egyptologists generally agree that this account reflects a memory of the traumatic rule of Amenhotep IV, who renamed himself Akhenaten and abolished the worship of the other Egyptian gods. In Manetho's account the traumatic rule of this Amenophis is mingled with the earlier traumatic memory of the Hyksos dynasty, who were of West Semitic heritage. As the Egyptologist Donald Redford observes, "The devotees of Akhenaten's sun cult are the historical reality underlying the 'lepers,' and this is confirmed by the iconoclastic nature of the lepers' legislation and the figure of thirteen years for the occupation, which corresponds to the period of occupation of Amarna [the capital city established by Akhenaten]."[96] Manetho identifies the leader of the lepers with Moses, so there is also some mingling with the story of the exodus. But the role of Amenophis is rooted in the cultural memory of the heresy of Amenhotep IV (contrasted in the story with his "good" father, Amenophis III). In sum, the standard interpretation of Manetho's account does not provide any support for Stripling's view that Amenhotep II was the pharaoh of the exodus.

---

96. Donald B. Redford, *Egypt, Canaan, and Israel in Ancient Times* (Princeton: Princeton Univ. Press, 1992), 415; Jan Assmann, *Moses the Egyptian: The Memory of Egypt in Western Monotheism* (Cambridge: Harvard Univ. Press, 1997), 29–34. This interpretation was first proposed by Eduard Meyer in 1904.

Tell el-Dab'a

Stripling says, "Bietak's stratigraphic analysis reveals a clear abandonment in the mid-Eighteenth Dynasty, during or after the reign of Amenhotep II." This is not so. Bietak states that the abandonment of Tell el-Dab'a occurred around 1530 BCE, because of the conquest of Ahmose, who defeated the Hyksos and founded the Eighteenth Dynasty.[97] This is nearly a century before Stripling's date for the exodus. This case is irrelevant to his early date.

Serabit el-Khadim and Wadi Nasb

Stripling cites Douglas Petrovich's readings of three proto-Sinaitic inscriptions to prove his case. In these three early alphabetic texts, Petrovich reads the personal names "Moses," "Ahisamach," and "Asenath." Stripling concludes that in these texts we have "the only contemporary extrabiblical reference to the historical Moses" and important testimony for "the exodus and associated people and events." But he adds a caveat: "If Petrovich's reading stands." The problem is that Petrovich's readings do not stand. As Christopher Rollston, an expert in inscriptions (and an evangelical scholar), says about these biblical names, "They are simply not there." Another evangelical scholar and expert in inscriptions, Alan Millard, says that Petrovich's claims are "irresponsible."[98]

Stripling reproduces Petrovich's drawing of Sinai 375a to prove his case. Here is a more reliable drawing, made by Gordon Hamilton from photographs by the West Semitic Research Project.[99]

---

97. Manfred Bietak, "From Where Came the Hyksos and Where Did They Go?" in *The Second Intermediate Period (Thirteenth–Seventeenth Dynasties): Current Research, Future Prospects*, ed. Marcel Marée, OLA 192 (Leuven: Peeters, 2010), 139–81.

98. Christopher A. Rollston, "The Proto-Sinaitic Inscriptions 2.0: Canaanite Language and Canaanite Script, Not Hebrew," www.rollstonepigraphy.com/?p=779; Alan R. Millard, "A Response to Douglas Petrovich's 'Hebrew as the Language behind the World's First Alphabet?'" *The Ancient Near East Today* 5 (2017), www.asor.org/anetoday/2017/04/response-petrovich.

99. Gordon J. Hamilton, *The Origins of the West Semitic Alphabet in Egyptian Scripts*, CBQMS 40 (Washington, DC: Catholic Biblical Association, 2006), 374, fig. A.43.

Courtesy of G. J. Hamilton

Sinai 375a drawing by Gordon Hamilton

Some of the letters that Petrovich claims to see in this inscription are not there (the first, third, and fifth letters of "Ahisamach"). Moreover, Petrovich connects letters from different lines to find his biblical names. David Falk (another evangelical scholar) sums up the problem in a recent review of Petrovich's book: "The translations are based upon an inadequate methodology, a doubtful epigraphy, and a poor understanding of ancient languages."[100] Unfortunately, this is an example of the pseudoarchaeology that Stripling warns about.

Amarna Tablets and Soleb Hieroglyph

These texts are important but irrelevant for the historicity or date of the exodus. The Habiru mentioned in the Amarna letters are rebels in the

100. David A. Falk, review of Petrovich, *The World's Oldest Alphabet: Hebrew as the Language of the Proto-Consonantal Script*, in *RBL* 10 (2018), www.bookreviews.org/pdf/12623_14068.pdf.

countryside (not exactly "nomadic marauders," but close). It is possible that some of them later became Hebrews, but this process sheds no direct light on the exodus. Similarly, the Soleb Inscription mentions the Shasu of Yhw. Yhw is probably a place-name.[101] This place-name may have something to do with the prehistory of the Israelite god YHWH, but the implications are unclear. (Does it have to do with the biblical memory of the Midianite worship of Yahweh? Maybe.) But Stripling's claim that "the group to which this inscription refers are the Israelites who are in Canaan just one generation after the early date places them there" is simply inaccurate. These are Shasu nomads, not Israelites, and they are in the region of Edom, not Israel.

Berlin Pedestal

Manfred Görg and some of his colleagues argue that one of the names on the Berlin Pedestal relief is "Israel." This is possible, since the other two names are "Canaan" and "Ashkelon." But other Egyptologists maintain that this reading is unlikely. James Hoffmeier points out that the sibilant is wrong—it's *š*, not *ś*—and some of the other letters are also unlikely to correspond to "Israel." He says there are several options for this place-name, "but none are Israel."[102] Stripling qualifies the relevance of this text with the caveat "If Görg's reading withstands scrutiny." It doesn't seem to. This too is a weak reed.

As my brief survey shows, Stripling has collected some interesting examples, but none of them helps his case. His use of these examples does not hold up to scrutiny. It seems to me that the case for the early exodus is based solely on one's convictions about biblical inerrancy. As Stripling's examples show, the attempt to find confirming evidence in the archaeological evidence is fruitless. As Gertrude Stein once wrote (about her childhood home of Oakland, which is nowadays more lively), "There is no there there."

---

101. Editor's note: The significance of the use of the proper name Yhw in this inscription is still debated. Hendel's mention of the word *probably* reflects this.

102. Hoffmeier, "What Is the Biblical Date for the Exodus?" 241–42.

REJOINDER

SCOTT STRIPLING

I appreciate the responses of my colleagues and found a number of helpful suggestions among their comments. Multiple authors raised similar issues, so I will attempt to clarify my position on these issues. I also will correct a few errors in their work.

Clarifications

Three authors expressed concerns that I take the Bible as a serious historical document and do not bifurcate my faith from my research. I wrote candidly about my presuppositions, but any implication that these presuppositions compromise my ability to evaluate literary and archaeological data dispassionately is incorrect, as Hoffmeier's response to Hendel's chapter later in this volume demonstrates. Hoffmeier's response demonstrates Hendel's longstanding bias against evangelicals engaging in scholastic debate.

My literal reading of 1 Kgs 6:1 bothers Hoffmeier, Feinman, and Rendsburg, who all believe that 480 should be taken figuratively. Hoffmeier suggests that 480 may be "what Assyriologists call a *Distanzangabe*" (57), an approximation of a previous period of time. However, the writer of 1 Kings carefully recorded historical events. The building of Solomon's Temple commenced in the 480th year after the exodus. He even provided the month. In other words, 479 years had passed, and the 480th (ordinal number) year had begun. Discussions of a *Distanzangabe* are quite unnecessary. The number of years in question is 479, not 480 (cardinal number). I do not hyperbolize the 480th year mentioned in 1 Kgs 6:1 because the exodus date that it yields (1446 BC) synchronizes with other biblical passages and archaeological evidences. Rendsburg stresses how such supposed round numbers functioned in the ancient Near East. If the author of 1 Kings intended the number to be understood metaphorically, he would not have undermined his own purpose by clearly documenting that only 479 years (and some months) had elapsed.

Feinman asks the following: "How exactly did Israel maintain such a detailed and precise chronological measurement for all those years?" (62). This question deserves an answer. There were two such methods: the use of the exodus era benchmark and the Jubilee/Sabbatical Year cycles. The exodus from Egypt marked the start of a new era for the Hebrew nation.

In Exod 12:2 the Lord told Moses, "This month is to be for you the first month, the first month of your year." What happened just one month later shows that the departure from Egypt launched a new calendar for Israel. Exodus 16:1 indicates that the people came to the Wilderness of Sin "on the fifteenth day of the second month after they had *come out [leṣēʾtām]* of Egypt" (emphasis mine). Passages like this one demonstrate that Israel used an exodus era calendar to mark the passage of time for events. The writer of the Pentateuch repeatedly alludes to the calendar's anchor date by mentioning an event's month, day, and year in association with a temporal expression like "after they had come out of Egypt" (Exod 16:1; 19:1; Num 1:1; 9:1; 33:38). That expression is implicit in Exod 40:17, Num 10:11, and Deut 1:3. Moreover, the calendar formula appears in 1 Kgs 6:1, where it functions as a literary allusion to show that 479 years had passed since the exodus; it was the 480th year of that era.

The second method of counting years is the system of Jubilee and Sabbatical cycles which Israel's priests tracked, even though the people generally ignored the stipulations such as not working their fields (Lev 25:1–7). The *Seder Olam* (ch. 11) and the Babylonian Talmud (ʿArak. 12a–b) state that Ezekiel's Jubilee was the seventeenth since the exodus. This harmonizes with Ezek 40:1, which indicates that it was both Rosh Hashanah and the tenth of the month. But only in a Jubilee Year was Rosh Hashanah observed on the 10th of Tishri (Lev 25:9–10); in all other years it was on the first of Tishri. The rabbinic passages correctly state that Ezekiel's vision in 574 BC was at the beginning of a Jubilee cycle. This establishes that 1406 BC would have begun a Jubilee cycle.[103] Despite the attempts to nullify the plain meaning of 1 Kgs 6:1 and despite the denial that Ezekiel saw the beginning of a Jubilee on Tishri 10 of 574 BC, Feinman and other critics have failed to explain this amazing "coincidence."

Three colleagues take umbrage with my interpretation of the Berlin Pedestal. Hendel cites Hoffmeier as proof that not all Egyptologists accept the reading of "Israel" on the Berlin Pedestal. In Hoffmeier's response to my chapter, he writes, "To read 'Israel' requires bending the standard rules for reading Semitic words in Egyptian, and there are a number of possible readings for the geographical term, including 'Ilshalir,' 'Ilsharil,' 'Irshalir,' 'Irsharil,' and 'Irshalil,' but not 'Israel'" (58–59). Both Hoffmeier and Hendel fail to address the challenge that I raised. None of these possible readings refers to a known toponym, whereas understanding the fragmentary name ring as a reference to Israel satisfies that expectation. Furthermore, the orthography of the Berlin Pedestal name ring suggests an Eighteenth Dynasty date, most likely during the reign of Amenhotep II.[104]

My final clarification deals with "the land of the Shasu of Yhw" mentioned on the Soleb Hieroglyph. Hendel believes that Yhw is "probably a place-name" but offers no evidence to support his belief. As I demonstrated, a strong case can be made that this inscription, likely from the time of Amenhotep III, shows that there were people who worshiped Yhw, the Israelite God, living outside of Egypt. Hendel sees that land as Edom, but as our coauthor Gary A. Rendsburg correctly wrote in his response to my chapter, the Shasu "were denizens of the great Southland, stretching across Sinai, modern-day southern Israel, and modern-day southern Jordan" (68). Since all of modern-day southern Israel lies within the boundaries of ancient Israel, then logically there were Shasu in Israel during the reign of Amenhotep III. According to the scribes of Amenhotep III, these Shasu worshiped Yhw. This is problematic for those who argue for an exodus in the thirteenth century (or later).

---

103. Rodger C. Young, "The Talmud's Two Jubilees and Their Relevance to the Date of the Exodus," *WTJ* 68 (2006): 77–82.

104. Zwickel and Van der Veen, "The Earliest Reference to Israel": 131–32; Manfred Görg, "Weitere Beobachtungen und Aspekte zur Genese des Namens 'Israel,'" *BN* 154 (2012): 57–68.

Corrections

Hoffmeier incorrectly believes that I miscounted the generations in 1 Chr 6:33–37. He states, "Since Korah was an adult at the exodus (cf. Num 16), only eighteen generations should be counted" (58). There are nineteen men mentioned in this genealogy, and I counted only eighteen generations. I then added a nineteenth generation to reach Solomon and synchronize with 1 Kgs 6:1. So it is Hoffmeier's misunderstanding, not mine.

Two parts of Hendel's response to my chapter need correction. First, he goes to lengths to establish that Manetho's Amenophis is Amenhotep IV (Akhenaten). I argue that in Josephus, Manetho refers to Amenhotep II—the likely pharaoh of the exodus, from my perspective. My primary point was that the name Amenhotep occurs only in the Eighteenth Dynasty, not in the Ramesside period, where Hendel might place it. Thus Hendel actually strengthens my argument. Second, in attempting to deal with the archaeological evidence at Tell el-Dab'a, Hendel asserts that I misdated the site's abandonment. To the contrary, Hendel conflates or confuses the partial abandonment during the time of Ahmose I with the later Semitic abandonment which I quite specifically describe. Bietak, as I assert, dates the fifteenth-century BC abandonment of Avaris (then known as Perunefer) to Amenhotep II.[105] Sometimes he favors *during* Amenhotep II's reign.[106] At other times he places it *after* Amenhotep II's reign.[107]

Finally, Rendsburg chides me for using the longer genealogy in 1 Chr 6:33–37 instead of the shorter genealogies in Ruth 4:18–22 and 1 Chr 2:5–15, upon which he relies to place the exodus in the twelfth century BC. He writes, "We have every reason to assume that David's genealogy is accurate and that Heman's has been artificially lengthened" (68). He bases this opinion on Henige's research, which indicates that lineage lengthening is more common than lineage telescoping.

105. See Petrovich, "Toward Pinpointing the Timing of the Egyptian Abandonment": 9–28.

106. Manfred Bietak, "Tell el-Dab'a in the Nile Valley," in *Beyond Babylon: Art, Trade, and Diplomacy in the Second Millennium B.C.*, ed. Joan A. Aruz, Kim Benzel, and Jean M. Evans (New Haven: Yale Univ. Press, 2008), 110–12.

107. Manfred Bietak, "The Aftermath of the Hyksos in Avaris," in *Culture Contacts and the Making of Cultures: Papers in Homage to Itamar Even-Zohar*, ed. Rakefet Sela-Sheffy and Gideon Toury (Tel Aviv: Tel Aviv Univ. Unit of Culture Research, 2011), 25.

However, Henige researched oral traditions in Africa. The genealogies in question here are written and non-African—profound differences to biblical genealogies. Thus Rendsburg overstates his case.

Conclusion

I encourage readers to consider the arguments in the essays, responses, and rejoinders. Besides the ad hominem missiles that Rendsburg launched at me, my coauthors made their cases fairly. In the end, I believe that the weight of evidence strongly supports a fifteenth-century BC exodus.

CHAPTER TWO

THE THIRTEENTH-CENTURY (LATE-DATE) EXODUS VIEW[1]

JAMES K. HOFFMEIER

Historicity and the Bible

"Did I not bring Israel up from Egypt?" This rhetorical question is posed by God in the book of Amos (9:7 NIV), the eighth-century Judean prophet. The obvious and clear answer is yes. The prophet's audience did not doubt this. Nor was there a reservation among the other writers of the Hebrew Scriptures. Consider the prominent words "I am the

1. Over the years I have written extensively on the Hebrew sojourn, exodus, and wilderness narratives. The current essay is largely culled from and abbreviated from these earlier works, including James K. Hoffmeier, *Israel in Egypt: The Evidence for the Authenticity of the Exodus Tradition* (Oxford: Oxford Univ. Press, 1997); idem, *Ancient Israel in Sinai: The Evidence for the Authenticity of the Wilderness Tradition* (Oxford: Oxford Univ. Press, 2005); idem, "What Is the Biblical Date for the Exodus? A Response to Bryant Wood," *JETS* 50 (2007): 225–47; idem, "Out of Egypt: The Archaeological Context for the Exodus," *BAR* 33, no. 1 (January/February 2007): 30–41, 71; idem, "These Things Happened–Why a Historical Exodus Is Essential for Theology," in *Do Historical Matters Matter to Faith? A Critical Appraisal of Modern and Postmodern Approaches to Scripture*, ed. James K. Hoffmeier and Dennis R. Magary (Wheaton, IL: Crossway, 2012), 99–134; idem, "Egyptologists and the Israelite Exodus from Egypt," in *Israel's Exodus in Transdisciplinary Perspective: Text, Archaeology, Culture, and Geoscience*, ed. Thomas E. Levy, Thomas Schneider, and William H. C. Propp, Quantitative Methods in the Humanities and Social Sciences (New York: Springer, 2015), 197–208; idem, "Egyptian Religious Influences on the Early Hebrews," in *"Did I Not Bring Israel out of Egypt?" Biblical, Archaeological, and Egyptological Perspectives on the Exodus Narratives*, ed. James K. Hoffmeier, Alan R. Millard, and Gary A. Rendsburg, BBRSup 13 (Winona Lake, IN: Eisenbrauns, 2016), 3–35; James K. Hoffmeier and Stephen O. Moshier, "Which Way out of Egypt? Physical Geography Related to the Exodus Itinerary," in Levy, Schneider, and Propp, *Israel's Exodus in Transdisciplinary Perspective*, 101–8.

Lord [YHWH][2] your God, who brought you out of Egypt, out of the land of slavery" (Exod 20:2 NIV). This assertion introduces the Ten Commandments. It is the opening section of the book of the covenant, in which, according to the Torah, God enters into a covenant relationship with the Hebrews at Mount Sinai after they fled Egypt under the leadership of Moses. Such an introductory formula, or historical prologue, is regularly employed in ancient Near Eastern treaty texts of the mid to late second millennium BC,[3] as it provides the historical rationale for why a nation should submit to the treaty or covenant of an overlord. The events leading up to Exod 20:2 justify YHWH's covenant demands on Israel. Because ancient treaties were initiated according to the historical dealings between the parties, Delbert Hillers argued that such prologues "had to be substantially accurate."[4]

The position taken in this essay is that real events stand behind the sojourn and exodus traditions. These events defined ancient Israel as a people, and her history would be forever marked by the exodus; after all, it is through this experience that the Lord became Israel's national deity. Hosea, the northern Israelite prophet of the eighth century, echoes Exod 20:2 to argue for Israel's exclusive relationship with the Lord, the God of the exodus: "I have been the Lord your God [who brought you] out of Egypt. You shall acknowledge no God but me, no Savior except me" (Hos 13:4 NIV). Recalling the exodus and using exodus motifs and themes is so constant throughout the Hebrew Bible that Graham Davies observed, "While it would be an exaggeration to say that the exodus story is mentioned in every part of the Old Testament, the exceptions are fairly few."[5] Likewise, Yair Hoffman affirms, "The exodus from Egypt is the most frequently mentioned event in the OT. Apart from the story

2. Throughout this essay, the writing Lord = the Divine Name, YHWH, following the practice of the NIV and other English translations.

3. For a review of all the treaty texts and law codes arranged diachronically, see Kenneth A. Kitchen and P. J. N. Lawrence, *Treaty, Law and Covenant in the Ancient Near East*, 3 vols. (Wiesbaden: Harrassowitz, 2012), esp. 3:259–63. The historical prologue portion of these treaty texts is absent in Assyrian and Aramean counterparts from the first millennium (3:264–66).

4. Delbert Hillers, *Covenant: The History of a Biblical Idea* (Baltimore: Johns Hopkins Univ. Press, 1969), 31.

5. Graham Davies, "Was There an Exodus?" in *In Search of Pre-Exilic Israel: Proceedings of the Oxford Old Testament Seminar*, ed. John Day (London: T&T Clark, 2004), 26.

itself in Exodus 1–15, it is mentioned about 120 times in stories, laws, poems, psalms, historiographical writings and prophecies."[6]

Given the ubiquity of attestations to the Egypt tradition in the Old Testament, one can understand John Bright's positive assessment, articulated in 1981, that "there can really be little doubt that the ancestors of Israel had been slaves in Egypt and had escaped in some marvelous way. Almost no one today would question it."[7] Before that decade ended, however, this optimistic assessment was widely questioned. The resurgence of historical minimalism that started with the Genesis narratives in the mid-1970s moved quickly to the books of Exodus through Joshua in the 1980s and 1990s in what became known as the minimalist versus maximalist debate.[8] The former sees little or no historical data in the Bible relative to Israel's origins and largely concludes that the Israelites were a people indigenous to Canaan who never had been in Egypt. They are exodus deniers. The latter, on the other hand, takes seriously the claims regarding Israel's beginnings and subsequent entry into the land of Canaan after a prolonged stay in Egypt.

Three basic approaches are presently employed in academe. They all fall into what I call the exodus-rejectionist camp. There are those who transmogrify the exodus, Israel's national founding story, into a small, trivial event that was subsequently inflated into a national founding myth. Some consider the Hebrew exodus motif to be appropriated from the Hyksos expulsion story in Josephus's *Against Apion*.[9] The idea of a literary fabrication is embraced by many Old Testament source-critical scholars. J. Maxwell Miller and John Hayes hold that the Torah's origin

6. Yair Hoffman, "A North Israelite Typological Myth and a Judaean Historical Tradition: The Exodus in Hosea and Amos," *VT* 39 (1989): 170.

7. John Bright, *A History of Israel*, 3rd ed. (Philadelphia: Westminster, 1981), 120.

8. For a review of these developments, see Hoffmeier, *Israel in Egypt*, ch. 1; William G. Dever, *What Did the Biblical Writers Know and When Did They Know It?* (Grand Rapids: Eerdmans, 2001), chs. 1–2.

9. Flavius Josephus connects the Hebrew exodus from Egypt and entry into Canaan with the Hyksos expulsion from Egypt. His aim is to show that Jews are one of the ancient nations who flourished prior to the Greeks (H. St. J. Thackeray, *Josephus: The Life; Against Apion*, LCL 186 [Cambridge: Harvard Univ. Press, 1966], I §39–40, see further §§73–94, 227–50). Donald B. Redford has championed the view that "'Israel' experienced no great exodus from Egypt," although "there was a great exodus from Egypt by *somebody* is a demonstrable fact; but the question is by whom" ("The Great Going Forth: The Expulsion of West Semitic Speakers from Egypt," in Levy, Schneider, and Propp, *Israel's Exodus in Transdisciplinary Perspective*, 437, emphasis in original).

traditions are "an artificial and theologically influenced literary construct."[10] Consequently, the biblical narratives were too ideologically and theologically shaped for reconstructing real history.

Postmodern hermeneutics denies authority and meaning to any text and so treats the biblical narratives as literary creations, with no memories on Israel's past. Israel Finkelstein and Neil Silberman maintain that the "saga" about Israel's origin is "a brilliant product of the human imagination."[11]

The latest trend in biblical scholarship is to view the exodus narratives through the lens of "cultural memory." Since Ronald Hendel advocates for this approach in this volume, readers can consult his summation. However, a quote from Jan Assmann, the progenitor of this hermeneutic in biblical studies,[12] suffices to illustrate this approach, opining that the departure from Egypt is "THE story, the story of stories, arguably the greatest, in any event the most consequential story ever told—though perhaps not literally experienced—in human history."[13]

How I Approach the Hebrew Bible / Old Testament

The foregoing leads one to ask, why this skepticism toward the Bible? The reason is straightforward—there is a general distrust of the Bible as a reliable source for history, a distrust that has been with us since the Enlightenment and has been renewed in the current postmodern milieu. If the Bible were not still held to be sacred by Jews and Christians, it probably would not be treated in such a condescending and dismissive manner. In some cases this is because of anti-religious bigotry. Because of this hermeneutic of suspicion, the Bible is not treated in the same way as are other historical sources.

Based on the scores of citations and allusions to the exodus, Hebrew writers at every stage of history were convinced of its authenticity.

---

10. J. Maxwell Miller and John H. Hayes, *A History of Ancient Israel and Judah* (Philadelphia: Westminster, 1986), 78. Editor's note: There is now a second edition of this, published in 2006.

11. Israel Finkelstein and Neil Asher Silberman, *The Bible Unearthed* (New York: Free Press, 2001), 1.

12. Jan Assmann, *Moses the Egyptian: The Memory of Egypt in Western Monotheism* (Cambridge: Harvard Univ. Press, 1997).

13. Jan Assmann, "Exodus and Memory," in Levy, Schneider, and Propp, *Israel's Exodus in Transdisciplinary Perspective*, 3.

Jeremiah taught that a new covenant would be made between God and Israel after the Babylonian captivity, but "it will not be like the covenant [God] made with their ancestors when [he] took them by the hand to lead them out of Egypt" (31:32 NIV).

The approach taken here is to treat the Hebrew Bible as one would treat any ancient source, following the dictum of the late William Hallo, who advised us to "treat the ancient sources critically but without condescension."[14] This is how I interpret ancient texts—Hebrew, Egyptian, Babylonian, or Assyrian. Further, I embrace the contextual reading of the biblical text that Hallo promoted: reading it in concert with commensurate ancient Near Eastern texts that shed light on the Hebrew narrative's background—culture, history, language, geography, environment, religion, and ideology.

Furthermore, I concur with Moshe Garsiel, whose understanding of the 1 Samuel narratives is applicable to those in Exodus, when he observes that "biblical historiography contains history that is intertwined with theological outlook and enriched with rhetoric and literary structures and literary devices."[15] Biblical Israel's religion and theology is based on history and intertwined with it. This is what distinguishes Israel's religion from those of her neighbors. The eminent historian of religion Mircea Eliade maintained that unlike the cyclical and cosmic patterns that characterized the religions of the Near East, "the idea of cyclic time is left behind, Yahweh no longer manifests himself in *cosmic time* (like the gods of other religions) but in *historical time*."[16] Ancient people did not bifurcate natural and supernatural phenomenon. Rather, historical events were interpreted through a religious lens. The Israelites were no different. The positivist historian must bear in mind this religious worldview when interpreting the Old Testament; the Israelites saw the hand of God in their origin story. Accepting the historicity of the exodus narratives, however, does not necessarily require one to believe in divine intervention in the plagues or parting the sea.

14. William W. Hallo, "The Limits of Skepticism," *JAOS* 110 (1990): 189.

15. Moshe Garsiel, "The Valley of Elah Battle and the Duel of David with Goliath: Between History and Artisitc Theological Historiography," in *Homeland and Exile: Biblical and Ancient Near Eastern Studies in Honour of Bustenay Oded*, ed. Gershon Galil, Mark Geller, and Alan R. Millard, VTSup 130 (Leiden: Brill, 2009), 393.

16. Mircea Eliade, *The Sacred and the Profane* (New York: Harcourt Brace Jovanovich, 1959), 110, emphasis in original.

Exodus and History

In the absence of direct archaeological evidence for the exodus, the historian has to rely on the background material, especially from Egypt, where the story is set. Even Assmann has to acknowledge that "archaeological, epigraphic, and other evidence may tell us about its historical background."[17] My contention is that if the stage on which the drama of the biblical story is acted out contains authentic sets and props that fit the geographical setting and the chronological parameters, then the plausibility of the narratives is enhanced. One cannot speak of "proof" with historic certitude, but neither can exodus agnostics or deniers prove the Bible's witness to be erroneous.

I. Did Levantine Semitic-Speaking People Live in Northern Egypt during the Second Millennium BC?

The flow of Egyptian history is a series of political, economic, and cultural highs and lows. The Old (ca. 2700–2200 BC), Middle (ca. 2000–1760 BC) and New (ca. 1525–1070 BC) Kingdoms were characterized by long, powerful royal dynasties whose influence reached south into Nubia and north through Canaan and into Syria. During the First Intermediate (2200–2000 BC) and Second Intermediate (1760–1550 BC) periods, however, central authority broke down and multiple kinglets flourished in a weakened Egypt, allowing Semitic-speaking pastoralists (known as *ꜥ3mw [Aamu]* in Egyptian texts) to infiltrate Egypt. During the second millennium, evidence of Levantine peoples has been discovered in the northeastern delta at Tell el-Dabʿa (Avaris), from which the Hyksos ruled.[18] Manfred Bietak describes these people as "Egyptianized" Canaanites.[19] In addition to the discovery of Levantine pottery, weapons, and burial types at Avaris, similar remains have been uncovered at other northeastern delta sites, including Tell el-Yahudiya, Inshas, Tell Farasha, and Tell el-Kebir, as well as sites in the Wadi Tumilat—Tell

17. Assmann, "Exodus and Memory," 3.

18. Manfred Bietak, *Avaris: The Capital of the Hyksos: Recent Excavations at Tell el-Dabʿa* (London: British Museum Press, 1996); idem, "The Many Ethnicities of Avaris: Evidence from the Northern Borderland of Egypt," in *From Microcosm to Macrocosm: Individual Households and Cities in Ancient Egypt and Nubia*, ed. Julia Budka and Johannes Auenmüller (Leiden: Sidestone, 2018), 73–92.

19. Bietak, *Avaris: The Capital of the Hyksos*, 48.

el-Maskhuta, Tell el-Rataba and Tell Kuaʿ—the latter three of which are presently being excavated.[20] These discoveries demonstrate that the delta during the Fourteenth–Seventeenth Dynasties was dominated by foreigners of Syro-Canaanite ethnicity. It does not stretch credulity to think that a Hebrew clan that migrated to Egypt during an extended drought in the Levant could be among these Semitic-speaking peoples. The Egyptians likely would have lumped the Hebrews into the same category as other foreign Semitic speakers, calling them *ꜥ3mw*, "Asiatics."

II. Is There Evidence That Foreigners Were Enslaved in Egypt?

After generations of sojourning in Egypt and tending flocks, herds, and cattle in the lush delta with the approval of a Hyksos (?) king (cf. Gen 47:1–12), who ruled from Avaris, conditions changed. "Then a new king, to whom Joseph meant nothing, came to power in Egypt" (Exod 1:8 NIV), marking the beginning of the oppression of the Hebrews. Why this change in fortunes? Between 1560 and 1540 BC, Theban kings from the south, starting with kings Seqenenre Tao II and Kamose, who attacked Hyksos positions, culminated with Ahmose's campaigns against Avaris. His troops pursued the Hyksos forces to Sharuhen in Canaan.[21] This expulsion marked the beginning of the Eighteenth Dynasty and the New Kingdom. Ahmose began an ambitious building program in Avaris, including a large mudbrick citadel to serve as Egypt's military base to launch campaigns into the Near East.[22] The presence of Egyptian rulers in the delta after more than a century of absence may account for the hostility toward the Hebrews in the delta, who would be associated with the hated Hyksos. Other major building projects at Avaris followed, possibly during the reign of Thutmose III (1479–1425 BC), when a massive palace complex, complete with storage facilities, was built, all of mudbrick.[23]

---

20. Anna-Latifa Mourad, *Rise of the Hyksos: Egypt and the Levant from the Middle Kingdom to the Early Second Intermediate Period* (Oxford: Archaeopress, 2015).

21. See Labib Habachi, *The Second Stela of Kamose and His Struggle against the Hyksos Ruler and His Capital* (Glückstadt: Augustin, 1972); "The Tomb Biography of Ahmose of Nekheb," trans. James K. Hoffmeier (*COS* 2.1:5–7).

22. Bietak, *Avaris: The Capital of the Hyksos*, 67–73.

23. Manfred Bietak, "A Thutmosid Palace Precinct at Peru-Nefer (Tell el-Dabʿa)," in *Ancient Egyptian and Ancient Near Eastern Palaces I*, ed. Manfred Bietak and Silvia Prell, Contributions to the Archaeology of Egypt, Nubia and the Levant 5 (Vienna: Univ. of Vienna, 2018), 231–57.

That the Hebrews were engaged in forced labor making brick for royal building projects is certainly the most remembered feature of the Israelites' labor in Egypt (Exod 1:8–14; 2:23–24; 3:7; 5:1–23). Beginning with the military campaigns to western Asia and Sudan of the fifteenth century, POWs were brought back to Egypt as slaves of the state, and individual warriors were rewarded by being allowed to keep captured humans as their personal slaves. The classic scene from the tomb of Rekhmire (ca. 1450–1400 BC) shows Levantine and African POWs making and hauling bricks for the construction of the Akh-menu Temple at Karnak. The caption over the tableau clarifies that the brickmakers were among the "plunder" *(ḥ3q)* taken by the king on his campaigns.[24]

Other Egyptian records mention Levantine peoples working on mining expeditions and corvée labor for the Egyptian state.[25] When Ramesses II was making his new capital, Pi-Ramesses, adjacent to Avaris, Papyrus Leiden 348 reports that foreigners called *ʿpr* (Habiru)[26] were dragging stone blocks for the construction of a "great pylon" in the new city.[27] Papyrus Anastasi V, dated to around 1200 BC, contains a letter that may be tied to Ramesses II's thirty-third year (ca. 1246 BC) and that reports on a military officer named Kakemwer who pursued a pair of runaway "workers" or "slaves" *(b3kw)* from Pi-Ramesses. They were escaping toward Sinai via the Wadi Tumilat (more on the geography of this follows). James Allen suggests that "although the fugitives are described only as 'workers,' their route suggests they were Asiatics rather than Egyptians, attempting to escape to Canaanite territory."[28] The obvious scenario is that these escapees were part of the foreign

24. Norman de Garis Davies, *The Tomb of Rekhmire at Thebes* (New York: Metropolitan Museum of Art, 1943), 47 and plates 56–57.

25. For a review of some of these texts, see Hoffmeier, *Israel in Egypt*, 59–61, 112–16.

26. The term *ʿpr*/*ḫāpiru*/*ḫābiru* (Habiru) corresponds to the word *Hebrew*; linguistically it is a match. The term, however, is widely used in the ancient Near East as a sociological term rather than an ethnic term. It is possible that some occurrences of the term *ʿpr*/*ḫāpiru*/*ḫābiru* (Habiru) could refer to the Israelites, but which one refers to Israelites is impossible to determine. Niels Peter Lemche believes the early Israelites were Habiru—uprooted migrants from one part of Canaan to the highlands (*Early Israel: Anthropological and Historical Studies on the Israelite Society before the Monarchy* [Leiden: Brill, 1985], 421–29). The Habiru in this stone building project at Pi-Ramesses could be biblical Hebrews, but there is no way of knowing for sure.

27. Alan H. Gardiner, *Late Egyptian Miscellanies*, Bibliotheca Aegyptiaca 7 (Brussels: Édition de la Fondation Égyptologique, 1937), 134.2.

28. "A Report of Escaped Laborers," trans. James P. Allen (*COS* 3.4:16). In addition to his comments, Allen's translation of the text is also provided.

forced labor gang at work in the area of Pi-Ramesses who hoped to free themselves and return to their homeland.

In addition to building operations described in the first chapter of the book of Exodus, the chapter also claims that the Hebrews were forced to do "all kinds of work in the fields" (1:14). Here too New Kingdom tomb paintings depict foreign men working in vineyards, harvesting grapes, treading them out for wine, and doing other fieldwork, such as plowing.[29] Papyrus Bologna 1086 contains a letter dated to the reign of Merenptah (1213–1203 BC), in which the scribe Bakenamon investigates the whereabouts of a field-worker or cultivator *(iḥwty)* who is identified as a Syrian *(ḫ3rw)*.[30] He had been consigned to the fields of the Temple of Thoth in Memphis after being brought on a cargo ship along with other slaves *(ḥmw)*.[31]

New Kingdom era texts and illustrations show that foreigners, typically prisoners of war, were forced into hard labor for the state. It is not unreasonable to believe that the Hebrews could have received similar treatment during the New Kingdom as various royal building projects were undertaken in the northeastern delta.

III. Is There Egyptian Evidence within the Torah to Support an Egyptian Sojourn?

The Torah reports that the Hebrews spent 400 (Gen 15:13) or 430 (Exod 12:40) years in Egypt, whereas, in the Septuagint, Exod 12:40 offers an alternative reading that shortens the stay to 215 years.[32] Thus a range from 200–400 years is possible. The Hebrews lived in the eastern delta of Egypt (the land of Goshen: Gen 47:27; Exod 8:22; 9:26), as many other Semitic-speaking peoples did.[33] Generations of

29. For a review of these scenes and others showing POWs working in various trades, see Ellen Morris, "Mitanni Enslaved: Prisoners of War, Pride, and Productivity in a New Imperial Regime," in *Creativity and Innovation in the Reign of Hatshepsut*, ed. Jóse M. Galán, Betsy M. Bryan, and Peter F. Dorman, SAOC 69 (Chicago: Oriental Institute of the Univ. of Chicago, 2014), 361–80.

30. The text is in Kenneth A. Kitchen, *Ramesside Inscriptions: Historical and Biographical*, 8 vols. (Oxford: Blackwell, 1976–1990), 4:78–80.

31. For a translation of the complete text, see Edward Wente, *Letters from Ancient Egypt* (Atlanta: Scholars, 1990), 124–26.

32. For a review of this textual problem, see Cornelis Houtman, *Exodus*, HCOT (Kampen: Kok, 1993), 1:175–76.

33. Bietak, "The Many Ethnicities of Avaris," 73–92.

Semites living in Egypt's delta would have experienced a high degree of cultural adaptation and assimilation. Sociologists recognize that when a people from one culture live as a minority group, in time a new blended culture emerges, a transcultural one. While the Hyksos were Egyptianized (inscriptions were written in hieroglyphs, kings adopted Egyptian throne names and wrote their Semitic and Egyptian names in cartouches, and administrators bore Egyptian titles), they retained many aspects of their Levantine culture even after many generations in Egypt. Nevertheless, the Egyptians called them *ꜥꜣmw* and *sṯtyw/styw*,[34] both terms for "Asiatics," or Semitic-speaking people. It stands to reason that the Hebrews were similarly Egyptianized. Hebrews, like other foreign communities in Egypt, no doubt adapted elements of Egyptian culture, language, and religion, as demonstrated archaeologically at Tell el-Dab'a.

The relevant question is, does the Torah preserve evidence for such Egyptianization among the Hebrews? It has been long recognized that among the Hebrews of the exodus generation, many bore Egyptian personal names, especially among the Levites.[35] These include Moses and Aaron (although these are linguistically challenging), Merari, Miriam, Phineas, Putiel, Assir, Ahira, Hur, Hori, and Harnepher.[36] Assir preserves the name of Osiris, while Ahira is theophoric, incorporating the name of the sun god, Re. The names Hur, Hori, and Harnepher use the name of the sky god Horus (e.g., *ḥr*). Horus is one of the most influential gods in the northeastern delta, as evidenced by his name appearing in a number of geographical features in that area.[37] This also is the very region where the Bible locates the Hebrews. This interconnection can hardly be a coincidence.

Further evidence of Egyptian religious influence in the Pentateuch can be seen in various cultic paraphernalia. The design of the tabernacle, Israel's mobile desert sanctuary, has long been linked to Egyptian

---

34. These terms are both used in the Kamose Stelae; see n.24.

35. Theophile J. Meek, *Hebrew Origins* (New York: Harper & Brothers, 1936), 31–32.

36. Hoffmeier, "Egyptian Religious Influences on the Early Hebrews," 18–27.

37. For recent treatment of the personal names in Exodus, see Hoffmeier, "Deities of the Eastern Frontier," in *Scribe of Justice: Egyptological Studies in Honour of Shafik Allam*, ed. Zahi A. Hawass, Khaled Abdalla Daoud, and Ramadan B. Hussein, Supplément aux Annales du Service des antiquités de l'Egypte 42 (Cairo: Conseil Suprême des Antiquités de l'Egypte, 2011), 197–99.

analogues. More than a century ago, Hugo Gressmann noticed striking parallels between the tabernacle of Yahweh and Ramesses II's tent encampment depicted on the walls of Luxor Temple, the Ramesseum and Abu Simbel, a point also recognized by more recent scholars.[38] Then too the description of the material used for the construction of the tabernacle and many of its utensils employed Egyptian technical terms. These include:[39]

1. The Hebrew word for Acacia wood, *šiṭṭâ*, plural *šiṭṭîm* (Exod 25:10, 13, 23; 26:15, 26, 32, 37), which was used in the tabernacle and other furnishings, derives from the Egyptian word for acacia, *šnḏt*.
2. Many of the wooden objects, such as the tentpoles, the ark of the covenant, and the table for bread offerings, were overlaid with gold foil, a technique mastered in Egypt. Behind the Hebrew term for this process, *paḥ*, stands the Egyptian word *pḫ(ꜣ)*. It occurs only in Exod 39:3 and Num 16:38.
3. The linen used in the tabernacle and in the priest's garments is *šēš* (Exod 26:1, 31, 36; 27:9, 16, 18; 39:27–29), which stems from *šs*, the Egyptian word for linen. Avi Hurvitz noted that *šēš* does not occur in datably later biblical texts; rather the common Hebrew word for linen, *bûṣ*, is employed, suggesting an "early origin" to the use of *šēš*.[40]
4. The menorah, the seven-branched lamp, has oil-holding "cups" (*gəḇiʿîm*—Exod 25:33–34); *gəḇiʿîm* is thought to be an Egyptian loanword, *qbḥw*.[41] Carol Meyers examined the menorah in light of different Near Eastern artistic motifs and goldsmith technology,

38. Hugo Gressmann, *Mose und Seine Zeit* (Göttingen: Vandenhoeck & Ruprecht, 1913), 240–42. See recently Michael M. Homan, *To Your Tents, O Israel! The Terminology, Function, Form, and Symbolism of Tents in the Hebrew Bible and the Ancient Near East*, CHANE 12 (Leiden: Brill, 2002); Kenneth A. Kitchen, "The Tabernacle––A Bronze Age Artifact," *ErIsr* 24 (1993): 119–29.

39. The Egyptian etymologies of the Hebrew terms discussed in this paragraph have been recognized by Thomas O. Lambdin, "Egyptian Loan Words in the Old Testament," *JAOS* 73 (1952): 146–55; Yoshiyuki Muchiki, *Egyptian Proper Names and Loanwords in North-West Semitic*: SBLDS 173 (Atlanta: Society of Biblical Literature, 1999); Hoffmeier, *Israel in Egypt*, 209–18; idem, "Egyptian Religious Influences on the Early Hebrews," 31–34.

40. Avi Hurvitz, "The Usage of *šēš* and *bûṣ* in the Bible and Its Implication for the Date of P," *HTR* 60 (1967): 117–21.

41. *HALOT* 173.

concluding that Egypt had some influence.[42] She also maintains that the origin of the tabernacle, along with the menorah, has its roots in the Sinai, concluding, "Its authentic place in the traditions of the wilderness period has been assumed in this study because the archaeological data that have been adduced in preceding chapters cannot allow us to do otherwise."[43]

5. The term *maḥtâ* refers to a type of censer (Lev 10:1; Num 16:6, 17–18), tray, or firepan used by priests (Exod 25:38; Num 4:9). Egyptian *ḫt* is the word for fire and is used in connection with burnt offerings and may be the Hebrew root for this offering device.
6. A number of items of the priestly regalia originated in Egypt. The Hebrew term for sash or cummerbund, *ʾaḇnēṭ* (Exod 28:4, 39–40; 29:9; Lev 8:7, 13; 16:4), derives from the Egyptian word *bnd*, which means "wrap" and is first found in New Kingdom texts.
7. Another sash associated with the priest's regalia, possibly worn on the turban, is called *pəʾēr*. This is an Egyptian loanword, *pry/pyr*, for various kinds of bands, including headbands.
8. The head opening on the priest's robe is called the *taḥrāʾ* (Exod 28:32; 39:23), which appears to derive from *tḫr*, the word for the circular openings on the side of chariot panels. Such a circular head opening may be in mind on the priest's robe. The text further states that "there shall be a woven edge like a collar around this *opening*, so that it will not tear" (28:32 NIV). This kind of needlework stitched around the neck has been found on Egyptian linen garments, such as one discovered in the tomb of Kha, a fourteenth-century BC architect from Deir el-Medina.[44]
9. The priests were to wear linen (*šēš/bad*, cf. Exod 39:28) undergarments *(miḵnāsayim)* that were designed to cover his private parts (Exod 28:42), lest he expose himself (cf. Exod 20:26).[45] Linen undergarments have been discovered in the tombs of

42. Carol L. Meyers, *The Tabernacle Menorah: A Synthetic Study of a Symbol from the Biblical Cult*, American Schools of Oriental Research Dissertation Series 2 (Missoula, MT: Scholars, 1976), 65–69, 107–11.

43. Meyers, *Tabernacle Menorah*, 182.

44. For a picture, see www.deirelmedina.com/lenka/TurinKha.html.

45. This reference prohibits the priest from climbing up steps to an altar "that your nakedness be not exposed on it" (Exod 20:26).

Tutankhamun and Kha. Because this piece of clothing was to cover the priests' private parts, the Egyptian root *kns* could be the word behind this garment. It refers to the sexual area or pubic region and thus fits *mik̲nāsayim* linguistically and semantically.

10. The priest was to wear a bejeweled breastplate *(ḥōšen)* with twelve gemstones (Exod 28:1–30; 39:1–21). *Piṭdâ* (submetallic hematite), *nōp̱ek* (turquoise), *lešem* (braided agate), and *ʾaḥlāmâ* (red jasper) are Egyptian words and known in New Kingdom period texts.[46] Turquoise is especially interesting, since Serabit el-Khadim in Sinai is the lone source for this valuable gemstone in the ancient Near East. When mining operations in Sinai end in the twelfth century, turquoise disappears from jewelry in Egypt and the Levant. So its presence in the priestly breastplate is significant. In the Iron II period and later times, turquoise was not available to biblical writers to include in the description of the breastplate in Exod 28 and 39.[47]

The data presented here concentrates on Egyptian personal names that can be tied to Hebrews who lived in Egypt, and on terms associated with the tabernacle and priestly regalia. Benjamin Noonan has analyzed the use of Egyptian terms in the exodus and wilderness traditions, documenting that there are 26 recognized Egyptian terms (excluding personal and geographical names; these will be treated next) used 381 times (1.172 percent of lexemes).[48] By way of comparison, he investigated the Persian (Old Iranian) loanwords in the corpora of Ezra, Nehemiah, and Esther, indubitably Persian period compositions. Remarkably, there are 26 terms used 82 times, 1.455 percent of distinct lexemes.[49]

46. James A. Harrell, James K. Hoffmeier, and Kenton E. Williams, "Hebrew Gemstones in the Old Testament: A Lexical, Geological, and Archaeological Analysis," *BBR* 27 (2017): 1–52.

47. *Nōp̱ek* occurs just twice outside of the two breastplate references (Exod 28:18; 39:11). In Ezek 28:13, it occurs as a gemstone in the royal baldachin of the prince of Tyre. Here *nōp̱ek* occurs along with eight other gemstones found in Exod 28. It is clear Exod 28 was the source for the Ezek 28 list. It is found again in Ezek 27:16 along with other luxury items traded by Aram (or Edom). See Harrell, Hoffmeier, and Williams, "Hebrew Gemstones in the Old Testament," 6–7.

48. Benjamin J. Noonan, "Egyptian Loanwords as Evidence for the Authenticity of the Exodus and Wilderness Traditions," in Hoffmeier, Millard, and Rendsburg, *Did I Not Bring Israel out of Egypt?* 52–53.

49. Noonan, "Egyptian Loanwords," 56.

Noonan rightly observes, "If we acknowledge Old Iranian linguistic influence on the books of Esther and Ezra-Nehemiah and the implications it has for these books' dates and composition, we should similarly acknowledge Egyptian linguistic influence on the exodus and wilderness traditions and implications it has for their date and composition."[50]

IV. Do the Topographical and Geographical Data Accord with That of Egypt?

The story of Moses being placed in the basket and set afloat in the Nile is often associated with the motif of Sargon the Great, who was placed in the Euphrates but was recovered by the gardener of the goddess Ishtar, who reared the lad who eventually became the king of Akkad (Mesopotamia).[51] Many Old Testament scholars believe that the biblical writers appropriated this legend for their hero, Moses. What has not been adequately explained, however, is the overwhelming number of Egyptian elements all compressed into one verse, Exod 2:3. Moses' mother "got a *papyrus basket* for him and coated it with tar and *pitch*. Then she placed the child in it and put it among the *reeds* along the *bank* of the *Nile*" (NIV, emphasis mine). The italicized words are of Egyptian etymology.

- Papyrus = *gōme'*, which corresponds to an Egyptian word for papyrus, *gmy*.
- Basket = *tēḇâ*, which represents the Egyptian term *ḏbꜣt*, meaning "box" and "coffin"—a rectangular container.
- Pitch = *zāp̄eṯ*, which possibly related to an Egyptian or Afro-Asiatic word, *śpt*, meaning "oil" or "resin."
- Reeds = *sûp̄*, which is the Hebrew writing for Egyptian *ṯwfy*. These reeds or rushes grow along the Nile, canals, inlets, and marshy areas/lakes. The sea through which the Israelites reportedly crossed on Egypt's frontier is *yam sûp̄*, "Reed Sea" (Exod 13:18; 15:4, 22; 23:31; Deut 11:4; Josh 2:10; 4:23).[52]
- Nile = *hayə'ōr*, which is the Egyptian term for the Nile. It is not the Hebrew generic word for river *(nāhār)*. This word occurs twice

50. Noonan, "Egyptian Loanwords," 56.
51. For a review of the literature on this story, see Hoffmeier, *Israel in Egypt*, 136–38.
52. More on this follows.

in 2:5; once it is translated "Nile" and the other "riverbank" when combined with *śāpâ* (next entry) in the NIV.

- Bank = *śāpâ*, which is a common Egyptian word *(spt)* for riverbank, but the word has Semitic cognates in Ugaritic, Hebrew, and Akkadian, meaning it is part of the Semitic substratum of Egyptian rather than a loanword.[53]

In Exod 2:5 when the princess discovered the baby in the basket, some of the same terms recur: Nile (twice), basket, reeds, as well as Pharaoh (Eg. *Pr-ʿȝ*).[54] This collocation of Egyptian words in verses 2–5, attested in Egypt during the second millennium, certainly reflects geographical and environmental realia of Egypt.

V. Do the Toponyms, or Place-Names, Fit Egypt and at What Period?

Early Egyptologists from the end of the nineteenth century and well into the twentieth were interested in locating sites mentioned in the exodus narratives.[55] Egyptologists tend to treat the toponyms as authentic, whereas lately some minimalist biblical scholars have argued in favor of a mythological geography as a way to undermine the historical foundation of the sojourn-exodus narratives.[56] To such a reading, Donald Redford retorts, "This is a curious resort, for the text does not look like mythology (at least on the definition of the latter as a timeless event set in the world of the gods). The Biblical writer certainly thinks he is writing datable history."[57] Redford maintains, however, that the geographical

---

53. *Spt* is attested in Egyptian as early as the Old Kingdom (ca. 2500 BC). Four other Hebrew words are known of a water's edge, brink, or bank. One of them, *yāḏ*, is used in Exod 2:5, but the writer's choice to combine the Egyptian words for Nile and bank is significant. There are other Egyptian words for riverbank that could have been used, *iḫmt*, *mȝʿ*, *mryt*, and *ḫfȝȝt* (see David Shennum, *English–Egyptian Index of Faulkner's Concise Dictionary of Middle Egyptian* [Malibu, CA: Undena, 1977], 10.) The author opted to use a common Egyptian term that would have been recognized to a Hebrew audience.

54. This Egyptian title for the monarch began sometime in the fifteenth century BC.

55. For a review of the biblical interests of early Egyptology, see Hoffmeier, "Egyptologists and the Israelite Exodus from Egypt," 197–208.

56. Batto and Ahlström argue that behind the current narratives lies an origin myth that was historicized during the exilic or postexilic periods; see Bernard Batto, "The Reed Sea: *Requiescat in Pace*," *JBL* 102 (1983): 27–35. See further idem, *Slaying the Dragon: Mythmaking in the Biblical Tradition* (Louisville: Westminster John Knox, 1992); Gösta W. Ahlström, *Who Were the Israelites?* (Winona Lake, IN: Eisenbrauns, 1986), 45–55.

57. Donald B. Redford, *Egypt, Canaan, and Israel in Ancient Times* (Princeton: Princeton Univ. Press, 1992), 409.

terms derive from the seventh century BC. Because of his influence, a number of Old Testament specialists and archaeologists have followed his lead.

While this understanding of the toponyms is possible, it is not the only way to date them, and this proposed late dating just happens to align with the theoretical dates for the composition of the exodus narratives. These toponyms indeed are also attested in Egyptian texts in the previous millennium.[58]

1. Could the Israelites Have Worked at Pithom and Rameses?

Exodus 1:11 names two places where the Hebrews were engaged in brickmaking and building projects as "they built Pithom and Rameses as store cities for Pharaoh" (NIV). Pithom is the Hebrew writing for *p(r)-itm*, the House or Domain of Atum (eg., *Ỉtm*), the name of the sun god, Re, whose origin cult center is On, located in Matariya, a northern suburb of Cairo. The Egyptian name *ʾōn* occurs as the home of Joseph's wife, Asenath, whose father, Potiphera, was the priest (Gen 41:45, 50). "Heliopolis" (city of the sun) is the translation found in the Septuagint. While some might be inclined to connect this cult center of Atum with Pithom, and this is a possibility, *p(r)-itm* is never used in texts for Heliopolis, the town or the temple.

Pithom is also equated with Tell el-Rataba in the Wadi Tumilat, the route that runs east from the delta to north-central Sinai. This identification is based on the occurrence of Pithom in Papyrus Anastasi VI within the region of Tjeku (Heb. *sukkôt*).[59] Ongoing excavations at Tell el-Rataba headed by Slawomir Rzepka[60] have proven what earlier generations of excavators concluded—that Pithom was the major military establishment of this frontier zone, with a large fort constructed by Ramesses II and expanded by Ramesses III.

The city of Rameses not only is associated with the building activity

---

58. Unless otherwise specified, the data in the following section is based on evidence presented in Hoffmeier, *Israel in Egypt*, 116–22, 176–98 and Hoffmeier, *Ancient Israel in Sinai*, 47–109.

59. "A Report of Bedouin," trans. James P. Allen (*COS* 3.5:16–17).

60. Slawomir Rzepka et al., "Tell el-Retaba 2007–2008," *AeL* 19 (2009): 241–45, and Slawomir Rzepka et al., "New Kingdom and the Third Intermediate Period in Tell el-Retaba: Results of the Polish–Slovak Archaeological Mission, Seasons 2009–2010," *AeL* 21 (2011): 139–84.

of the Hebrews but also was the place from which the exodus was launched. Both the exodus narrative and the Num 33 itinerary agree on this point (Exod 12:37; Num 33:3, 5). Rameses has long been associated with Ramesses II's (1279–1213 BC) delta capital. A century ago Sir Alan Gardiner conducted an exhaustive investigation of texts known in his day that mentioned Pi-Ramesses.[61] He resolved, "Whether or no [*sic*] the Bible narrative be strict history, there is not the least reason for assuming that any other city of Ramesses existed in the Delta besides those elicited from the Egyptian monuments. In other words, the Biblical Raamses-Rameses is identical with the Residence-city of Pi-Ramesse."[62] This identification has largely been accepted by scholars.

Locating the ancient city with certainty took nearly a century of explorations. After alternatives, such as Tell el-Rataba, Pelusium, and Tanis, proved they were not Pi-Ramesses, its location has been fixed at Qantir (Sharkiya Provence), a couple miles north of the old Hyksos capital at Avaris (Tell el-Dab'a).[63] Since 1980 Edgar Pusch, and now Henning Franzmeier, have undertaken excavations and regional magnetometer surveys at Qantir. This work revealed a massive city that included a vast stable complex where royal chariotry was stationed.[64] Eric Uphill described this impressive city as "probably the vastest and most costly royal residence ever erected by the hand of man."[65] This bustling delta capital was abandoned toward the end of the twelfth century as the Nile distributary near which Pi-Ramesses was built started desiccating because of lower volume of water in the Nile.[66] Perhaps around 1130 BC the final Ramesside kings relocated to Memphis.[67] Shortly thereafter,

61. Alan H. Gardiner, "The Delta Residence of the Ramessides," *JEA* 5 (1918): 127–38, 179–200, 242–71.

62. Gardiner, "The Delta Residence," 266.

63. This identification was advanced by Labib Habachi beginning in the 1950s; see *Tell el-Dab'a I: Tell el-Dab'a and Qantir: The Site and Its Connection with Avaris an Piramesse* (Wien: Österreichischen Akademie der Wissenschaften, 2001), 23–127.

64. In addition to scores of preliminary reports and studies, Edgar Pusch and his team have now published ten volumes: *Die Grabaungen des Pelizaeus-Museums Hildesheim in Qantir-Piramesse* I–X (Mainz: Philipp von Zabern, 2009–2017).

65. Eric Uphill, *The Temples of Per Ramesses* (Warminster: Aris & Phillips, 1984), 1.

66. Karl Butzer, *Early Hydraulic Civilization in Egypt: A Study in Cultural Ecology* (Chicago: Univ. of Chicago Press, 1976), 56; Rushdi Said, *The River Nile: Geology, Hydrology and Utilization* (New York: Pergamon, 1993), 150.

67. Kenneth A. Kitchen, *On the Reliability of the Old Testament* (Grand Rapids: Eerdmans, 2003), 255.

by 1070 BC a new dynasty began with Tanis as its capital, located fifteen miles (twenty-four kilometers) north of Qantir. The huge temple area at Tanis was constructed with inscribed stone blocks and pillars transported from Pi-Ramesses, and statues, obelisks, and stela from the old capital adorned the precinct.

Exodus 1:11 explicitly identifies these building projects as "store cities" *('ārê miskənôṯ)*. In Egypt, every administrative center, palace, temple, and fort had a walled-off storage area consisting of long, narrow, adjacent rectangular mudbrick structures with vaulted roofs. Possibly the Hebrews were engaged in such building efforts at Pithom and Pi-Ramesses. To summarize, the archaeological evidence shows conclusively that both cities experienced major building efforts and flourished during the thirteenth and twelfth centuries.

References to Rameses in the Torah are crucial for dating purposes in that this metropolis had a limited history. While it was Seti I (1294–1279 BC) who built a small residence at Qantir, it was his son Ramesses II who transformed it into a megalopolis that was deserted less than a century after his death.

2. The Route of the Exodus

The narratives in Exodus, complemented by the list in Num 33, provide an itinerary of the travels of the Israelites from the departure at Pi-Ramesses to the famed crossing of the Reed/Red Sea, then to Mount Sinai and on to the land of Moab. Our concern here is only with the Egyptian segment of their journey.

"The Israelites journeyed from Rameses to Sukkoth" (Exod 12:37 NIV).

With the starting point established at Pi-Ramesses, there were two routes out of Egypt to Sinai and on to Canaan. The northerly route hugs the northern coast of Sinai and is known as the Way(s) of Horus in Egyptian texts. Exodus 13:17 calls it "the road [to] the Philistine country" (NIV), and the Israelites are told to avoid it. The other means of egress from Egypt is via the Wadi Tumilat, which in Egyptian texts is called Tjeku, corresponding to Hebrew Sukkot. The "tum" element in "Tumilat" preserves the name of the aforementioned Atum. The name Tjeku/Sukkot survives in the name of the village, Tell el-Maskhuta, situated eight miles (fourteen kilometers) east of Tell el-Rataba. This is the route taken by two runaway slaves in Papyrus Anastasi V, who fled from Pi-Ramesses to the Wadi Tumilat.[68] The slaves were pursued by a "troop commander" *(ḥry pḏt)* named Kakemwer. His rank places him just below a general,[69] suggesting that this was an important operation which was not undertaken without a substantial force accompanying him. Minimally, it suggests that apprehending runaway slaves was important. Interestingly, Kakemwer reached "the fort at Tjeku (Sukkot)" from Pi-Ramesses the next day, just as the Hebrews did apparently following the same route.[70]

"After leaving Sukkoth they camped at Etham on the edge of the desert" (Exod 13:20 NIV).

Moving east past the area of the fortress of Tjeku, the Hebrews find themselves at the limits of Egypt, about to enter Sinai at a place called Etham *(ʾēṯām)*. As with Pithom, located about sixteen miles (twenty-seven kilometers) to the west in the Wadi Tumilat, Etham also preserves the name of Atum, even though presently a specific site has not been identified for it. The Egyptian name is indisputable.

"Tell the Israelites to turn back and encamp near Pi Hahiroth, between Migdol and the sea. They are to encamp by the sea, directly opposite Baal Zephon" (Exod 14:2 NIV).

A shift in direction from the east is suggested by the word *šwḇ* ("turn back"), which takes the Israelites on a more northerly route out of Egypt. This cluster of toponyms is situated in the vicinity of "the sea," the body of water associated with the sea crossing. This "sea" elsewhere is called *yam sûp̄*, Reed Sea (cf. Exod 13:18; 15:4, 22; 23:31; Deut 11:4; Josh 2:10; 4:23). As with Exod 2:3, *sûp̄* means reeds or rushes and is linguistically related to the Egyptian word *ṯwfy*, which shares the same meaning. Most English Bibles render *yam sûp̄* as "Red Sea," reflecting the Septuagint text. On Egypt's northeastern frontier sat a marshy region called *pꜣ ṯwfy*, known largely from Ramesside era texts. In 1975, based on analysis of

68. "A Report of Escaped Laborers," (*COS* 3.4:16).

69. Alan R. Schulman, *Military Rank, Title and Organization in the Egyptian New Kingdom*, Münchner Ägyptologische Studien 6 (Berlin: Hessling, 1964), 53–54.

70. "A Report of Escaped Laborers," (*COS* 3.4:16).

Egyptian texts and delta geography, Bietak connected *pꜣ ṯwfy* with the Ballah Lakes (now defunct) and with biblical *yam sûp̱*.[71]

Recent geological investigations of the Ballah depression reveal that the lake was thriving in New Kingdom times (and earlier). The southern section of the lake is just north of the Wadi Tumilat, while its northern reach extends about twelve miles (twenty kilometers) toward the Mediterranean, just south of a frontier town and forts at Tjaru.[72] The Onomasticon of Amenemope (ca. 1150 BC) situates Tjaru as Egypt's northernmost toponym, south of which is *pꜣ ṯwfy*.[73] Now that the location of Tjaru's double fort system was found at Tell Hebua I and II,[74] Bietak's theory that the Ballah depression corresponds to *pꜣ ṯwfy* in Egyptian texts and *yam sûp̱* of the Bible is established.

With the location of *yam sûp̱/pꜣ ṯwfy* fixed, the other toponyms in Exod 14:2 can be investigated, assuming this collocation is intended to help pinpoint the location of the sea in this narrative. Indeed, Benjamin Scolnic has called this group of toponyms "a precise set of referents."[75]

---

71. Manfred Bietak, *Tell el-Dabʿa II: Der Fundort im Rahmen einer archäologisch-geographischen Untersuchung über das ägyptische Ostdelta* (Vienna: Österreichischen Akademie der Wissenschaften Wien, 1975), 137 and plates 10, 23. See his most recent study: idem, "On the Historicity of the Exodus: What Egyptology Today Can Contribute to Assessing the Biblical Account of the Sojourn in Egypt," in Levy, Schneider, and Propp, *Israel's Exodus in Transdisciplinary Perspective*, 27–28, esp. the map on p. 28, fig. 2.3.

72. Stephen O. Moshier and Bahaa Gayed, "Geological Investigation of the Ballah Depression, Northern Suez Canal Zone, Egypt," in *Tell el-Borg II*, ed. James K. Hoffmeier (University Park, PA: Eisenbrauns, 2019), 5–20.

73. Alan H. Gardiner, *Ancient Egyptian Onomastica II* (London: Oxford Univ. Press, 1947), 201–2. See also James K. Hoffmeier and Stephen O. Moshier, "New Paleo-Environmental Evidence from North Sinai to Complement Manfred Bietak's Map of the Eastern Delta and Some Historical Implications," in *Timelines: Studies in Honour of Manfred Bietak*, ed. Ernst Czerny et al., OLA 149 (Leuven: Peeters, 2006), 2:169–70.

74. See Mohamed Abd el-Maksoud, *Tell Heboua (1981–1991): Enquête archéologique sur la Deuxième Période Intermédiaire et le Nouvel Empire à l'extrémité orientale du Delta* (Paris: Éditions Recherche sur les Civilisations, 1998); Mohamed Abd el-Maksoud and Dominique Valbelle, "Tell Héboua–Tjarou l'apport de l'épigraphie," *RdÉ* 56 (2005): 1–44. Regarding Hebua II, see Mohamed Abd el-Maksoud and Dominique Valbelle, "Tell Héboua II: Rapport Préliminaire sur le décor et l'épigraphie des elements architectoniques découverts au cours des campagnes 2008–2009 dans la zone centrale du Khétem de Tjarou," *RdÉ* 62 (2011): 1–39.

75. Benjamin Scolnic, "A New Working Hypothesis for the Identification of Migdol," in *The Future of Biblical Archaeology*, ed. James K. Hoffmeier and Alan R. Millard (Grand Rapids: Eerdmans, 2004), 98.

"Migdol" is a New Kingdom period Semitic loanword into Egyptian.

This is the case with a number of military architectural terms; the word means "tower" or "watchtower" and can be rendered "fort."[76] Ramesside period documents note a fort on Egypt's eastern frontier named "Migdol + the current king's name." The names of Seti I, Ramesses II, and Ramesses III (1184–1153 BC) are all associated textually with this fort. Recent archaeological work in northwest Sinai allows for a plausible location for this strategic fort. The Karnak reliefs of Seti I, which display a string of forts from Tjaru to Gaza, also depict Tjaru (two forts separated by a body of water), which corresponds to Hebua I and II, followed by the Dwelling of the Lion (Tell el-Borg).[77] The next in the sequence is the Migdol of Seti I, which has been identified with Migdol of Exod 14:2. Four kilometers to the southeast of Tell el-Borg is an archaeological site discovered by Eliezer Oren, identified by its survey number as T-211. Potsherds recovered on the surface date the site to the New Kingdom.[78] It is located at the southern tip of the paleo-lagoon into which two Nile branches debouched. Today the site has been covered (possibly destroyed!) by agricultural development. But 1960s era CORONA satellite images and aerial photos of the 1950s clearly show the form of a large feature surrounded by a depression that appears to be a moat.[79] Because of its location as the third fort in the sequence after Hebua and Borg, it is likely Ramesside Migdol.

"Pi Hahiroth" has been interpreted to be an Egyptian name as well as a Semitic one.

As for Pi Hahiroth, there is no agreement about what Egyptian words it represents, nor does it correspond to any known toponym on Egypt's frontier. A Semitic meaning could be rendered "Mouth of the Canal."[80] Indeed, geologists have discovered traces of a canal in north Sinai.

---

76. *HALOT* 543–44.

77. James K. Hoffmeier and Stephen O. Moshier, *Excavations in North Sinai: Tell el-Borg I* (Winona Lake, IN: Eisenbrauns), 34–61.

78. This survey from 1972–1982 remains unpublished. The information I have on T-211 was provided by Professor Oren himself, for which I am grateful.

79. James K. Hoffmeier, "The Search for Migdol of the New Kingdom and Exodus 14:2: An Update," *BurH* 44 (2008): 3–12; idem, "A Possible Location in Northwest Sinai for the Sea and Land Battles between the Sea Peoples and Ramesses III," *BASOR* 380 (2018): 1–25.

80. *HALOT* 925; Hoffmeier, *Israel in Egypt*, 164–75.

It passes just south of T-211 (Migdol) and is visible on CORONA images.[81] The juxtaposition of these two features is intriguing, but a date for the canal has not been established archaeologically, although Papyrus Anastasi III states that "the Lake of Horus has salt, the Canal has natron. Its ships set out and dock . . ."[82] The Lake of Horus has been equated with the same lagoon on whose southern tip sits the proposed site of Migdol.[83] The word James Allen renders as "canal" in Egyptian is *pꜣ ḥw-ir*, which he relates to a Semitic word, *ḫarru*, which refers to a dug-out watercourse, and *ḫerūtu* in the Babylonian/Kassite period (ca. 1600–1200) means "canal."[84] When one considers geographical proximity of an ancient canal trace to the eastern lagoon, and association of a canal—*pꜣ ḥw-ir* of Papyrus Anastasi III and meaning of Pi Hahiroth in Exod 14:2— with the location of the fort at T-211 (Migdol), the toponym and the geographical features correlate nicely.

"Baal Zephon" is the name of the Syro-Canaanite storm god.

The name literally means "Baal of the North." This foreign deity was worshiped in Egypt. A cylinder seal with his image was discovered at Avaris from the Hyksos period.[85] A shrine to Baal Zephon is listed among those of other deities at Memphis in the late Ramesside period Papyrus Sallier IV.[86] The meanings of *yam sûp̱*, Migdol, and Pi Hahiroth are suggestive of the nature of those toponyms. The same is not true of Baal Zephon. What kind of place was it? A town, lake, fort, or something else? Papyrus Anastasi III describes the lacustrine northeastern frontier and specifically mentions the Lake of Horus and *pꜣ ṯwfy* (Reed Sea), as well as another watery feature called "the waters of Baal," but the proximity of those waters to the two lakes is unclear.[87] The nature and location of Baal Zephon in Exod 14:2 remains uncertain, but Baal was

---

81. Amihai Sneh, Tuvia Weissbrod, and Itamar Perath, "Evidence for an Ancient Egyptian Frontier Canal," *American Scientist* 63 (1975): 542–48.

82. "Praise of Pi-Ramessu," trans. James P. Allen (*COS* 3.4:15).

83. Bietak, *Tell el-Dab'a II*, 2:137, and plates 10, 23; Bietak, "On the Historicity of the Exodus," 28, fig. 2.3.

84. "Praise of Pi-Ramessu" (*COS* 3.15), and see n. 4. See further James E. Hoch, *Semitic Words in Egyptian Texts of the New Kingdom and Third Intermediate Period* (Princeton: Princeton Univ. Press, 1994), §322; Hoffmeier, *Ancient Israel in Sinai*, 105–8.

85. Bietak, *Avaris: The Capital of the Hyksos*, 25–29, fig. 25.

86. Gardiner, *Late Egyptian Miscellanies*, 89.6–7.

87. Gardiner, *Late Egyptian Miscellanies*, 22.8.

revered in Egypt throughout the second millennium. There apparently was a watery feature with Baal's name somewhere in the northeastern frontier near the Lake of Horus and *pꜣ ṯwfy* that might correspond to Baal Zephon.

Some Concluding Thoughts on §§ I-IV

What is the significance of this? In my judgment many of the details reviewed here, from types of gemstones, priestly garb, to geographical, environmental, and toponymic specificities, would not and possibly could not have been known to the Hebrew author(s) had the biblical texts been composed in the seventh through fifth centuries BC. And if they were somehow known, these seemingly trivial Egyptian minutiae would have been meaningless to a Jewish audience in the Babylonian-Persian period. All of this is relevant as we seek to date the writing of the text and the date of the exodus itself.

The Date of the Exodus

The previous sections concentrated on various details in the narrative of Exodus 1–14, which suggest to me that we are dealing with the genuine experiences of early Israelites that were foundational to their religious and social development. The raison d'être of the covenant, particular laws, various religious practices and rites, the message of the prophets, and certain praises contained in psalms make no sense without a historical exodus. This is why much of my essay has focused on these authenticating details.

I have argued that the biblical data and supportive archaeological evidence for a sojourn and exodus is compelling, and without these events, the remainder of Israel's history is incomprehensible. As interesting as the date of the exodus is, it is a secondary issue. The first half of my academic career, I was sympathetic with (but not dogmatic about) the fifteenth-century date (see Scott Stripling's chapter). In the past twenty years, I shifted to the thirteenth-century date.[88] The main reason for my switch was that I started framing the question differently, asking how one would date the exodus event using only the book of Exodus. Naturally, if the book had contained the name(s) of the pharaoh(s)

88. Hoffmeier, "What Is the Biblical Date for the Exodus?" 225–47.

involved in Exod 1–14, establishing the date of the events would be straightforward. Some believe that the absence of the pharaoh's name demonstrates that the narratives were not historical. I believe there is a better explanation for the absence of the king's name. The narratives of Exod 1–4 and 5–14 telescope events and pharaohs over a period of time, spanning perhaps several centuries. In 5:2 the king made an incalculable blunder when he responded to Moses' request, "Who is the LORD, that I should obey him and let Israel go? *I do not know the LORD* and I will not let Israel go" (NIV, emphasis mine). The narrative demonstrates throughout that YHWH is the God of the exodus; the crucial matter is not the identity of Pharaoh(s), and the omission of the king's name helps make that point. By way of contrast, Exodus names the Hebrew midwives, Shiphrah and Puah (1:15), women of lowly status when compared with Pharaoh. Why are they named in Exod 1, while Pharaoh is not? They feared God (1:17, 21); the recalcitrant king did not. Clearly, the author elevates or diminishes the characters by naming the former and using anonymity for the latter according to his theological purposes.

There are two additional reasons for detailing the toponyms in the previous section. First, it is clear that some of these place-names have been located or possibly identified (see above). Others possibly correspond to toponyms occurring in Egyptian sources or are based on Egyptian terms, even if their location presently eludes us (Baal Zephon, Etham). Second, all the geographical names reviewed previously are attested in Egyptian documents dating to the period 1300–1150 BC. The four references to Rameses in Exodus are critical for dating the narrative, because this city flourished only during the same time span that these texts did,[89] and this city is not mentioned again in the Bible after Num 33:5. When a later psalmist sang about the exodus wonders, he placed them in the "region of Zoan[/Tanis]" (Ps 78:12, 43 NIV). The reason seems evident. The Ramesside metropolis was gone, and nearby stood the largest east delta city from 1070 BC down to Roman times. The psalmist preferred to use the name of the current delta

89. The title the "gods of Pi-Ramesses" continues into the next millennium, indicating that some of the cults from the defunct city were honored elsewhere. It is quite a stretch to believe that from these small, obscure cults the Hebrews derived the name Rameses in the seventh–sixth centuries, as Egyptologist Edward F. Wente has theorized ("Rameses," *ABD* 5:617–18), a view warmly embraced by some biblical scholars.

capital—a city known to first-millennium Israelites—rather than the long-departed Rameses counterpart.

A final chronological datum is the reference to Israel in Merenptah's famous stela. Ramesses II's son and successor launched a military campaign into Canaan no later than his fifth regnal year (ca. 1208 BC), meaning that Israelites were in the southern Levant in sufficient numbers for Merenptah to target.[90] Considering that the construction of Pi-Ramesses began under Seti I and was completed by Ramesses II (ca. 1294 and 1260 BC) and that Merenptah's Asiatic campaign falls ca. 1208 BC, 1270–1240 BC seems like a plausible window of time for the exodus.

Logistical Matters

One of the perplexing problems about the exodus is the size of the group. Exodus 12:37 reports there were six "hundred thousand men" *(šēš mēʾôṯ ʾelep̱)*. This figure seems to derive from the tribe-based military census taken in Sinai in Num 1 of those older than twenty who could fight. Six hundred thousand men, plus women and children, could easily total around three million to four million. Logistically, this is impossible. Egypt's entire population in the New Kingdom is estimated to be just three million,[91] while Pi-Ramesses' has been reckoned to be three hundred thousand, based on the surveys of its size (ten square kilometers), including the data offered by geophysical prospection.[92] Then too, during the Ramesside era, Egypt's military is thought to range from twenty-five thousand to forty thousand troops.[93] Therefore six hundred thousand able-bodied Hebrew men would have outnumbered the entire Egyptian army by a rate of between fifteen and twenty-four to one. The Israelites could have walked off the job and easily overwhelmed their masters!

Then too, had three million to four million Israelites arrived in Canaan en masse, they would have vanquished the entire land in short

---

90. For translations, see "The (Israel) Stela of Merneptah," trans. James K. Hoffmeier (*COS* 2.6:40–41); "The Poetical Stela of Merneptah (Israel Stela)," in Miriam Lichtheim, *Ancient Egyptian Literature* (Berkeley: Univ. of California Press, 1976), 2:73–77.

91. Butzer, *Early Hydraulic Civilization in Egypt*, 76–77.

92. Edgar Pusch, Helmut Becker, and Jörg W. E. Fassbinder, *Einblicke in die Struktur der Ramses-Stadt durch magnetische Prospektion und Grabung*, Grabungen des Pelizaeus-Museums Hildesheim in Qantir—Pi-Ramesse 9 (Hildesheim: Roemer-und Pelizaeus-Museum, 2017).

93. Hoffmeier, *Ancient Israel in Sinai*, 154–55; Anthony J. Spalinger, *War in Ancient Egypt* (Oxford: Blackwell, 2005), 203–4.

order. But Josh 13:1–7 and Judg 1 offer a different picture. During the prosperous days of the Middle Bronze Age, which ended around 1500 BC, 140,000 people are thought to have been scattered around the city-states that constituted Canaan.[94] In the Late Bronze Age (ca. 1500–1200 BC), the population declined as Egypt's empire dominated the region,[95] especially the Mediterranean coastal regions and major travel routes via Megiddo and Beit Shean, home to Egyptian garrisons.

Such a small population in Canaan would have been overwhelmed by a multimillion-person Israelite juggernaut, and the population of the southern Levant would have increased twenty-five-fold. There is no archaeological evidence for such a population explosion at any time between 2000 and 1200 BC. When all is considered, a much smaller population of Israelites must necessarily be envisioned. What about the "six hundred thousand" reference?

Numbers in the Hebrew Bible do not utilize numerals. So one cannot dismiss this as a scribal error by someone adding too many zeros. Rather the number is written alphabetically, and the critical word is *ʾelep̱*, which has commonly been translated "thousand" but can also be rendered "clan." Gideon lamented, "My clan *[ʾelep̱]* is the weakest in Manasseh" (Judg 6:15). A third meaning for *ʾelep̱* is "military unit." David brought food to his brothers on the battlefront with the Philistines, along with some cheese "to the commander of their unit *[ʾelep̱]*" (1 Sam 17:18 NIV). Given the military context of the Num 1 census, the nature of the soldierly march out of Egypt (cf. Exod 12:51; 13:18; 14:8), and the fact that the six hundred *ʾelep̱* are made *gibbôrîm*, which can mean "warriors"[96] (the standard word for men, *ʾănāšîm*, is not used), "military unit" is a sensible reading of *ʾelep̱*. One could translate this expression *(šēš mēʾôṯ ʾelep̱)* as "six hundred units," with the exact number of men per unit remaining unknown.[97] The precise total of the census occurs in Num 1:46 (and is repeated in 2:32) and is "six hundred thousand and three thousand and five hundred and fifty" (my translation). So one possible interpretation of this, using the

94. For a review of the demographic data for Canaan from the third through first millennia, see Hoffmeier, *Ancient Israel in Sinai*, 155–56.

95. Shlomo Bunimovitz, "On the Edge of Empires—Late Bronze Age (1500–1200 BCE)," in *The Archaeology of Society in the Holy Land*, ed. Thomas E. Levy (London: Leicester Univ. Press, 1995), 326–27.

96. *HALOT* 172.

97. For an extensive discussion of these issues, see Hoffmeier, *Ancient Israel in Sinai*, 155–59.

foregoing reasoning, is: 600 units [of] 3,550 (warriors). If we multiply this figure three or four times (to account for women and children), a more manageable and plausible population is in view.

Theology and History

I have argued in this essay that the Bible itself views the exodus as a real event with profound theological significance that shaped many aspects of Israel's religious life (Passover, the Feast of Unleavened Bread, the Feast of Tabernacles, redeeming the firstborn). Israelites were not to abuse immigrants in their midst, because they knew what it was like to be oppressed as sojourners when they were in Egypt (Exod 22:21; 23:9; Lev 19:33–34; Deut 10:19).

We return now to Israel's eighth-century prophets, who recall the exodus and wilderness traditions to make theological points in their day. Micah, from Judah, appeals to the ancient story:

> "I brought you up from the land of Egypt
> and redeemed you from the house of slavery,
> and I sent before you Moses,
> Aaron, and Miriam.
> O my people, remember what Balak king of Moab devised,
> and what Balaam the son of Beor answered him,
> and what happened from Shittim to Gilgal,
> that you may know the righteous acts of the LORD."
> (Mic 6:4–5 ESV)

Gerhard Maier explains that in this pericope Micah "runs very briefly through the Exodus from Egypt, Moses, Aaron, Miriam, Balak, Balaam, Shittim, and Gilgal—in the chronological sequence found in the Pentateuch, incidentally—and speaks of God's actions encountered by Israel at each of these stages in its history, without needing to clarify any elements of this history."[98] These prophets unambiguously believed that Israel's relationship with God was tied to historical events from

98. Gerhard Maier, "Truth and Reality in the Historical Understanding of the Old Testament," in *Israel's Past in Present Research: Essays on Ancient Israelite Historiography*, ed. V. Philips Long, Sources for Biblical and Theological Study 7 (Winona Lake, IN: Eisenbrauns, 1999), 204.

centuries earlier. Indeed, Jerry Hwang has argued that the exodus and wilderness passages in Hosea illustrate "that Hosea is well versed in an ancient tradition of Yahweh's deliverance from Egypt" and that "the declaration 'I am Yahweh your God from the land of Egypt' would have been both widely known and accepted as historically true in the 8th century BC."[99] It stands to reason that if the eighth-century audiences did not fully embrace this narrative, the prophets would not have called attention to it. Finally, as Hwang has cogently argued, "It would be illogical for Hosea to assail his hearers for not knowing what they had never known and for forgetting a past that had never happened."[100] So I maintain there was a real exodus and that the evidence in the book of Exodus points to the thirteenth century BC, although I am willing to be persuaded otherwise should compelling extrabiblical evidence come to light.

---

99. Jerry Hwang, "'I Am Yahweh Your God from the Land of Egypt': Hosea's Use of the Exodus Traditions," in Hoffmeier, Millard, and Rendsburg, *Did I Not Bring Israel out of Egypt?* 252.

100. Hwang, "I Am Yahweh Your God," 252.

RESPONSE TO JAMES K. HOFFMEIER (THE FIFTEENTH-CENTURY EXODUS VIEW)

SCOTT STRIPLING

Professor Hoffmeier sets forth a strong case for the historicity of the exodus. Those who value the relationship between ancient Egypt and the pentateuchal narratives will find much to further their study in both the text and the footnotes. The faith community will certainly appreciate the respect with which Hoffmeier handles the biblical text, and the academic community will value his scholarly attention to details. Both groups will encounter a wealth of well-documented information which establishes a cultural milieu in the New Kingdom period that harmonizes with the exodus account. Surprisingly, Hoffmeier devotes almost his entire essay to this very thing, with less focus on the case for a thirteenth-century BC exodus. In the following, I respond in order to each of Hoffmeier's sections.

Historicity and the Bible

After briefly explicating Amos 9:7 and Exod 20:2, Hoffmeier discloses his view that "real events stand behind the sojourn and exodus traditions." He cites scholars such as Graham Davies, Yair Hoffman, and John Bright who hold similar views and J. Maxwell Miller, John Hayes, Israel Finkelstein, Neil Silberman, and Jan Assmann who advance more liberal paradigms. With this juxtaposition established, Hoffmeier moves next to his approach.

How I Approach the Hebrew Bible / Old Testament

First, Hoffmeier makes clear to the reader that since the Enlightenment there has been a "hermeneutic of suspicion," and as a result "the Bible is not treated in the same way as are other historical sources." This is a sad but true reality. Like Hoffmeier, I agree with William Hallo that we should treat ancient sources like the Bible "critically but without condescension" and in light of other ancient texts which can often illuminate the background to help the reader understand the intent of the ancient writer. A knowledge of the mythology of ancient Near Eastern cultures is essential to understanding how and why Israel did what it did.

Exodus and History

Hoffmeier addresses historiography and rightly reminds readers to be cautious in light of the absence of direct archaeological evidence that substantiates the exodus. He presciently observes that the decentralization which occurred in the First and Second Intermediate periods allowed "Semitic-speaking pastoralists . . . to infiltrate Egypt." Evidence of a significant Semitic population at numerous sites in the Egyptian delta (biblical Goshen), especially Tell el-Dab'a (Avaris) and Tell el-Maskhuta, is helpful, since Hoffmeier later links these to important sites mentioned in the exodus itinerary. He informs readers that Hebrews may have been a part of the Semitic population that dominated the region during the Fourteenth–Seventeenth Dynasties. While I appreciate his caution, to me it seems almost certain that Hebrews dwelt in the delta. As I note in my contribution, stratigraphic analysis at Tell el-Dab'a reveals that the Semites living there abandoned the site in the mid-fifteenth century BC (Eighteenth Dynasty). This abandonment could be evidence of the exodus at the time of the early exodus date (ca. 1446 BC, not the thirteenth-century BC date favored by Hoffmeier).

After explaining the events which led to the formation of the Eighteenth Dynasty, Hoffmeier gives three examples of forced labor by foreigners. The first example, the tomb of Rekhmire, "shows . . . POWs making and hauling bricks" immediately prior to the time of the early-date exodus. The other examples come from the Nineteenth Dynasty. He notes that Papyrus Leiden 348 documents *'pr* (Habiru) in Egyptian servitude during the time of Ramesses II, and then he explores in a footnote the possibility that these slaves were Hebrews. The term *'pr* (Habiru) linguistically points to Hebrews, some of whom may have been recaptured by the Egyptians and returned to forced servitude. We know that Amenhotep II rounded up slaves in southern Palestine in

November of his ninth year in his Second Asiatic Campaign—just after the exodus, in my view.[101] As I discuss in my contribution, the Amarna letters portray Habiru sieging the city-states of Canaan early in the Late Bronze IIA period (1400–1300 BC), the same time that the early exodus date places the Israelites' struggle to establish hegemony in Canaan. In this section Hoffmeier successfully establishes the Egyptian practice of enslaving foreigners.

Next Hoffmeier looks at evidence within the Torah from a sociological perspective. Over time the Hebrew language blended with Egyptian language, as to be expected of a minority population's language. This can be seen in personal names such as Miriam, Phineas, and Assir. He notes that some names are theophoric. Ahira incorporates the name of the sun god, Re, and Hur is certainly a form of Horus, the sky god. Hoffmeier correctly cites scholars Hugo Gressmann, Carol Meyers, and Benjamin Noonan to demonstrate Egyptian linguistic influence on the tabernacle and its implements. Even raw materials such as acacia wood and turquoise connect the Hebrews to Egypt. Hoffmeier demonstrates the pervading influence of the Egyptian language on the Hebrew language, including numerous cognates in Exod 2:3. His establishment of verisimilitude in this section is effectively done.

Hoffmeier presents Donald Redford's perspective that the geographical terms in the exodus narrative point to a seventh-century BC writing, but he makes sure that his readers know that the Egyptian toponyms "are also attested in Egyptian texts in the previous millennium." Next Hoffmeier presents a summary of the research on the locations of Pithom and Rameses, followed by a fifteen-hundred-word discussion on the exodus route. While this is interesting research, it does not address his task of dating the exodus. He spends more than twice the number of words on the exodus route as he does on evidence to support his thirteenth-century BC exodus view.

The Date of the Exodus

Clearly, Hoffmeier's top priority is establishing that the exodus actually happened. When it happened is a secondary matter to him. While I

---

101. "The Memphis and Karnak Stelae of Amenhotep II," trans. James K. Hoffmeier (*COS* 2.3:21–22).

agree with Hoffmeier that the date of the exodus is less important than establishing that the event occurred, I was surprised that he presented only three lines of evidence, two of them very briefly, to support a thirteenth-century BC exodus.

First, Hoffmeier argues that only the book of Exodus should be used to determine the date of the exodus. He adopted this methodological approach twenty years ago, presumably around 2000. Prior to this, he was "sympathetic with (but not dogmatic about) the fifteenth-century date." Hoffmeier's own account indicates that when the entirety of the Bible is allowed into evidence, the early date increases in viability. He does not explain the reason for shifting his hermeneutical approach. I see value in studying the exodus in isolation before comparing and contrasting the findings with other biblical books, but isolated study should be only one step in the interpretive process.

Second, Hoffmeier argues that the store cities of Pithom and Rameses fit best in the thirteenth century BC. Hoffmeier writes, "The four references to Rameses in Exodus are critical for dating the narrative, because this city flourished only during the same time span that these texts did." In my essay I argue that the references to Rameses in Exodus are intentional anachronisms meant to direct later readers to the correct site, which was ancient Avaris, the site from which the exodus began in the mid-fifteenth century BC. Two centuries later Ramesses II rebuilt the northern part of Avaris (modern Qantir), naming it after himself.

A New Testament scholar interested in the chronology of Jesus' ministry would rightly study each gospel in isolation, but that would not be the final step. He or she would then seek to synchronize Johannine chronology with that presented by the other gospel writers. Likewise, an Old Testament scholar studying the conquest might study Joshua in isolation and get the impression that after seven years Israel had subdued most of Canaan. Judges, however, presents a much more nuanced and protracted process of subjugation. Only by studying both books together would a full picture emerge. Scripture illuminates Scripture.

I earned a master of arts degree in English and taught American literature for many years. If I wanted my students to understand the worldview of Nathaniel Hawthorne, I might ask them to limit their initial analysis to his greatest novel, *The Scarlet Letter*, but the students' understanding would be incomplete if they never read Hawthorne's other novels and short stories. A late-date exodus diminishes in appeal when the data in Exodus is read in light of 1 Kgs 6:1, Judg 11:26, 1 Chr 6:33–37, Ezek 40:1, and Acts 7:29–30. Strong extrabiblical and archaeological data, like these passages, point to the exodus occurring in the mid-fifteenth century BC, during the Eighteenth Dynasty.

Hoffmeier bases his third argument on the Merenptah Stela. This famous relief mentions Israel among those defeated by Merenptah. The stela dates to about 1210 BC, and Hoffmeier's "plausible window of time for the exodus" is 1270–1240 BC. In 1270 BC it is plausible, but not likely, that Israel would have become powerful enough to merit inclusion on Merenptah's list of vanquished nations. If the exodus occurred in 1240 BC, Israel would not even have arrived in Canaan, as the Bible records a forty-year wilderness sojourn between the exodus and conquest. In 1250 BC Israel would have just arrived in Canaan and been marching around Jericho's walls. So the Merenptah Stela better fits the early exodus date, since Israel was already a well-established nation by the time of Merenptah.

Importantly, the Berlin Pedestal, which Görg dates to a time earlier than that of the Merenptah Stela, has a partly effaced toponym that is in the same sequence of vanquished enemies as where "Israel" appears on the Merenptah Stela, and for which no satisfactory reading other than "Israel" has been offered by the scholarly community.[102] Hoffmeier's three reasons to place the exodus in the thirteenth century BC fail to persuade me. If there is more evidence, I would love to examine it.

Logistical Matters

Hoffmeier makes a strong case for an exodus of thousands, not millions. He demonstrates that the semantic range of the Hebrew word *ʾelep* includes "clan" (Judg 6:15) and "military unit" (1 Sam 17:18). Translating *ʾelep* as "one thousand" presents several problems. With an army of around six hundred thousand fighting men, the entire nation would have numbered around three million to four million, according to Hoffmeier. The number would have been even larger in my estimation. Hoffmeier points out that the entire population of Egypt was about three million, and the Egyptian army numbered between twenty-five

102. Manfred Görg, "Israel in Hieroglyphen," *BN* 106 (2001): 21–27.

thousand and forty thousand men. The total population of Canaan was about fifty thousand when the Israelites arrived. If Israel numbered in the millions, there would have been no need for miraculous deliverance from Egypt or for divine help with the conquest. They would have overpowered Egypt and crushed the Canaanite city-states.

Conclusion

Hoffmeier succeeded in proving beyond a reasonable doubt that there was a historical exodus. He places this watershed event in the thirteenth century BC, but he remains open-minded "should compelling extrabiblical evidence come to light." I applaud Hoffmeier's excellent research and his willingness to be persuaded, but I regret that so little of his essay dealt with the actual date of the exodus.

RESPONSE TO JAMES K. HOFFMEIER (THE THIRTEENTH-CENTURY HYKSOS/LEVITE-LED EXODUS VIEW)

PETER FEINMAN

Hoffmeier's contribution complements my own. We both believe in a historical exodus in the time of Ramesses II. In effect he defines the stage, while I write the story. If there was a performance of the exodus, then Hoffmeier would be responsible for the set, the props, the costumes, the vocabulary, and fact-checking the dialogue: "My contention is that if the stage on which the drama of the biblical story is acted out contains authentic sets and props that fit the geographical setting and the chronological parameters, then the plausibility of the narratives is enhanced."

So while it may not be possible to prove the occurrence of the exodus with "historic certitude," similarly it cannot be disproved because of inauthentic or erroneous background information.

My contribution to the performance would be the action, the actual story. I do not mean to suggest that Hoffmeier agrees with my historical reconstruction of the exodus. As I write this response to his contribution, I have not yet had the opportunity to read his response to mine. Nonetheless, I consider the two contributions to work together.

Hoffmeier begins with a question from Amos in the eighth century BC about the exodus. While I agree with both Hoffmeier and Amos that eighth-century Judah believed there had been an exodus, I would not use that claim to prove the case that there had been one five centuries earlier. I do agree with him that the overwhelming number of references to the exodus reflects a widespread belief that the exodus had occurred, but belief is not proof. Still, why would anyone in Amos's audience take him seriously if he was making up a story from scratch?

In the next paragraphs, Hoffmeier surveys the various interpretations in biblical scholarship. He notes the antipathy toward the Bible from those who study and distrust it (probably in part because of what people have done in its name). He is correct to observe that if the Bible were simply a secular book (like the *Iliad*), "it probably would not be treated in such a condescending and dismissive manner." As a result, the standard of proof for an event contained in the Bible is not beyond a reasonable doubt: there has to be no alternative explanation even possible before a biblical event can be considered true. While these are my words, I think they reflect the frustration Hoffmeier has with biblical scholarship as it is often practiced today.

As a point of clarification, Hoffmeier notes the expulsion of the Hyksos in the sixteenth century as an explanation for the exodus (such as by Egyptologist Donald Redford, his own teacher). The Hyksos have been an irresistible lure for people seeking a historical exodus (like the Thera volcano, which passed unnoticed in these contributions). People are right to consider the Hyksos but wrong to limit that consideration to the sixteenth century BC. My historical reconstruction recognizes this earlier occurrence of the Hyksos defeat but focuses on their continued presence in Egypt into the thirteenth century BC.

In his section on enslaved foreigners in Egypt, Hoffmeier comments on "Hebrews in the delta, who would be associated with the hated Hyksos." Here we disagree. My contention is that the Hebrews were warriors from across the river Nile and therefore are to be equated with the Hyksos. Some of these Hebrews/Hyksos later led people out of Egypt and became Levites. The equation of Hebrews with Hyksos necessitates an excursus on the slavery and brickmaking aspects of the exodus story, elements which do not appear in my historical reconstruction. I do not question that some of the people the Hyksos led out of Egypt were non-Hyksos slaves.

Unfortunately, within the parameters of the length of the contributions to this book, it is not possible to deal with all the issues involved. The forced labor for the building projects of "Pharaoh" Solomon and Pharaoh's daughter, the king and queen of Israel, seemed to indicate that the conditions warranting another exodus had occurred. That realization contributed to a going forth from the kingdom a generation later to create the northern kingdom of Israel. Numerous biblical scholars have commented on the similarities of the golden calves of Jeroboam to the golden calf of the exodus. The exodus story was retold at this time as part of the cultural memory of the event, a perspective that is related to the contribution to this book by Ronald Hendel. As Americans, we continually retell the stories of Thanksgiving, the American Revolution, and the Civil War and Lincoln to address contemporary issues. Similarly, the period of forced labor in the tenth century BC would have been an ideal time to retell the story of the exodus.

Hoffmeier also notes the Hebrew/Habiru issue. Like Sterling, he considers the words *ʿpr/ḫāpiru/ḫābiru* (Habiru) and *Hebrew* to be a linguistic match. However, he goes on to define the former as a sociological reference and not an ethnic one in the ancient Near East. He recognizes that it "is impossible to determine" if there were Israelites in the Habiru. Unfortunately, he discusses this point in a footnote, so it may be missed by readers of his contribution.

The next several pages are devoted to the realia of Egyptian life. Hoffmeier examines toponyms, personal names, vocabulary, technical terms, and physical items. These sections represent about half of his contribution and relate directly to his stated intention to document the stage on which the exodus occurred.

Part of this section is devoted to the route of the exodus. Here he draws on his own archaeological excavations in the delta and northern Sinai. He seeks to link biblical names and Egyptian names on the Egyptian Ways of Horus and the biblical "way [to] the land of the Philistines" (Exod 13:17). I would like to add one consideration which reflects a different view regarding the writing of the biblical text. Hoffmeier does not directly address that question here. Based on his previous contribution to this series in a book on Gen 1–11, he rejects the traditional documentary hypothesis. I have problems with it too. But one thought which comes to mind for me is that the route detailed in Exod 13 (vv. 17–22) is not from Moses writing about the route in his present. Rather it is by someone later who wondered about the route of the exodus and drew on his knowledge in his present. Someone was trying to figure out how Moses did what he did, and in effect conducted research: how do people travel from Egypt to Canaan *now*? The result is the same because the basic road across Sinai with its fortifications had not changed. But he was writing at a time when the name "way [to] the land of the Philistines" existed, whereas it did not in the time of Moses.

Some of the issues addressed by Hoffmeier are similar to those in the Stripling contribution. This similarity should not be surprising, as these two contributors are evangelical Christians. Hoffmeier states that the unnamed king of Egypt "made an incalculable blunder when he responded to Moses' request, 'Who is the LORD, that I should obey him and let Israel go? *I do not know the LORD* and I will not let Israel go' [Exod 5:2 NIV, emphasis added]." But did the historical pharaoh of the exodus utter these words, or did the exodus storyteller put these words in the mouth of the character? Hoffmeier leaves open who the author was and when he lived. If you choose to think Moses is the author, then you believe he has firsthand knowledge of what Pharaoh said. If you choose to believe that the narrative was written centuries later, then the words are the creation of the storyteller, an "Israelite Homer." Hoffmeier finesses the question by using the anonymous "author," allowing readers to draw their own conclusions. I can accept that a historical Miriam sang a song of victory and that it was remembered. As for the dialogue, I would look to what it meant at the time it was written, a time when Israel had both king and prophet.

Hoffmeier's interpretation of the Merenptah Stela is more consistent with my own position than with that of Stripling. The latter postulates that a "mid-thirteenth century [exodus] followed by a forty-year wilderness sojourn and an initial conquest of six years does not allow adequate time for the development and recognition of national Israel at the end of the same century [as required by the Merenptah Stela]." Putting aside Stripling's overreliance on the purported biblical-chronological literalness, the Merenptah Stela is quite compatible with the time frames Hoffmeier and I suggest. Hoffmeier proposed a 1270–1240 BC window, while I propose the seventh year of the reign of Ramesses II. Either dating provides sufficient time for an Egyptian departure, a wilderness wandering, and a Canaanite arrival.

Hoffmeier and Stripling reach similar conclusions on the definition of *ʾelep*. It refers to a military unit like a platoon and not to "thousand." I agree. However, I disagree that an organized twelve-tribe structure even existed prior to Solomon, with his taxes and forced labor. I would add that *ʾelep* is not so much an exodus term as an Iron I

(1200–1000 BC) term from the time of Deborah. The time of mustering troops by tribes occurred in the period of the judges prior to the monarchy and a professional or permanent military force under the direct control of the king. It also reflects a time when Israel had expanded beyond the people who had participated in the exodus, to include those who had not. These newcomers still wanted and needed to be connected to the foundational event of the people to whom they now belonged. Including all the tribes by name in the exodus story was part of the way the cultural memory was maintained (see my Hendel response), and that practice was developed in the time of Deborah (see my Rendsburg response).

Hoffmeier's observation about the purported Babylonian-Persian period origin of the exodus story applies to the Merenptah Stela as well, although he does not state this. He questions how people in the seventh to fifth centuries BC would know such Egyptian minutiae as evidenced in the exodus story: it "would have been meaningless to a Jewish audience in the Babylonian-Persian period." The same observation applies to the Merenptah Stela. The Egyptian audience already knew the name Israel. Merenptah was not introducing a strange term that would cause his Egyptian audience to scratch their heads in bewildered confusion and ask, "Who are they?" They remembered the name from the exodus in the time of Ramesses II. Egypt had a cultural memory of the exodus too, a factor Hendel does not seem to consider (see my Hendel response).

As in Stripling's contribution, there is no human element in Hoffmeier's contribution. I am guessing this is because both contributors rely on the biblical text and its dialogue to present that story. Hoffmeier makes a point of identifying the stage, with its props, on which the narrative occurred. But once having done so, he stops. His contribution does not address the narrative itself. He simply provides the backdrop for a historical exodus, without breathing any life into that background. I am not criticizing the validity of the stage Hoffmeier has depicted, simply noting the absence of any story. The implication is that we should accept the biblical story as inerrant since there is no suggestion of any historical alternative. I want to know why real people risked their lives in defying the most powerful person in their known world.

Hoffmeier concludes his contribution with the assertions that the exodus occurred as a historical event and that ancient Israel believed it had occurred. I agree. He ends by stating he is willing to be persuaded that it did not occur in the thirteenth century BC "should compelling extrabiblical evidence come to light." In my contribution I present not new evidence but new interpretations of existing evidence that I think provide the story that played out on the stage Hoffmeier describes.

RESPONSE TO JAMES K. HOFFMEIER
(THE TWELFTH-CENTURY EXODUS VIEW)

GARY A. RENDSBURG

Of the five main contributors to the present volume, James Hoffmeier is the unsurpassed master of the historical geography of the eastern delta and the north Sinai coast. He devotes much of his article, accordingly, to issues relating to the toponyms mentioned in the biblical account: Pithom, Rameses, Sukkot, Migdol, Pi Hahiroth, and the Sea of Reeds. I defer to Hoffmeier on all these matters and accept his conclusions, which are well argued and are in conformity with the archaeological reports produced by Manfred Bietak, Edgar Pusch, Henning Franzmeier, and others.

As indicated in the next section, I also concur with Hoffmeier's judicious use of Egyptian sources such as Papyrus Anastasi VI, Papyrus Leiden 348, and Papyrus Anastasi V. These documents, in said order, provide very close parallels to the basic narrative of the Bible: arrival in Egypt, corvée labor, and escape from Egypt.

A good portion of Hoffmeier's article is devoted to Egyptian words which appear in the Bible, especially in the tabernacle account, with special attention to precious stones, clothing items, and the like. I might prefer a tighter linguistic argument for one or two of these items, but in the main the presentation is sound. That said, the presence of these Egyptian words within Biblical Hebrew does not guarantee that the Israelites were resident in Egypt for any length of time. Clearly, per my own main essay in this volume, I believe that they were, but in theory any Shasu group of the Southland could have borrowed these terms for high-status items from ancient Egyptian, given the general Egyptian cultural influence over the Sinai, modern-day southern Israel, modern-day southern Jordan, and indeed Canaan as well.

Semites were busy at work in the turquoise mines in western Sinai, while Egyptians were present at copper mines and foundries in southern Israel (Timnaʿ) and southern Jordan (Khirbet en-Naḥas). One will assume, accordingly, that Semites across the region interacted with Egyptians throughout the period under discussion (and probably long before and long after). As a literary vignette indicative of such interaction, note how Reuel's daughters refer to Moses as an *ʾîš miṣrî*, "an Egyptian man" (Exod 2:19).

Somewhat oddly, only a small portion of Hoffmeier's article is devoted to the subject adumbrated in the title. I refer to his opinion that the exodus occurred during the thirteenth century BCE, about which Hoffmeier has comparatively little to say. Perhaps he felt no need to argue the point, since the thirteenth century BCE remains the standard date proposed by those who hold to the historical exodus. In addition, and to be fair, Hoffmeier adds, "As interesting as the date of the exodus is, it is a secondary issue." Nevertheless, one would have hoped for some defense of the thirteenth-century date.

A few questions are raised here, accordingly. Not regarding the exodus per se but in the lead-up thereto, Hoffmeier writes, "Thus a range from 200–400 years [for the sojourn of the Israelites in Egypt] is possible." I did not address this issue in my essay, but using the same methodology that I employed there yields a very different reconstruction. Moses and Aaron are the great-grandsons of Levi: note the genealogy of Levi-Kohath-Amram-Moses presented in Exod 6:16–20. According to the biblical tradition, since Levi and Kohath emigrated from Canaan to Egypt (Gen 46:11, etc.), and since Moses and Aaron represent the older segment of the generation which left Egypt (Exod 12:50, etc.), the entire sojourn in Egypt could have lasted only fifty years or so. See further the tradition recorded in Gen 15:13–16, which states that Abra(ha)m's descendants would be strangers in a foreign land but would return to the land of Canaan in the fourth generation—a pronouncement consistent with the genealogy presented in Exod 6:16–20. All of this speaks to a much shorter time span of Israelite residency in Egypt than is normally posited, including by Hoffmeier here.

The fuller statement by Hoffmeier is as follows: "The Torah reports that the Hebrews spent 400 (Gen 15:13) or 430 (Exod 12:40) years in Egypt, whereas, in the Septuagint, Exod 12:40 offers an alternative reading that shortens the stay to 215 years. Thus a range from 200–400 years is possible." This statement suffers from the same difficulty as does Stripling's attempt to date the exodus to the fifteenth century BCE (see my response): both rely on a literal acceptance of the years presented in the Bible (in either its Hebrew or its Greek forms, in Hoffmeier's case). But as I showed in my response to Stripling's essay, and as I argued forcefully (I hope) in my own essay, the years used by the early Hebrew prose writers bear little or no reality and cannot be used for chronological reconstruction. By contrast, the genealogical information conveyed in the Bible (save the doctored material in Chronicles) reflects an internal consistency.

Using the same methodology for the date of the exodus, I would ask my good friend and learned colleague: how does he arrive at the thirteenth-century date for the exodus? As I argue in my chapter, the genealogy of David (admittedly, the only one that we possess[103]) points to a twelfth-century date for the exodus. What real evidence is there for the thirteenth century? Hoffmeier, like almost everyone else, uses the Merenptah Stela to bolster the proposal. In his words, "A final chronological datum is the reference to Israel in Merenptah's famous stela. Ramesses II's son and successor launched a military campaign into Canaan no later than his fifth regnal year (ca. 1208 BC), meaning that Israelites were in the southern Levant in sufficient numbers for Merenptah to target." To repeat what I have argued in my essay, though, does the Merenptah Stela really imply that the Israelites—a people without a land (per the classifier/determinative) ca. 1208 BCE—mean that they were resident in Canaan at this time? Too many questions remain, and not enough answers are provided.

Hoffmeier ends his essay with the following open—and honest—statement: "So I maintain there was a real exodus and that the evidence in the book of Exodus points to the thirteenth century BC, although I am willing to be persuaded otherwise should compelling extrabiblical evidence come to light." The evidence that I have provided is not necessarily extrabiblical, but it does coordinate a reasonable interpretation of the Merenptah Stela, the evidence of the Bible, and the archaeological data from twelfth-century Canaan. Might I convince my friend and colleague of the correctness of my stance?

---

103. Apart from the doctored ones in the book of Chronicles, for which see my essay and my critique of Stripling.

RESPONSE TO JAMES K. HOFFMEIER
(THE EXODUS AS CULTURAL MEMORY VIEW)

RONALD HENDEL

James Hoffmeier has a more complicated and subtle approach than does Scott Stripling. He advocates a thirteenth-century date, which puts him within the mainstream of modern biblical scholarship. Like Stripling, he also holds that the Bible is "a reliable source for history." But, he adds, it does not seem to be wholly reliable. He writes, "Accepting the historicity of the exodus narratives, however, does not necessarily require one to believe in divine intervention in the plagues or parting the sea." Hoffmeier's position, if I understand it correctly, takes a flexible view of biblical inerrancy. The historical backdrop is accurate, but the writers took some license in their representation of the events. As he says, "Historical events were interpreted through a religious lens."

In this view the exodus is basically historical, but its events have been revised and interpreted to make them more religiously meaningful. Hoffmeier agrees with Moshe Garsiel that the Bible contains "history that is intertwined with theological outlook and enriched with rhetoric and literary structures and literary devices." This is a sophisticated approach to biblical history and the concept of inerrancy. It allows for the nonhistoricity of some miracles, which may be the product of writers' interpretation of events and not the events themselves. It is an approach that includes the writers' accommodation of events to their ancient worldview. This is similar to the approach of John Calvin (especially in his commentary on Genesis), but I assume it draws the ire of some conservative evangelicals.

There are two areas where I wish to disagree with Hoffmeier. These have to do with parts of his position that are close to the standard doctrine of inerrancy. First is his view that verisimilitude implies historical accuracy. Second is his view that the biblical text of Exodus must have been written very shortly after its thirteenth-century date, possibly by Moses, although he does not say this. He argues that it could not have been written hundreds of years later, when most biblical scholars—myself included—date the text of Exodus. These are complicated issues, which I can only touch on briefly here.

Verisimilitude and History

Hoffmeier writes, "My contention is that if the stage on which the drama of the biblical story is acted out contains authentic sets and props that fit the geographical setting and the chronological parameters, then the plausibility of the narratives is enhanced." This may be true, but the "fit" of these details to the geography and historical setting of the exodus can have a variety of implications. As Hoffmeier's dramaturgical language indicates, the sets and props on a stage can be "authentic" even if some or all of the characters and events are fictional. Anyone who has seen a play or movie about past events—let's say Shakespeare or *Gone with the Wind*—can bear this out.

As the theologian Hans Frei has emphasized, verisimilitude in biblical narrative isn't the same thing as history. Biblical narrative tends to be "history-like" in its representation of events—as does the modern novel—but that doesn't mean that the persons and events are historical. As Frei observes, one should not conflate realism with reality.[104] Of course, a history-like or realistic narrative *may* be historically accurate, but the style, the setting, and the props do not make it so. Hoffmeier's learned investigation concerns, as he says, the "authentic sets and props" and shows the degree to which the biblical narrative is history-like. But it is a more complicated and difficult task to establish that the *events* are historical. Hoffmeier seems to take this on faith, with allowance for the interpretive influence of the writers' "religious lens."

Hoffmeier makes a further claim about the sets and props. He writes that many of the details that he discusses "would not and possibly could not have been known to the Hebrew author(s) had they been composed

---

104. Hans W. Frei, *The Eclipse of Biblical Narrative: A Study in Eighteenth and Nineteenth Century Hermeneutics* (New Haven: Yale Univ. Press, 1974), 1–16.

in the seventh through fifth centuries BC." Since I date the prose narratives of the exodus to around the ninth to sixth centuries BCE, I should explain why I disagree with his position on these details. This has more to do with the date for the composition of the book of Exodus than with the date of the exodus itself.

Hoffmeier says that many of the details in the text would have been forgotten after the thirteenth or twelfth century BCE. I agree that there are memories of Egyptian slavery and Canaanites in Egypt that probably stem from the era of the Egyptian Empire, so I will limit my remarks to cases in his sections III–V. Some of the details that he addresses in these sections may be authentic early memories, but others are not. His position is marred by the availability of many of these details during the first millennium BCE.

Personal Names and Place-Names

There are several personal names in Exodus that are originally Egyptian, including Phineas, Hophni, and Merari. These give a touch of verisimilitude to the story. But Egyptian elements in personal names are known throughout the monarchic period. The names of Egyptian gods occur in personal names in Hebrew inscriptions of the eighth to sixth centuries BCE, including Isis, Bes, and Horus. People knew Egyptian names in this period, and some of the Egyptian or Egyptian-like names in the Pentateuch may have been formulated then. Others may derive from the earlier period. It's hard to tell which is which. A case for the date of the exodus cannot rely on these names, since they can date from anytime in this span. They do not prove or eliminate an early or late date.

The place-name Rameses is a good example (Exod 1:11). As Hoffmeier says, the city of Rameses in Exod 1:11 is a memory of the great city of Pi-Ramesses, built by Ramesses II at the beginning of his reign (ca. 1279 BCE) and abandoned at the end of the Ramesside period (1069 BCE). But as Egyptologists have shown, the memory of this city persisted through much of the first millennium. The Ramesside literary tradition of praising the city of Pi-Ramesses continued up to the eighth century BCE.[105] And as Hoffmeier notes, the god Amun of Pi-Ramesses

105. Bernd U. Schipper, "Raamses, Pithom, and the Exodus: A Critical Evaluation of Ex 1:11," *VT* 65 (2015): 269–72.

was worshiped in Thebes until Ptolemaic times. The biblical reference to the city of Rameses bears on the antiquity of the memory of this city, but it doesn't mean that the text could have been written only in the second millennium BCE. The memory of this great city lingered for many centuries. It may have lingered in Israelite memory from the time of the Egyptian Empire or been rekindled by Egyptian influence during the first millennium, perhaps during a time of Egyptian hegemony over Israel, as occurred in the late seventh century BCE.[106] In any case, the memory of the great city of Rameses persisted.

Loanwords, Linens, and Precious Stones

There are many Egyptian loanwords in Hebrew, including words for ink, linen, boat, and monkey. This does not mean that the people of the exodus carried these words from Egypt to Israel, and it does not mean that all of these words entered Hebrew early. As Hoffmeier shows, there are two Hebrew words for linen (*šēš* and *bûṣ*) and both come from Egyptian, but one is used in Classical Biblical Hebrew and the other in Late Biblical Hebrew. Clearly, one of them entered Hebrew much later than the thirteenth century. Other loanwords may have entered Hebrew later too. But even if many entered early, this says nothing about the date or historicity of the exodus or the composition of the book of Exodus. It only shows that Egyptian administrators and soldiers lived in Canaan during the Egyptian Empire, and through them Egyptian words entered the local language. Egyptian was a prestige language during this period, and Egyptian emulation was a strong cultural factor.

Hoffmeier makes a strong point about the words for precious stones in the priestly breastplate, in particular turquoise *(nōpek)*, which is an Egyptian loanword. Turquoise was a prestige item mined by Egypt in the Sinai. Hoffmeier says, "Its presence in the priestly breastplate is significant. In the Iron II period and later times, turquoise was not available to biblical writers to include in the description of the breastplate in [Exodus]." But this is not so. Turquoise was known in the first millennium BCE, even after the Sinai mines ceased. As Hoffmeier notes, the word occurs in Ezek 27:16, where it is a commodity in the prince of Tyre's trade network. Hoffmeier argues that Ezekiel is dependent on the

106. This is the thesis of Schipper's article.

priestly breastplate in Exodus for this idea. But turquoise was a prestige commodity in the Iron II period and after. The best evidence is from the recent excavation of an eighth-century tomb of Assyrian queens from Calah, whose crowns, bracelets, and other jewelry are inlaid with turquoise.[107] Turquoise was also inlaid in the wings of Egyptian *ba* statues in the seventh century and later. So Ezekiel is probably accurate about turquoise in the Tyrian trade. Biblical writers knew about turquoise—and much else—in this period. This word—and the precious stone it designates—was known over a long period and so can't serve as evidence for a date for the exodus or the biblical text.

These examples show that the influence and prestige of Egypt (and things with Egyptian names, like turquoise and ink) affected Israel both early and late. In the book of Exodus, the Egyptian touches add to the verisimilitude of the story. But none of them has a direct bearing on the historicity of the exodus. They are, as Hoffmeier says, props and sets in a religious drama about great events of the past. Nor do they have direct bearing on when the book of Exodus was written. But there are other evidences of language that do help, such as the linguistic history of Hebrew, as I have tried to show elsewhere.[108]

---

107. Muzahim Mahmoud Hussein, *Nimrud: The Queens' Tombs*, Oriental Institute Miscellaneous Publications (Chicago: Oriental Institute of the Univ. of Chicago, 2016). Some of these stones may be faux turquoise, but the implications for turquoise as a precious stone in this period are the same.

108. Ronald Hendel and Jan Joosten, *How Old Is the Hebrew Bible? A Linguistic, Textual, and Historical Study*, ABRL (New Haven: Yale Univ. Press, 2018).

REJOINDER

JAMES K. HOFFMEIER

Chronology and Historicity: The Focal Point of Rameses/Pi-Ramesses

Critical to the thirteenth-century date of the exodus is the toponym Pi-Ramesses ("Rameses" in Exod 1:11). This name corresponds to the thirteenth-century delta capital that Stripling believes is a later textual gloss for the earlier city, Avaris. One can reconstruct history only by working with the texts as they are rather than speculating about what was written in an earlier version. Thus the mention of Rameses in Exod 1:11 should be given its due weight as the primary chronological marker.

But the stakes regarding Pi-Ramesses are even higher than chronology as it impacts historicity. Thus I must address Bernd Schipper's recent article in *Vetus Testamentum*,[109] which is embraced by Hendel. Schipper argues that many inscribed blocks from Pi-Ramesses were transferred to build Tanis and that cults centered at Pi-Ramesses enjoyed renewed veneration, causing the name to survive in later periods. Hendel therefore challenges the antiquity of the toponym Pi-Ramesses, suggesting that its use reflects a first-millennium writing, not one from the thirteenth–twelfth centuries.

There are good reasons to question Hendel's and Schipper's view. Pi-Ramesses was deserted between 1140–1130 BC, according to Kenneth Kitchen, the foremost Ramesside scholar.[110] The Bible never

109. Even though I strongly disagreed with his interpretation of the data and believe he misconstrued the linguistic evidence, I recommended the paper for publication. However, I plan to challenge Schipper's interpretation in the second edition of my *Israel in Egypt* (now in preparation).

110. Ramesses VI (1143–1136 BC) is the last pharaoh whose name appears on monuments at Pi-Ramesses; cf. Kenneth A. Kitchen, "Egyptians and Hebrews, from Ra'amses to Jericho," in *The Origin of Early Israel—Biblical, Historical and Archaeological Perspectives*, ed.

uses "Rameses" (Gen 47:11; Exod 1:11; 12:37; Num 33:3, 5) to mean "Tanis/Zoan" (Heb. *ṣōʿan*); however, in the first millennium, Tanis occurs in lieu of Pi-Ramesses for obvious reasons (e.g., Ps. 78:12, 43). Pi-Ramesses did not exist during Israel's monarchy, but twelve miles north stood its replacement, Avaris. If the authors of the Torah wrote in the mid-first millennium, Tanis would likely be used in the Torah. Bietak has recently argued that the late period cults begin in the fourth century and therefore are too late to have influenced the biblical writers. He concludes, "The start of the itinerary in Exodus (13:17–18; 14:2) reflects the topographical conditions of the Ramesside Period."[111] I concur, as does Kitchen.[112]

Merenptah Stela Redux

Stripling claims that a thirteenth-century exodus is ruled out because Israel would not be "powerful enough to merit inclusion" in the Merenptah Stela. This is a curious argument, since he believes that "Israel" occurs on the Berlin Pedestal (for issues with his view on this, see my response to him), dating to Amenhotep III (1390–1353 BC) or slightly earlier.[113] Such dating does not allow sufficient time for Israelites who entered Canaan in ca. 1406 to be included on this inscription, so if a set period of time is required for an entity to gain power before being mentioned in an Egyptian text, the argument cuts both ways!

Genealogies and the Length of the Sojourn

Rendsburg spurns the biblical figures for the length of the sojourn because that entails treating the figures literally, and in his judgment they "bear little or no reality." I too recognize that large figures in the Hebrew Bible—and in ancient Near Eastern texts—can be used for different reasons and not just for chronology, such as a *Distanzangabe*

Shmuel Aḥituv and Eliezer D. Oren, Beer-Sheva Studies by the Department of Bible and Ancient Near East 12 (Beersheva: Ben-Gurion Univ. of the Negev Press, 1998), 81.

111. Manfred Bietak, "On the Historicity of the Exodus: What Egyptology Today Can Contribute to Assessing the Biblical Account of the Sojourn in Egypt," in Levy, Schneider, and Propp, *Israel's Exodus in Transdisciplinary Perspective*, 30.

112. Kitchen, "Egyptians and Hebrews," 80–84.

113. Robert Ritner, "The Supposed Earliest Hieroglyphic Mention of Israel (Berlin AM 21687): A Refutation," in *Semitic, Biblical, and Jewish Studies in Honor of Richard C. Steiner*, ed. Aaron J. Koller, Mordechai Z. Cohen, and Adina Moshavi (New York: Yeshiva Univ. Press, 2020), 37.

(see my response to Stripling).[114] Nevertheless, it seems inconceivable that the tradition of a period of tranquility followed by an era of bondage can be reduced to just two generations.

The weight of Rendsburg's argument rests on taking genealogies literally. He maintains that Moses' genealogy in Exod 6 corresponds to Gen 15:13, where Abraham is told that his offspring would be sojourners *(gēr)* and slaves *('ebed)* for four hundred years but would return in the fourth generation (15:16). Since Levi and Kohath went to Egypt, this leaves just two generations to be born in Egypt before the exodus. The "fourth generation" in Gen 15:16, however, minimally suggests that four generations were born in Egypt (not two). However, because four hundred years and four generations *(dôr)* occur together in parallelism, they likely "are equated."[115] *Dôr* can refer to longer blocks of time than the twenty to twenty-five years (literal generation) or forty years (a symbolic generation).[116] Thus the four hundred years and the fourth *dôr*, or cycle of time, represent the same block of time.

Rendsburg argues that David's genealogy in Ruth 4:18–22 also favors a twelfth-century exodus. This conclusion requires one to treat this list literally and exhaustively and to dismiss the longer genealogical lists as "doctored" (expanded), like Heman's in 1 Chronicles. But this is not always the case in the ancient world. Egyptian genealogies and king lists at times omit individuals (e.g., Hatshepsut), portions of a dynasty, or even entire dynasties. The Abydos King List removed both Amarna period rulers and the Hyksos dynasties. I cannot cite a single case in which nonhistorical figures were added to embellish an Egyptian king list.[117]

Rendsburg believes that the period covered in the book of Judges can be drastically abbreviated, thus accommodating to his twelfth-century exodus. The literary-structural of Judges compares with Assyrian summary texts, in which campaigns or events are arranged not necessarily

114. I suggested this understanding of 480 in Hoffmeier, "What Is the Biblical Date for the Exodus?" 237–38.

115. Gordon Wenham, *Genesis 1–15*, WBC (Waco, TX: Word, 1987), 332.

116. See Nahum Sarna, *Genesis: The JPS Torah Commentary* (Philadelphia: Jewish Publication Society, 1989), 116; Kitchen, *On the Reliability of the Old Testament*, 256; James K. Hoffmeier, "Egyptian Religious Influences on the Early Hebrews," in Hoffmeier, Millard, and Rendsburg, "Did I Not Bring Israel out of Egypt?" 4.

117. "King Lists," trans. James K. Hoffmeier (*COS* 1.37:68–73).

chronologically but geographically and ideologically.[118] Judges uses a similar scheme, meaning the order of events described therein is not chronologically arranged. Thus their value in chronological reconstructions is tenuous at best.

I have a great deal of respect for Gary A. Rendsburg. Ultimately, I find there are problems with his understanding of genealogies. Crucially, I simply cannot ignore the writing "Israel" in the Merenptah Stela and its implications for the origins of Israel or Proto-Israel in Canaan before the end of the thirteenth century.

Of Turquoise and Gems

The gemstone turquoise (Heb. *nōp̱eḵ*), mentioned in the high priest's breastplate (Exod 28:18; 39:11), indisputably derives from the Egyptian term *mfkꜣt*.[119] Egyptian mining operations in Sinai lasted for more than two millennia and ended when Pi-Ramesses was deserted (ca. 1140–1130 BC).[120] After that turquoise is rare to nonexistent in Egypt and the Levant. This is background to my claim that "in the Iron II period and later times, turquoise was not available to biblical writers." Thus Hendel's criticism is valid to a point; I should have more carefully nuanced my claim, as was done in the collaborative and multidisciplinary study of gemstones in the Hebrew Bible. In that study my colleagues and I concluded that turquoise was *rare* in the Levant and Mesopotamia in the Late Bronze Age and "is *virtually absent* in the archaeological record of Egypt and the Near East after the 12th century BC."[121] True, turquoise appears in a few cases of later jewelry in Egypt, in which it may have been reused from earlier ornaments or heirlooms. The source of the turquoise in the Assyrian queens' tombs at Nimrud, mentioned by Hendel,

118. K. Lawson Younger, "Judges 1 in Its Near Eastern Literary Context," in *Faith, Tradition, and History: Old Testament Historiography in Its Near Eastern Context*, ed. James K. Hoffmeier, Alan R. Millard, and David W. Baker (Winona Lake, IN: Eisenbrauns, 1994), 207–27.

119. Yoshiyuki Muchiki, *Egyptian Proper Names and Loanwords in North-West Semitic*, SBLDS 173 (Atlanta: Society of Biblical Literature, 1999), 251.

120. Ramesses VI is the last pharaoh whose name appears at the Serabit el-Khadim turquoise mining area; see A. H. Gardiner, T. Eric Peet, and Jaroslav Černý, *The Inscriptions of Sinai*, 2 vols. (London: Egypt Exploration Society, 1952–1955), 2:38–39.

121. James A. Harrell, James K. Hoffmeier, and Kenton E. Williams, "Hebrew Gemstones in the Old Testament: A Lexical, Geological, and Archaeological Analysis," *BBR* 27 (2017), 17–18, 31–32. Quote from p. 44.

is unknown, but it possibly came from Iran.[122] A survey of Babylonian and Assyrian lexica, including the *Chicago Assyrian Dictionary*, indicates that there is no known word for turquoise.[123]

The reality is, archaeological discoveries from the Levant in the Iron II–III periods are devoid of turquoise, and linguistic evidence offered by Lambdin shows that *nōp̱eḵ* entered Hebrew before the first millennium.[124] So I stand by my earlier conclusions that the use of *nōp̱eḵ* in Exodus points to the time and space (Sinai) where turquoise was readily available.

Philosophical Issues and Concluding Remarks

I agree with Dr. Feinman that "it may not be possible to *prove* the occurrence of the exodus with 'historic certitude.'" Historians don't use the word "prove" when it comes to ancient history, and they use it even less with biblical history. It has been said that "a historian cannot know what *really* happened, but he/she has a duty to try."[125]

"Critical" biblical scholars typically are averse to speaking of possibilities or probabilities when it comes to the Pentateuch as a witness to history, owing to modern and postmodern skepticism. These scholars often believe that conservative scholars err because of flawed philosophical or theological assumptions. This seems highly unfair, as everyone interprets texts, especially the Bible, through their political, theological, worldview, and experiential lenses. Anyone assuming that they approach the text dispassionately succumbs to the Baconian fallacy—"the idea that a historian can operate without the aid of preconceived questions, hypotheses, ideas, assumptions, theories, paradigms, postulates, prejudices, presumptions, or general presuppositions of any kind."[126] Hendel does a disservice to our dialogue and advancing knowledge by thinking

---

122. Edward Gübelin, "A Visit to the Ancient Turquoise Mines in Iran," *Gems and Gemology* 12, no. 1 (1966): 3–13; Mohsen Manutchehr-Danai, "On the Turquoise Deposits of Nishabur (N. E. Iran)," *Gems and Gemology* 15, no. 10 (1977): 315–19; Peter Bancroft, *Gem and Crystal Treasures* (Fallbrook: Western Enterprises and Mineralogical Record, 1984), 285–88.

123. I am grateful for the assistance of my colleague, K. Lawson Younger, with this search.

124. Thomas O. Lambdin, "Egyptian Loan Words in the Old Testament," *JAOS* 73 (1952): 152.

125. David Hackett Fischer, *Historians' Fallacies* (New York: Harper, 1970), 43, emphasis in original.

126. Fischer, *Historians' Fallacies*, 4.

my scholarship and conclusions are tainted by my theology (even though I never appeal to it when advancing an argument). Our assumptions notwithstanding, we need to focus our efforts on the actual data and their implications for "proof."

Mark Lanier, one of the premier trial lawyers in the U.S., acknowledges that court cases must meet the burden of proof. But those verdicts are typically rendered according to the preponderance or "greater weight" of evidence, and this includes circumstantial evidence.[127] The same holds for historical research. With ancient texts and other archaeological data, one has to examine carefully all the details in a text or a piece of iconography to determine authenticity, and place them on the scale to see which way it tips as the data piles up. I believe that the preponderance of biblical and extrabiblical evidence tilts the scale in favor of a historical exodus. I try to achieve this in my chapter by using the image of a stage on which the drama is played. A historically authentic stage does not prove that the drama was acted out, but if the props were all wrong and anachronistic, the story would surely be dismissed by Biblicists.

---

127. Lanier is the founder and owner of the impressive Lanier Theological Library in Houston, Texas, and is a biblical scholar in his own right.

CHAPTER THREE

THE THIRTEENTH-CENTURY HYKSOS/LEVITE-LED EXODUS VIEW

PETER FEINMAN

In the seventh hour of the last night of the seventh year in the reign of Ramesses II, the Hebrew/Hyksos Levite Moses led people out of Egypt against the will of Ramesses II. He later constituted them as the people Israel and told stories that became the basis of the Hebrew Bible. These sentences express my claim that a historical exodus occurred during the reign of Ramesses II. My contribution to this book will not address the biblical account of the exodus. Instead it will focus on the Egyptian record, archaeological, textual, and historical evidence. In some cases it will show how the biblical account derives from and is consistent with such evidence. This claim that the exodus happened is at significant variance with biblical scholarship that denies it occurred or claims that any departure was minor in nature and would not have been noticeable.

One guiding methodological principle is the concept that literature is politics / politics is literature.[1] Conceptually, the idea of history as it actually was is irrelevant to ancient Egyptian and Israelite narrative-writing. Outside of business or sale contracts, writings were not meant

1. As reflected in the title of David S. Vanderhooft and Abraham Winitzer, eds., *Literature as Politics, Politics as Literature: Essays on the Ancient Near East in Honor of Peter Machinist* (Winona Lake, IN: Eisenbrauns, 2013).

to be biologically, literally true. In modern terms these writings were political in nature to serve the needs of the king or the political leaders. The challenge for us is to recognize what texts meant in the time they were composed. That means even if a smoking gun for the exodus existed, we might not recognize it. The issue is not how we would express the departure from Egypt against the will of Pharaoh but how Pharaoh, who had been publicly defied, would express it. What would you expect Ramesses to say—for the record—after the exodus?

In this essay we will focus on three issues: the Levites, the Hyksos, and a proposed historical reconstruction. More specifically, we'll ask, "Who were the Levites?" and examine the understanding of the identity and history of the Levites according to current scholarship. The goal is to determine if a location for them within the Egyptian world can be identified. Then we will ask, "Who were Hyksos?" and examine the understanding of the identity and history of the Hyksos according to current scholarship. The goal in this section is to determine if the Hyksos were somehow connected to the exodus. Then we'll propose a historical reconstruction for the exodus primarily based on the Egyptian archaeological data. The goal in this section is to determine if the Hyksos Levites, but not necessarily *all* Hyksos, had motive, means, and opportunity to depart Egypt against the will of Ramesses II. My hope is that this reconstruction will be considered possible, plausible, and reasonable judging by the archaeological record and will stand on its own merits regardless of one's personal religious beliefs.

Who Were the Levites?

The identity of the Levites is critical to the historical reconstruction of the exodus. Most obviously, Moses is a Levite in the biblical account. Therefore it is essential to clarify who the Levites were in an Egyptian context if one is to propose that a Levite-led exodus historically occurred. Traditionally, biblical scholarship on the Levites has not focused on this issue. The primary areas of interest have been:

1. Their role in the writing of the Hebrew Bible.
2. Their relationship to the Aaronide and Zadokite priesthoods.
3. Their political involvement with the creation and division of the Israelite kingdom.

4. Their connection to Moses, the Mushite priesthood, Nebo, and the Yahweh tradition.
5. Their propensity to violence.

In this contribution I suggest that it is the final item, the propensity to violence, that provides a starting point for situating the Levites in Egypt as leaders of the exodus (that includes leading non-Levites as well). To do so, I begin with the scholarship on Levite violence, then propose a link of the Levites to Egypt, and finally offer my interpretation of the Levite-Hyksos connection.

To begin with, these are the verses typically cited to illustrate that violent aspect of the Levite identity:[2]

- *Genesis 34:25:* "Three days later, while all of them were still in pain, two of Jacob's sons, Simeon and Levi, Dinah's brothers, took their swords and attacked the unsuspecting city, killing every male."
- *Genesis 49:5–7:* "Simeon and Levi are brothers—their swords are weapons of violence. Let me not enter their council, let me not join their assembly, for they have killed men in their anger and hamstrung oxen as they pleased. Cursed be their anger, so fierce, and their fury, so cruel! I will scatter them in Jacob and disperse them in Israel."
- *Exodus 32:27–28:* "Then he [Moses] said to them, 'This is what the Lord, the God of Israel, says: "Each man strap a sword to his side. Go back and forth through the camp from one end to the other, each killing his brother and friend and neighbor."' The Levites did as Moses commanded, and that day about three thousand of the people died."
- *Deuteronomy 33:8–11:* "About Levi he [Moses] said: 'Your Thummim and Urim belong to your faithful servant. You tested him at Massah; you contended with him at the waters of Meribah. He said of his father and mother, "I have no regard for them." He did not recognize his brothers or acknowledge his own children, but he watched over your word and guarded your covenant. He teaches your precepts

2. All citations are from the NIV.

> to Jacob and your law to Israel. He offers incense before you and whole burnt offerings on your altar. Bless all his skills, LORD, and be pleased with the work of his hands. Strike down those who rise against him, his foes till they rise no more.'"

Exactly how it came to be that the Levites and violence are so closely linked is not clear.[3]

In his oral presentation titled "The Fightin' Mushites" two years prior to his published paper, Mark Leuchter stated in his abstract, "The priestly line founded by Moses (the 'Mushites,' following [Frank Moore] Cross and others) stands out most prominently in this regard in premonarchic tradition and, subsequently, in the northern kingdom. . . . But how did the Mushites establish themselves as a dominant priestly house, and at what point did Moses himself become a typological symbol of the Levites more broadly?"[4]

Leuchter finds his answers in the violent Mushite legacy of Moses slaying the Egyptian taskmaster who beat a Hebrew (Exod 2:11–22). In that episode Moses flees to Midian, where he marries Zipporah and they have a son, Gershom. Leuchter dismisses the biblical "stranger in a strange land" explanation for the name of Gershom as its true meaning. Citing various scholars, Leuchter links the shared root *grš* to the action of the shepherds who "drove away" the women watering at the well before Moses turned the table on them. Thus the son was named after the action whereby his parents met. Leuchter then suggests that the term Gershom was less a name than a title signifying a Mushite who acts to defend the weak, be it the Hebrew man in Egypt or the Midianite women in the wilderness. In the remainder of the article, Leuchter elaborates on the continuity of this marital prowess tradition. Levite violence may well have been against Egypt, but it was against imperial Egypt in Canaan. The Levites originate in the

---

3. For the Levites and violence, see Joel S. Baden, "The Violent Origins of the Levites: Text and Tradition," in *Levites and Priests in Biblical History and Tradition*, ed. Mark A. Leuchter and Jeremy M. Hutton, AIL 9 (Leiden: Brill, 2012), 103-16; Mark A. Leuchter, "The Fightin' Mushites," *VT* 62 (2012): 479–500.

4. Mark A. Leuchter, "The Fightin' Mushites" (paper presented at the Columbia Hebrew Bible Seminar, Columbia, NY, March 17, 2010). The published article dates the presentation to February 2010.

twelfth century BC and have no connection to a Transjordanian or Egyptian Moses.[5]

It remained for Richard Elliott Friedman to firmly push the Levite identity back to the origin of Israel in Egypt itself. In his book *Who Wrote the Bible?* (1987), Friedman suggests that perhaps among the people who became Israel only the Levites had been slaves in Egypt. He cites the Egyptian names of key Israelites such as Moses and Aaron's grandson Phinehas. Years later he returned to that subject online and at a Society of Biblical Literature conference (2014). Finally, he published *The Exodus* (2017). It repeats and elaborates on his previous scholarship in a forty-one-page section titled "The Levites and the Exodus." However, Friedman does not extensively engage Egyptological scholarship on the place of Asiatics in Egypt in the second millennium BC, including the Hyksos. As a result, he is unable to situate the Levites in Egypt or to suggest how the marginalized slaves developed their literary and violent proclivities.[6]

He then offers a suggestion that bears similarity to Leuchter's analysis of the name Gershom. Friedman posits that the people who became Levites probably were not known by that name in Egypt. He cites the work of William Propp, who stated the personal name Levi most probably means "attached" or "joined" person, in the sense of a "resident alien."[7] He acknowledges that "we don't have any idea what they would have been called here [in Egypt]."[8] So just as there is no point in seeking a people named Israel living in Egypt, Friedman claims there is no point in seeking a people there named Levites either. The challenge then is to identify a Semitic people in Egypt who would choose to defy Pharaoh and then come to be known for their status as resident aliens in the exodus.

---

5. Leuchter, "The Fightin' Mushites," 489–94. He shares the mnemohistory approach of Ronald Hendel, who is a contributor to this book.

6. Richard Elliott Friedman, *Who Wrote the Bible?* (San Francisco: HarperSanFrancisco, 1987), 82; idem, "The Exodus Is Not Fiction: An Interview with Richard Elliott Friedman," *Reform Judaism* (Spring 2014), 6–8, 60, https://reformjudaism.org/exodus-not-fiction; idem, "Levites and Priests in History and Tradition" (paper presented at the annual conference of the Society of Biblical Literature, San Diego, CA, November 24, 2014); idem, "The Historical Exodus: The Evidence for the Levites Leaving Egypt and the Introduction of YHWH into Israel," *TheTorah.com*, January 2015, www.thetorah.com/article/the-historical-exodus; idem, *The Exodus* (New York: HarperCollins, 2017), 31–71, 72–74. See also Richard Elliott Friedman, "Love Your Neighbor: Only Israelites or Everyone?" *BAR* 40, no. 5 (September/October 2014): 48–52.

7. Friedman, *The Exodus*, 63.

8. Friedman, *The Exodus*, 67.

Who Were the Hyksos?

If one accepts Friedman's insight of a Levite-in-Egypt origin for the exodus, then that acceptance leads to the quest to identify within Egypt the Semitic resident aliens who were associated with violence. For violent Semites in the time of Ramesses II, there are two primary choices: the Hyksos and the lesser-known *n'rn*.[9] *N'rn* is a Semitic word. It refers to soldiers who served in the Egyptian army. Generally, they are considered to be Canaanites from multiple locations now fighting on behalf of Egypt, but their ethnicity is under debate among Egyptologists. However, Merenptah's Karnak Inscription clearly differentiates the *n'rn* from the victorious Egyptian troops as they are contrasted with each other.[10] One might even inquire why Merenptah chose to compare his Egyptian troops to the *n'rn* in the first place. Evidently, their fighting reputation was well known.

The military participation of Semites in the Egyptian army dates back to the Twelfth and Thirteenth Dynasties. Semitic warriors participated in an internal political conflict during the early part of the Thirteenth Dynasty. In the Egyptian artistic depictions of Levantines during this period, the most frequently attested goods carried by them are weapons. So even before the arrival of the Hyksos or the captives from the campaigns of the New Kingdom pharaohs, there already was a Semitic military presence within the Egyptian military.[11]

The most significant action involving these Semitic warriors fighting on behalf of Egypt occurs with the *n'rn* in the battle of Qadesh, year 5, in the reign of Ramesses II. Not only did this division participate in the battle; the *n'rn* rescued the headstrong commander in chief who had marched into a Hittite trap and barely escaped with his life. In the Egyptian account the *n'rn* appear out of nowhere without

---

9. For the *n'rn*, see Alan R. Schulman, "The *N'rn* at the Battle of Kadesh," *Journal of the American Research Center in Egypt* 1 (1962): 47–52; idem, "The *N'rn* at Kadesh Once Again," *JSSEA* 11 (1981): 7–19.

10. Merenptah's Karnak Inscription is to be differentiated from the more famous Merenptah's Stela, which mentions Israel. For the inscription, see Colleen Manassa, *The Great Karnak Inscription of Merneptah: Grand Strategy in the 13th Century BC*, Yale Egyptological Studies 5 (New Haven: Yale Univ. Press, 2003).

11. Anna-Latifa Mourad, *Rise of the Hyksos: Egypt and the Levant from the Middle Kingdom to the Early Second Intermediate Period* (Oxford: Archaeopress, 2015), 32, 82, 84, 124–30, 200–202.

explanation. They function like the cavalry coming to the rescue. Naturally, Ramesses, who was very meek, more than all men who were on the face of the earth, was eager to give credit where credit was due. He praised the *n'rn* for saving him. At least he did once, when he was not otherwise taking credit for having won the battle all by himself.[12]

Were the Levites of *n'rn* origin? Friedman's violent slave resident aliens makes more sense if they had a military background. Levite *n'rn* would have had a military heritage, but there is more to the Levite heritage than violence. They also are closely associated with the writing of the Hebrew Bible.[13] The *n'rn* did not have the writing, cultural, and leadership experience of the Hyksos, who had once ruled Egypt (Fifteenth Dynasty, ca. 1650–1550 BC) and remained a more elite and educated group. One may speculate that the commanding officers of this Semitic division were Hyksos. One should also note that such a domestic military force would have posed a threat if they became disgruntled over their treatment by Ramesses II. In a real-world scenario this consideration is important in a historical reconstruction. It is intriguing to consider the possibility that some Hyksos and Semitic warriors left Egypt against the will of Ramesses after having rescued him in the battle of Qadesh.

The Hyksos of Manetho

If the resident aliens were not *n'rn*, then were they Hyksos? The Hyksos have been associated with the exodus for more than two millennia. The connection is best known from Manetho. He was a third-century BCE Egyptian priest who wrote a history of Egypt in Greek, possibly during the reign of Ptolemy II Philadelphus (285–246 BCE). He does not appear to have originated the linkage but was drawing on an older and accepted tradition. If this dating is correct, it means that at the same time he was writing his Egyptian history in Greek, Jews in Egypt were translating the Hebrew Bible into Greek in what became known as the Septuagint. It is very likely these two scholarly ethnic groups

12. The battle of Qadesh between Ramesses II and the Hittites is one of the best-documented battles in the history of the ancient Near East. For its impact on the exodus, see below.

13. For the Levites and writing, see Karel van der Toorn, *Scribal Culture and the Making of the Hebrew Bible* (Cambridge: Harvard Univ. Press, 2007).

were aware of one another, as they were both competing for the favor of the Ptolemaic king. Manetho was not an Egyptologist in the current sense of the term but was more of a political player seeking to impress a foreign ruler.

We no longer have a copy of Manetho's history. All that survives are excerpts quoted by other writers. The critical excerpts relating to the exodus are by Josephus, the first-century CE Jewish historian. Besides the more familiar writings about himself, the Jewish war against Rome (the Masada incident), and a Jewish history, Josephus authored *Against Apion*.[14] As the title suggests, Josephus wrote this in response to the writings of another individual, Apion, who had written derogatively about the Jews. He sought to counter these anti-Semitic slurs with his own publication, and in doing so, he included references to other anti-Semitic writers, including Manetho. One should remain cognizant of the political objectives of these writings even though they contain historical information about both the time of the writer and the time that the writings are about.

The texts cited in this analysis represent the words of Manetho and not an analysis or comment by Josephus. He introduces Manetho's account about the Hyksos by stating it is about "us" (*Ag. Ap.* 1.74). By so doing, Josephus indicates that he accepts the connection between the Hyksos and the Jews. He then pledges that he will report Manethos's words as if he were the participant in a court proceeding (*Ag. Ap.* 1.74). Evidently, Josephus believes this testimonial tactic will lend credulity to his own words, contra this witness.

The account begins with Manetho disparaging the achievements of the Hyksos, whom he identifies by that name (*Ag. Ap.* 1.82). Instead of their being conquerors of Egypt, as Alexander the Great had been, these people are of ignoble origin. Manetho describes their entrance into Egypt as not being one of glorious conquest by exalted warriors. Instead an unnamed Egyptian deity, who sought to punish Egypt for an unstated reason, allowed these Hyksos to enter the land (*Ag. Ap.* 1.75). It should be noted that contrary to Manetho, there is no archaeological evidence of a Hyksos "expedition" or campaign to conquer Egypt (see

14. See *The Complete Works of Josephus*, trans. William Whiston (Grand Rapids: Kregel, 1981), 607–22.

the following). Manetho is denying a heroic history to the ancestors of the people of the exodus, who are the ancestors of the Jews in his present. He is doing so as part of his anti-Semitic campaign, so his depiction of the Hyksos cannot be relied on as valid. As will be seen, Manetho did not invent this technique of skewing the historical past to deliver a message in the present. The same technique was employed by an unnamed Egyptian about the exodus (see the following).

Manetho continues his assault on the Hyksos by describing their rule in Egypt as horrific. According to him, they committed multiple atrocities. These actions included the burning of cities, the demolishing of temples, and the mistreatment of people, such as the imposition of slavery (*Ag. Ap.* 1.76). Assuming Manetho is aware of the biblical account of the exodus, he has turned the story upside down. He makes the Hyksos, the ancestors of the people of the exodus, the ones who enslaved others. The Hyksos arrival into the land of Egypt was ignominious, and their conduct once there was also despicable. Again, based on the archaeological record, the Hyksos did none of what Manetho claims they did.

Manetho then turns to the Hyksos military administration of Egypt. He claims that the Hyksos established garrisons throughout the land. The reason for this action is revealing. It was to secure the eastern borders from invasion by the Assyrians (*Ag. Ap.* 1.77). The Hyksos did not do this either. The reference made to the Assyrians (who did invade Egypt in the seventh century BC) indicates the actual time period with which Manetho was more familiar. The Assyrians were destructive, and their actions shocked Egypt. It was inconceivable to the Egyptians that these ignoble eastern foreigners could violate their land as they had. It is likely Manetho has retrojected the cause of that trauma onto the Hyksos nearly one thousand years earlier.

Manetho locates the Hyksos capital at Avaris (*Ag. Ap.* 1.78). While the Hyksos did not found that city, they did rule from it. So did the Nineteenth Dynasty pharaohs. The next three verses are devoted to the listing of Hyksos kings. The key name mentioned here is that of Apophis. He will appear in the Egyptian writings of the Eighteenth and Nineteenth Dynasties and is a crucial figure for my historical reconstruction of the exodus (see the following).

At this point, Manetho switches perspectives. Instead of recounting the story of the arrival and rule of the Hyksos, he focuses on the cessation of Hyksos rule because of heroic Egyptians (*Ag. Ap.* 1.84–86). If we ignore the names and numbers of years detailed in these verses, Manetho seems to be referring to the Thebans of the late Seventeenth and early Eighteenth Dynasties, who did displace the Hyksos from rule in the sixteenth century BC. Pharaohs Kamose and Ahmose battled with the Hyksos against Apophis and at the capital city of Avaris.[15] Manetho concludes his description of the Theban-Hyksos confrontation with his version of the departure from Egypt (*Ag. Ap.* 1.87–90). Pharaoh allows them to depart. They do so and journey through the wilderness. Out of fear of the Assyrians who rule over Asia, the Hyksos then build a city called Jerusalem in a country called Judea.

Further on, Manetho provides an extensive description of the exodus departure itself (*Ag. Ap.* 1.228–320). Suffice it to say, his lengthy account heralds the actions of the Egyptian pharaohs, who cleansed the land of lepers. The departure was an expulsion and not an exodus, and it included all the Hyksos and only the Hyksos. Their departure from the land reflected their degenerate identity, as had their arrival. Here one may observe the true purpose of Manetho's anti-Hyksos diatribe: he wants the current pharaoh to expel the leper Jews to cleanse the land just as Egypt had done once before. He is using a historical memory to recommend an action in the present. That begs the question, what was his historical source that linked the Hyksos to the exodus?

The Hyksos of Bietak and Beyond

Until the archaeology of the 1800s and onward to today, this account from Josephus was almost all that was known about the Hyksos. In the nineteenth century Egyptologists began to discover texts about the Hyksos. These texts will be used in the historical reconstruction in the next section. Then, in the 1960s, the Austrian archaeologist Manfred Bietak began excavating what was later determined to be the capital city of the Hyksos when they ruled much of Egypt.[16] While

15. Labib Habachi, *The Second Stela of Kamose and His Struggle against the Hyksos Ruler and His Capital* (Glückstadt: Augustin, 1972); T. G. H. James, "Egypt: From the Expulsion of the Hyksos to Amenophis I," in *The Middle East and the Aegean Region, c.1800–1380 BC*, ed. I. E. S. Edwards et al., 3rd ed., vol. 2/1 of *The Cambridge Ancient History* (Cambridge: Cambridge Univ. Press, 1973), 289–312.

16. Manfred Bietak, *Avaris: The Capital of the Hyksos: Recent Excavations at Tell el-Dab'a* (London: British Museum Press, 1996).

these excavations did not permit the Hyksos to speak to us in their own words, the material remains discovered at the site spoke volumes to our understanding of this people. In the 1990s various scholars working individually and at conferences began to produce book-length studies on the Hyksos, and the scholarship has continued to this day.[17]

Bietak's excavations at Tell el-Dab'a have provided us with a new understanding of the Hyksos, one that is at variance with the view promulgated by Manetho. Anna-Latifa Mourad's book *Rise of the Hyksos* may be considered the most thorough and up-to-date summary of the present state of Hyksos scholarship and is the basis for the following interpretations and conclusion. Avaris was established as a trading depot between Egypt and the Levant following the Asiatic assistance in securing the establishment of the Twelfth Dynasty. The city became a melting pot of Egyptians, Semites, and people of mixed background, with a commercial and military focus. Mourad ends her book specifically with a rewrite of Manetho: "'From the regions of the east,' an elite group of Northern Levantines entered Tell el-Dab'a and Egypt as allies and diplomats, and formed vocational and commercial opportunities with the Egyptians. After some internal socio-political conflicts, the 'elites' seized independence from their city . . ."[18]

That elite became the Fifteenth Dynasty of the Hyksos. One likely location of origin for these "rulers of foreign lands" was Retjenu, possibly in eastern Lebanon. The term appears in the Tale of Sinuhe, and the Hyksos ruler Apophis is identified as being from there.[19] There was no invasion and no hostility between the Egyptians and the Semites in general or the Hyksos in particular.[20]

These discoveries should lead to a reevaluation of both the Semites and the Hyksos in Egyptian history. This process of digesting the information from the archaeological investigations is ongoing. The more one learns about the Hyksos, the more one learns about the people the ancient Egyptians linked to the exodus. The more one learns about the

17. See Marcel Marée, ed., *The Second Intermediate Period (Thirteenth–Seventeenth Dynasties): Current Research, Future Prospects*, OLA 192 (Leuven: Peeters, 2010); Mourad, *Rise of the Hyksos*; Eliezer D. Oren, ed., *The Hyksos: New Historical and Archaeological Perspectives* (Philadelphia: Univ. of Pennsylvania, 1997).

18. Mourad, *Rise of the Hyksos*, 218.

19. Mourad, *Rise of the Hyksos*, 199, 201, 217.

20. Mourad, *Rise of the Hyksos*, 215.

Hyksos, the more one learns about the background of the people who led the exodus and became Levites. The more one learns about the Hyksos, the more one learns about the texts from the time of Ramesses II and Merenptah that are related to that departure from the land.

The Exodus in the Time of Ramesses II

In this section I want to propose a possible historical reconstruction of the exodus based on some Hyksos defying Ramesses II and later becoming known as Levites, or "resident aliens." To do so, there are two considerations to take into account. First, there are four key historical figures involved in this proposed historical reconstruction. Second, there are three Egyptian texts which were produced directly as a result of the historical exodus. These three texts are known to Egyptologists. They are studied separately, and their connections have not been realized. Only by putting the pieces together can one see that these people and texts provide Egyptian documentation of the exodus. Admittedly, without the Hebrew Bible it probably would not have occurred to me to combine these people and texts into a singular exodus narrative. So while the Hebrew Bible is not a direct source in the proposed reconstruction, the biblical story of the exodus does provide the background for making these connections.

There are four historical people involved in this historical reconstruction.

1. *Seqenenre* was a Theban-based Seventeenth Dynasty pharaoh who fought the Hyksos and lost. Seqenenre's legacy lives on through his traumatized skeleton and the Quarrel of Seqenenre and Apophis, also known as the Quarrel Story or the Tale of Apophis and Seqenenre, one of the three texts in the reconstruction.[21] The sole extant copy of the story is from the time of Merenptah, the son and successor to Ramesses II, more than three centuries after Seqenenre lived.
2. *Apophis* was the last Hyksos ruler. Apophis triumphed over Seqenenre and apparently inflicted head wounds to his skull.

21. For a translation of the story, see Adolf Erman, *Ancient Egyptian Poetry and Prose* (New York: Dover, 1995), 165–67.

By contrast Kamose and especially Ahmose were triumphant over him. As is evident from the Quarrel of Seqenenre and Apophis, the historical Hyksos king lived on in the cultural memory of Egypt as both a victor and a defeated adversary.

3. *Ramesses II* is the traditional pharaoh of the exodus and had connections to both the Hyksos and Apophis. His father, Seti I, had reestablished the Hyksos capital at Avaris as the capital for the new Nineteenth Dynasty. Ramesses also experienced defeat or performed below expectations at Qadesh against the Hittites in year 5. The impact of the consequences of that battle against the Hittites has not been adequately factored into understanding the political context in which the exodus occurred. As previously noted, the *n'rn* had rescued Ramesses II when he was trapped in this battle. The aftermath of this battle will be expanded on in the reconstructed context of the exodus.
4. *Merenptah* was the son and successor to Ramesses II and claimed to have destroyed the seed of Israel in the famous stela that now bears his name. As part of his responsibility to restore the cosmos after the exodus, he would have had to explain first how the chaos occurred and then how he ended it. The restoration and maintenance of *ma'at*, the Egyptian sense of cosmic harmony and order, was an essential component of the Egyptian royal ideology. It was paramount that the king show that the world was operating as it should be, as it had been created to be, and that all threats to the cosmic order, both mythical and historical, had been defeated.[22] The ability to do so was foundational to the legitimacy of the king. Failure to do so meant the dissolution of the Egyptian world. After the exodus, Merenptah faced such a cosmological situation. He, like Ahmose, claimed to have restored order through a text, in his case the Quarrel of Seqenenre and Apophis.[23]

Now that we have listed the major characters, let me propose a historical reconstruction that brings them together. The three texts

22. Antonio Loprieno, "The King's Novel," in *Ancient Egyptian Literature: History and Forms*, ed. Antonio Loprieno, Probleme der Ägyptologie 10 (Leiden: Brill, 1996), 277–95.

23. Peter Feinman, "The Tempest in the Tempest: The Natural Historian," *Bulletin of the Egyptological Seminar* 19 (2014): 253–62.

will be introduced in reverse chronological order. The first text will be the aforementioned Quarrel of Seqenenre and Apophis, containing Merenptah's spin on the exodus. The second will be Leiden Hymn 30 by Ramesses II, in which he claimed to have restored *ma'at* by harpooning chaos, a conventional Egyptian motif. The third will be the 400-Year Stela, also from Ramesses II, written after the exodus when he sought to shore up his political support with the Hyksos who had not joined the "resident alien" Hyksos in the exodus.

Seqenenre and Apophis

The Story of Seqenenre and Apophis was a literary creation based on historical figures, intended to deliver a political message about the author's present. There is no constructive purpose served in analyzing the story as a historical document of the sixteenth century BC, in which the story is set. Its historicity is in its expression of concerns of the thirteenth century BC, the time of its composition, through historical figures from the earlier time. The story expresses the Egyptian perspective on the exodus, which had only recently occurred. The Egyptians dealt with the trauma of the exodus in their own terms.[24]

Merenptah did not have the option of naming names, as one would do in writing a history. Then again, he did not commission a history; he needed a political polemic. The story expresses the classic confrontation between cosmos and chaos, between order and disorder, between Egypt and foreigner, that one would expect to find in Egyptian literature, but with the orientation reversed. In the Egyptian tradition, Pharaoh always triumphed, so how could Merenptah write about a pharaoh who had failed? In Egyptian culture, one honored one's father, so how could he write about his father Ramesses II as the one who failed? The technique an unnamed Egyptian author developed was to write a story set in the past about real people but make it about real people in the present. The author counted on the audience to make the connections.[25]

To begin with, why did the author pick Seqenenre to be the defeated

24. Christopher Eyre, "Is Egyptian Historical Literature 'Historical' or 'Literary'?" in *Ancient Egyptian Literature: History and Forms*, ed. Antonio Loprieno, Probleme der Ägyptologie 10 (Leiden: Brill, 1996), 415–33.

25. For the story as a play, see Anthony J. Spalinger, "Two Screen Plays: 'Kamose' and 'Apophis and Seqenenre,'" *Journal of Egyptian History* 3 (2010): 115–35.

pharaoh of his story? The Quarrel of Seqenenre and Apophis was observed in 1828, but the skeleton of Seqenenre was not discovered until 1881, and then it was unrolled in 1886. It had multiple holes in its skull.[26] The visible blunt trauma to the head immediately engendered an effort by Egyptologists to understand what had happened to this individual. Unfortunately, this effort was undertaken with little consideration for the story about Seqenenre.

Gaston Maspero, who led the effort to uncover the mummy, believed Seqenenre had died in battle, surrounded by Hyksos. The Egyptians then recovered and hastily embalmed the partially decomposed body before bringing it to the family tomb in Thebes. In his review of the five wounds to the skull, G. Elliot Smith in 1912 rendered his verdict that Seqenenre had been attacked while lying down by two or more people with probably three or more weapons.[27] Herbert Winlock continued this discussion by noting, "The preparation of the corpse for burial was hasty, the process of embalming most summary, and no attempt was made to lay the body out in orthodox position. It was left contorted as it lay in its death agony."[28]

He then suggested a third possibility: assassination.[29] Winlock suggested that the manner in which Seqenenre had died made him "one of the romantic figures of Egyptian history," likely referring to the Quarrel of Seqenenre and Apophis.

Since the story is not a literal rendering of an event in history but a metaphorical expression of one in cosmological terms, one must scrutinize each element chosen by the author to understand the meaning of his creation. The story begins when the land was in a state of pestilence; one may reasonably conclude that the story will end with the cessation of pestilence and the restoration of *ma'at*. The Hyksos ruler, Apophis,

---

26. For the discovery of the skeleton and the story, see Peter Feinman, "The Quarrel Story: Egypt, the Hyksos, and Canaan," *Conversations with the Biblical World* 35 (2015): 94–127.

27. G. Elliot Smith, *The Royal Mummies* (1912; repr. London: Duckworth, 2012), 1–2, 4–6, quotation from p. 6.

28. H. E. Winlock, "The Tombs of the Kings of the Seventeenth Dynasty of Thebes," *JEA* 10 (1924): 217–77, here p. 249.

29. Winlock, "The Tombs of the Kings," 250. The presumed assassination of Amenemhet I as recounted in the Instruction of Amenemhet is perhaps the most famous literary example in Egyptian history. The assassination of Ramesses III occurred subsequent to the writing of the Quarrel Story.

is in Avaris, and Seqenenre is in the south, meaning Thebes. According to the story, Apophis worships Seth. There comes a time when Apophis sends couriers to Seqenenre to deliver the message that he, Apophis, cannot sleep because of the noise of the hippopotami in the southern capital. Seqenenre is rendered speechless by the message and weeps. An exchange of messages appears to ensue, and the story comes to an abrupt halt, unresolved. There is no indication of how many messages were sent, what actions were taken, or whether any new characters were introduced in the story. It does present Apophis as the initiator of the action, and Seqenenre as the somewhat passive, befuddled, and indecisive receiver of the message. The rest of the story has been lost to history.

Egyptologists have been quick to fill the lacuna from the missing ending by deploying the standard Egyptian paradigm. That template postulates that "Pharaoh smites the enemy." As Egyptologist Jan Assmann describes it, "If there is one iconic image, an emblematic expression of Egyptian political self-identification, it is the image of Pharaoh smiting his enemies."[30] That image is ubiquitous in Egyptian culture, stretching from the dawn of the dynasties through the triumphs of various alien rulers who mimicked/adopted the standard Egyptian iconography. The scenes of this conventional expression of Egyptian triumphalism have been collected and are readily available today.[31]

That very image presented Egyptologists with a conundrum. This Seventeenth Dynasty pharaoh is an anomaly in Egyptian history. Here was a skull of a pharaoh with a plethora of holes in it. Egyptologists were obligated to reconcile these disparate facts. They did so in a way that perpetuated a rut. One has here a textbook case of the need to think outside the box, by recognizing that Seqenenre was not the hero of the story; rather, he was selected for the story because he was a failure. It is in this omission by Egyptologists that the historicity of the exodus in the Egyptian record has been missed. Egyptologist John Wilson provides a typical example of how Egyptologists made Seqenenre the hero of the story despite the blunt-trauma-to-the-skull evidence suggesting

30. Jan Assmann, *Of God and Gods: Egypt, Israel, and the Rise of Monotheism* (Madison: Univ. of Wisconsin Press, 2008), 28.

31. For the ubiquity of the motif "Pharaoh smites an enemy" in Egyptian culture, see Emma Swan Hall, *The Pharaoh Smites His Enemies: A Comparative Study* (Berlin: Deutscher Kunstverlag, 1986).

otherwise: "Unfortunately the story breaks off in the middle of a sentence, so we do not know how the Theban king extricated himself from this embarrassment (of the arrogant and insulting message from Apophis 400 miles away)."[32]

When in doubt, the safest recourse is to apply the conventional template.

The missing ending has continued to be a tantalizing void drawing Egyptologists to fill it in the quest to understand the purpose of the story. There is insufficient space to examine or even list all the scholars who have wrestled with this dilemma. It seems more likely that the original Quarrel Story was consistent with the historical record known today and to the ancient Egyptian audience. Seqenenre was not the person historically who restored *ma'at*, and he was not the hero of the story; Kamose and Ahmose, who did succeed, were. Literary Seqenenre suffered a humiliating death at the hands of the ignoble foreigner from the north, just as historical Seqenenre had. Literary Seqenenre was avenged by literary Kamose and Ahmose, the Theban heroes from the south who rose up to defeat Apophis, just as historical Kamose and Ahmose did. The Quarrel Story was not ancient Egypt's Alamo or Masada, and Seqenenre was no martyr seeking the rewards of virgins in paradise. If the entire Quarrel Story had survived, it would end with a triumphant Kamose or Ahmose restoring the cosmic order. Again, it is vital to understand that the author of the story is using it to comment on sensitive events from his time period, the thirteenth century, so Seqenenre is a literary foil for a thirteenth-century pharaoh (more to follow).

With that understood, there is sufficient information to provide the basis for a conclusion consistent with the historical record even though the ending is missing. In the Egyptian culture the hippopotamus is an animal to be harpooned by the heroic warrior-leader; it is a representation of the forces of chaos.[33] One would expect the Egyptian to be the one to harpoon the hippopotamus that represented chaos in the conflict.

---

32. John A. Wilson, *The Culture of Ancient Egypt* (Chicago: Univ. of Chicago Press, 1951), 160, originally published as *The Burden of Egypt*.

33. For the role of the hippopotamus in the Egyptian version of cosmos and chaos, see Torgny Säve-Söderbergh, *On Egyptian Representations of Hippopotamus Hunting as a Religious Motive* (Upsala: Gleerup, Lund, 1953). Säve-Söderbergh suggested that a real harpooning in the hippopotamus ritual in Thebes underlay this story (pp. 44–45). J. Gwyn Griffiths considered allegory to be a critical element in the storytelling, with the religious dimension of

Instead the story sets up the Egyptian leader as the defender of chaos and makes Apophis the one who threatens the beast. It's as if the Hyksos king is more Horus in the Egyptian myth of Osiris than the literary Seqenenre is. The author deliberately has turned Egyptian conventions topsy-turvy; that is part of his message.

These animals are not beasts of silence; that too is part of the author's message. Hans Goedicke characterized the noise of the beasts as an "insane message."[34] But the inclusion of this purported insanity is because of the sanity of the author, and its function in the story needs to be determined. In the Myth of Atrahasis, fragments found at Ugarit contemporary with the time of the writing of the Quarrel Story, noise is the disruptive motif which eventually led to a deluge destroying almost the entire human race.[35]

> Enlil heard their noise
> and addressed the great gods:
> The noise of humankind has become too intense for me,
> with their uproar I am deprived of sleep.[36]

Deluge itself is a cosmological term which need not necessarily be taken literally. In the Assyrian royal monuments, the deluge represents the overpowering onslaught of the onrushing Assyrian king and army that overwhelms and sweeps away the old order so the new order centered on the Assyrian king can be built.

Adad-nirari II A.0.99.2 (911–891 BCE)

> *I overwhelm like the deluge—*
> *[I laid] traps as strong as the destructive deluge for him.*

---

the harpooning of the hippopotamus representing the triumph of Horus over Seth being the key ("Allegory in Greece and Egypt," *JEA* 53 [1967]: 79–102, here p. 96).

34. Hans Goedicke, *The Quarrel Story of Apophis and Seqenenre* (San Antonio, TX: Van Sicklen, 1986), 3.

35. W. G. Lambert and Alan R. Millard, *Atra-ḫāsis: The Babylonian Story of the Flood* (Oxford: Clarendon, 1969), 131–33.

36. Bill T. Arnold and Bryan E. Beyer, eds., *Readings from the Ancient Near East: Primary Sources for Old Testament Study*, Encountering Biblical Studies (Grand Rapids: Baker Academic, 2002), 26.

Assurnasirpal II A.0.101.1 (883–859 BCE)

Ninurta . . . king of battle . . . whose attack is a deluge . . .
Ashurnasirpal . . . mighty flood-tide which has no opponent.[37]

Flooding waters, then, were a metaphor for military victory. If the Quarrel Story followed this scenario, then it would have transformed the flood into a weapon against Egypt. The land that was the gift of the Nile now would experience its wrath. The "absurd" request of Apophis to Seqenenre should be understood instead not as an absurdity or battle of wits but as a reversal of Egyptian convention, delivering the message of "tomorrow you die" . . . and by a flood! For thematic purposes, the power of the story would have been enhanced if the flooding which destroyed the hippopotami had occurred at night, precisely when mythical Apophis was to be vanquished in the performance of the daily Amduat ritual supporting the reappearance of the sun.

According to this reconstruction, in the next episode of the story, literary Seqenenre would be killed either in battle or in a ritual execution, quite likely the fate of historical Seqenenre. In 705 BC Sargon II died in battle and suffered the humiliating fate of not having his body recovered—a sign to all the peoples ruled by Assyria that something was amiss in the heavens. The death of a king on a battlefield in Mesopotamian history was unparalleled. Sennacherib had to determine the hidden reasons of his father's death to know what his sins were.[38] Such an unusual occurrence had repercussions. "The circumstances of Sargon's death haunted the son. It was most unusual for an Assyrian king to die in battle and it was inevitably interpreted by the Assyrians as a bad omen, particularly because the royal corpse could not be buried at home."[39]

The Assyrians were capable of holding the deceased king responsible for his own demise for violating the cosmic order, thereby obligating the

---

37. A. Kirk Grayson, *Assyrian Rulers of the Early First Millennium BC I (1114–859 BC)* (Toronto: Univ. of Toronto Press, 1991), 148, 151, 193, 194.

38. Hayim Tadmor, "The Campaigns of Sargon II of Assur," *JCS* 12 (1958): 22–40, 77–100, here p. 97.

39. A. K. Grayson, "Assyria: Sennacherib and Esarhaddon (704–669 B.C.)," in *The Assyrian and Babylonian Empires and Other States of the Near East, from the Eighth to the Sixth Centuries B.C.*, ed. John Boardman et al., 2nd ed., vol. 3/2 of *The Cambridge Ancient History* (Cambridge: Cambridge Univ. Press, 1991), 103–41, 765–68, here p. 118.

successor to right the wrong.[40] On the other hand, this unexpected death of the ruler of the world led Isaiah of Judah to taunt Sargon's fate. Isaiah 14:4–21 depicts the fall from power to the depths of Sheol of the world ruler who previously had sought to ascend to the heavens.

The Bible weighs in on this issue with other examples as well. King Josiah of Judah dies at Megiddo after meeting Pharaoh Neco, in circumstances that remain unclear. His body is brought back by chariot to the capital, Jerusalem, where he is buried (2 Kgs 23:29–30). Joshua hanged the kings of five cities after triumphing in battle against them (Josh 10:22–27), a very public display which might qualify as a ritual execution. In perhaps the closest parallel to the proposed ritual execution of Seqenenre, the Philistines nailed the body of the already-dead Saul to the wall at Beth Shan, the former Egyptian military post in Canaan. The next day, the men of Jabesh Gilead rescued his body and gave the dead king a proper burial (1 Sam 31:8–13). David mourned the deaths of Saul and Jonathan (2 Sam 1). The death of a king in battle or following a battle was of considerable importance to Assyria and Israel.

Undoubtedly, the most famous example of slain royalty in battle was Achilles' dispatch of Hector (*Iliad*, book 24; Goliath was not royal). The treatment of Hector before the walls was the ultimate degradation of him. Even if Saul and Hector did not die exactly as portrayed, their stories demonstrate that storytellers knew how to grab the attention of the audience. While historical Seqenenre's battlefield death was not as devastating as that of Sargon II, who had ruled for more than fifteen years and whose body never was recovered from the battlefield, it still would have been traumatic for Thebes. It was a humiliating cultural legacy. The "Pharaoh smites the enemy" society had been turned topsy-turvy in violation of *ma'at*. That was the pivotal memory with which Egypt had to live. Egypt endured in part because of the heroics of Seqenenre's successors Kamose and then Ahmose. It did not forget the trauma of Seqenenre's brutal death.

The author of the Quarrel Story used this sixteenth-century BC historical legacy to deliver his message in the thirteenth century BC. Seqenenre is defending the symbol of chaos, and Apophis restores order

40. Hayim Tadmor, Benno Landsberger, and Simo Parpola, "The Sin of Sargon and Sennacherib's Last Will," *SAAB* 3 (1989): 3–51.

by killing the bellowing beasts through a flood. The Egyptian leader is not the restorer of *ma'at*; he is a defender of chaos and was defeated. That was the point of the story: the disruption to *ma'at*. Regardless of how the historical Seqenenre was killed by the Hyksos, literary Seqenenre was likely to have been ritually killed in a ceremony that reversed the normal order and humiliated Egypt. In a society that so valued Pharaoh smiting the enemy, Seqenenre could not be a hero. The story was much more powerful, dramatic, and effective when the author deliberately used conventional Egyptian iconography but with reverse polarity. The literary inversion helps deliver the message regardless of the historical details of Seqenenre's death. This does not mean that a thirteenth-century BC pharaoh died in battle, but one is being mocked for having failed just as Seqenenre had against the Hyksos.[41]

This interpretation of the Quarrel of Seqenenre and Apophis means Merenptah was audacious and subtle. He was audacious in that he was declaring that his father Ramesses II had been a humiliated, defeated failure in a Hyksos confrontation led by Apophis. He was audacious in declaring that the Hyksos leader, following an exchange of messages, had defeated the Egyptian pharaoh in a water-related event that turned the Egyptian world topsy-turvy. He was audacious in declaring that he, Merenptah, was the one who succeeded and who restored *ma'at*, the Egyptian sense of cosmic order. The story needed to expose Apophis as a false Horus. Apophis was not a legitimate pharaoh (or prince of Egypt), and Merenptah would destroy his seed.

The Quarrel Story in its current form and its proposed conclusion resonates with the biblical account of the exodus. They share the following common traits.

1. Conflict between the Egyptian pharaoh and a Semitic leader (Moses and Pharaoh).
2. Exchange of messengers (Aaron and the magicians).
3. Disruption of cosmos (plagues).

---

41. For the instability of the thirteenth century BCE, see Peter Brand, "Ideology and Politics of the Early Ramesside Kings (13th Century BC)," in *Prozesse des Wandels in historischen Spannungsfeldern Nordostafrikas/Westasiens: Akten zum 2. Symposium des SFB 295, Mainz, 15.10.–17.10.2001*, ed. Walter Bisang, Kulturelle und sprachliche Kontakte 2 (Würzburg: Ergon, 2005), 23–38.

4. Defeat of Pharaoh at the waters of Egypt.
5. Semites leave the land.

According to Manetho's version the departure was an expulsion and not an exodus. Merenptah's spin is likely to have delivered the same message and quite possibly was a source for Manetho.

The Quarrel Story is a smoking gun for the exodus, expressed in Egyptian terms.

Leiden Hymn 30

Ramesses II's take on the exodus is likely to have been different from Merenptah's. His depiction of Apophis portrays a more conventional Egyptian approach: the king harpoons the forces of chaos and restores *ma'at*. As a Baal-Seth king, he may even have drawn on the imagery of the Astarte Papyrus.[42] It is an Egyptian retelling of the Ugaritic myth of Baal triumphing over Yam, the sea. Pharaoh is supposed to be triumphant over the waters, not be flooded by them. The closest text I can find consistent with a triumphant-Ramesses-over-Apophis confrontation in this tradition is Leiden Hymn 30.

> The harpoon is deep in Apophis, the Evil,
> he falls by the sword;
> and those who chose war are huddled for slaughter—
> Death cuts the hearts of God's demon enemies,
> who groan as outlaws,
> apostate forever . . .
> He has ridden the waves unscathed
> and the rebels are no more! . . .
> You have won, Amun-Re![43]

Ramesses II employs the mythical Apophis, a cosmological being of chaos, rather than the historical Hyksos Apophis of the Quarrel Story. I conjecture that Ramesses's use of Apophis is not simply another mythical hymn but his claim of restoring cosmos.

---

42. A. H. Sayce, "Astarte Papyrus and the Legend of the Sea," *JEA* 19 (1933): 56–59.

43. John L. Foster, *Echoes of Egyptian Voices: An Anthology of Ancient Egyptian Poetry* (Norman, OK: Univ. of Oklahoma Press, 1992), 67.

Typically, the attempts to understand the exodus in a historical setting suggest a small-scale, underneath-the-radar, below-the-fold event that no one in Egypt even would have noticed. Such efforts to compare it to runaways who have been captured at the border represent a refusal to come face-to-face with the biblical account. The biblical story involves a direct Moses-Pharaoh confrontation. Even Cecil B. DeMille knew that. The Quarrel Story and Leiden Hymn 30 as interpreted here match the biblical account. These confrontations occur at the highest level. In this hymn Amun-Re triumphs at the waters just as he had in the battle of Qadesh. The rebels are outlaw demon enemies. Contra the Song of the Sea, Leiden Hymn 30 sings to the victory of Pharaoh at the waters.

Ramesses II's spin on the exodus more likely occurred not at the moment of the departure but sometime later. Perhaps this hymn from around year 52 sings to the demise of the Hyksos Apophis who had challenged his rule: Moses in the wilderness is dead; he will never threaten Egypt again. But the anti-Egyptian people he had created did not die. They continued to be a threat, thereby necessitating Merenptah's claim to have finished the job.

The 400-Year Stela

The third piece of textual archaeological data in this reconstruction is the 400-Year Stela of Ramesses II, honoring the legacy of the Hyksos.[44] The stela commemorates the action of his father, Seti I, fusing the Baal-Seth identity in the new Egyptian capital at Avaris in the Nineteenth Dynasty. The time period of four hundred years is a familiar one from the biblical account of the exodus. Yahweh informs Abram that his descendants will experience oppression in Egypt for four hundred years (Gen 15:13). Biblical scholar Baruch Halpern suggests that if the Israelite scribes knew of the 400-Year Stela, such knowledge is evidence of the portrayal of Israel as Hyksos and therefore the identification of Ramesses II as the pharaoh of the exodus. I agree. Halpern then asserts that the Israelites linked themselves to the memory of the Hyksos in Egypt probably during the time of Solomon, when relationships between the two countries were good and monuments were being relocated

44. For the 400-Year Stela, see Peter Feinman, "The Hyksos and the Exodus: Two 400-Year Stories," in *What Difference Does Time Make?* ed. Richard Beal and Jo Ann Scurlock (Oxford: Archaeopress, 2019), 136–51.

from the region of Goshen/Avaris to Tanis, where the 400-Year Stela was found. Here I disagree. Halpern does not appear to consider the possibility that some Hyksos (Levites) led the people who left Egypt in the time of Ramesses II and that therefore these linkages had always been part of the Israelite cultural heritage, my position here.[45]

Assmann similarly notes the connection between the two four-hundred-year traditions. First, he calls attention to the often-overlooked uniqueness of the Egyptian stela: "It represents the first and for a long time remained the only instance of a historical anniversary recorded in the annals of history."[46]

Next, he questions whether the two four-hundred-year traditions in Egypt and Israel are coincidental. He calls this noncoincidence a "resonance phenomenon." Assmann links the stela to Ramesses II's celebration of the establishment of the Baal-related cult of Seth at Avaris. He probably is correct. Israel was aware of both the four-hundred-year tradition and its honoring Baal. But for Israel in the land of Canaan, the four hundred years was a time of oppression and not celebration. Going forth from Ramesses is equated to going forth from Baal-Seth. The people who became Israel would base their religious identity on a deity who was in opposition to Egypt, one who surpassed Baal. Israel was already anti-Baal before it arrived in Canaan, because Baal was linked to Pharaoh and was the deity of Egyptian oppression in the exodus and in the promised land.

Why did Ramesses II choose to erect this stela? I suggest he did so because after some Hyksos led people out of Egypt, he needed to reaffirm the loyalty of the Hyksos who remained. Manetho's statement of a total expulsion should not be treated as gospel. Even the Babylonian exile did not include all the peoples of the land. A more realistic view is that the leadership and its army were the ones who left the land when Ahmose triumphed. Other Hyksos remained.

---

45. Baruch Halpern, "The Exodus from Egypt: Myth or Reality," in *The Rise of Ancient Israel*, ed. Hershel Shanks (Washington, DC: Biblical Archaeological Society, 1992), 86–117, here pp. 98–101; idem, "Fracturing the Exodus, as Told by Edward Everett Horton," in *Israel's Exodus in Transdisciplinary Perspective: Text, Archaeology, Culture, and Geoscience*, ed. Thomas E. Levy, Thomas Schneider, and William H. C. Propp, Quantitative Methods in the Humanities and Social Sciences (New York: Springer, 2015), 293–304, here p. 299.

46. Jan Assmann, *The Invention of Religion: Faith and Covenant in the Book of Exodus* (Princeton: Princeton Univ. Press, 2018), 36.

Ramesses II did not erect this stela because he was a historian who suddenly discovered an event that had occurred four hundred years ago. He recognized it just as Americans in 2019 commemorated the beginning of slavery in the British colonies four hundred years earlier. The people involved were still around. The audience for Ramesses's stela were the Hyksos in the land, Hyksos whose support Ramesses needed.

At this point, it is critical to examine the context in which Ramesses II was operating, according to the archaeological record. As previously noted, during the battle of Qadesh, Ramesses had been rescued by the timely arrival of the *n'rn*. Despite Ramesses's claims of victory, the facts on the ground meant there were people who knew better. Egyptologist Donald Redford claims that after the battle of Qadesh, "headmen of Canaanite towns, vassals of Egypt, were impressed by what they divined as inherent weaknesses in Pharaoh's forces: poor intelligence and a tendency to panic. Rebellion was possible; Egypt *could* be beaten. . . . In the wake of the retreating Egyptians, all Canaan flared into open revolt. . . . It was Ramesses's darkest hour."[47]

Redford limits this awareness to Canaanites in the land of Canaan. Redford is correct about Canaanites revolting in the land of Canaan following Ramesses's poor performance as commander in chief. The destruction of Hazor is simply the most prominent example of the "Canaanite spring," the unrest Ramesses now had to face in the land of Canaan.

Meanwhile all was not quiet on the home front. Biblical scholar Thomas Thompson astutely comments on the significance of the battle of Qadesh beyond the battle itself: "After this defeat, Ramesses II's army was racked with revolts. It had borne the brunt of the cost of his expensive misadventure. . . . Civil unrest and religious opposition at home was doubly encouraged. . . . A series of plots and intrigues by court factions bitter over the military failure at Kadesh effectively paralyzed royal authority and its control of important groups within the army."[48]

One might take issue with the extent to which unrest and intrigue occurred, but the basic thrust of the observation appears valid. Qadesh exposed the shortcomings of the leader of the country, and people

---

47. Donald B. Redford, *Egypt, Canaan, and Israel in Ancient Times* (Princeton: Princeton Univ. Press, 1992), 185, emphasis in original.

48. Thomas L. Thompson, *The Mythic Past: Biblical Archaeology and the Myth of Israel* (New York: Basic, 2000), 153.

responded to that weakness. Thompson has honed in on the precise time when the potential for disruption of *ma'at* in the political arena had occurred, leading to the exodus. It was in this gap between Ramesses II's failure at Qadesh in year 5 and his campaign into Canaan in year 8 when the exodus occurred.

It is reasonable to conclude that Canaanites in the land of Egypt were equally capable of recognizing the shortcomings of the Egyptian commander in chief, especially if they had rescued him in the battle of Qadesh. Canaanites in the delta could revolt as well. Not all of them, just some. Perhaps led by a Hyksos Apophis who was very great in the land of Egypt, in the sight of Pharaoh's servants, and in the sight of the people. Instead of a battle between the Hyksos in the north and the Thebans in the south, the battle had shifted to one within the capital city the Hyksos and the Nineteenth Dynasty shared. These Hyksos and their allies lost, of course, since Ramesses II obviously was not removed from the throne. What did some of those resident aliens in the land of Egypt do after their revolt against Ramesses failed and they no longer had a home there? Did they disappear from history? The memories of those actions can be found in the Quarrel of Seqenenre and Apophis, Leiden Hymn 30, the Merenptah Stela, and the book of Exodus.

Conclusion

The secular reality of a Hyksos-led exodus has significant implications for Egyptian history, Israelite history, and the formation of the Hebrew Bible. Karel van der Toorn calls the exodus a charter myth for the northern kingdom of Israel in the tenth century BC. He postulates a historical exodus of some kind in the thirteenth century BC by a limited group. He identifies the Levites, or "consecrated" clergy of Yahweh, according to their name as the bearers of this tradition and heirs to Moses, their founder. Then he states that "the origins of the Exodus motif are still an unsolved riddle." The recognition that Moses was a Hyksos and that the people who perpetuated his legacy were called Levites solves the riddle and puts tenth-century Israel in a new historical context.[49] The exodus really happened regardless of whether God exists or Israel was chosen.

---

49. Karel van der Toorn, *Family Religion in Babylonia, Syria and Israel: Continuity and Change in the Forms of Religious Life*, Studies in the History and Culture of the Ancient Near East 7 (Leiden: Brill, 1996), 287–315.

RESPONSE TO PETER FEINMAN
(THE FIFTEENTH-CENTURY EXODUS VIEW)

SCOTT STRIPLING

Like Professor Hoffmeier, Dr. Feinman believes that the exodus occurred in the thirteenth century BC, but Feinman strays far from the standard late-date view. Feinman's title, "The Thirteenth-Century Hyksos/Levite-Led Exodus View," covers the three points that he attempts to establish in his chapter: Moses was a Levite, Moses was of Hyksos descent, and the exodus occurred after Ramesses II's fifth year, when he was weakened because of his near defeat at the battle of Qadesh. Feinman makes no attempt to explain why the thirteenth century BC is the best time in which to find evidence of the exodus. He presupposes that his readers accept this dating scheme. I do not. I argue in my contribution that the weight of evidence favors placement of the exodus in the fifteenth century BC, during the reign of Amenhotep II. This will become relevant as I examine how well Feinman has proved his theses.

Was Moses a Levite?

The Bible is clear about Moses' tribal affiliation, and I am not aware of anyone who challenges his pedigree, but what the typical Bible reader understands a Levite to be is quite different from how Feinman sees a Levite. In his view Levites are the remnant of Hyksos who remained in Egypt even after Ahmose expelled them early in the sixteenth century BC. I am not aware of any source which documents Hyksos in Egypt in the thirteenth century BC.

Feinman devotes significant space in his chapter to proving the violent nature of the Levites. He presents four passages which demonstrate

Levitical violence: Gen 34:25, Gen 49:5–7, Exod 32:27–28, and Deut 33:8–11. I believe Feinman's point is that Moses, as a Levite, was violent (he killed an Egyptian, and he lost his temper when he struck the rock in the wilderness), so he was an ideal candidate to deliver the Israelites. If there was a larger point, I missed it. In a sort of syllogism, Feinman's logic goes something like this:

- Major premise: the Hyksos were violent people.
- Minor premise: the Levites were violent people.
- Conclusion: the Levites and the Hyksos were the same people.

I was also left wondering if Levites were more violent than the people from other Israelite tribes. The acts of the men of Benjamin come to mind. While he does not explicitly state it, Feinman appears to agree with the views of Richard Elliott Friedman when Feinman opines that "perhaps among the people who became Israel only the Levites had been slaves in Egypt" and "the people who became Levites probably were not known by that name in Egypt." In this Friedman/Feinman paradigm, readers must jettison the historicity of the patriarchal narratives. The sons of Jacob, if they existed, never sojourned in Egypt or experienced slavery. This seems a high price to pay, especially absent any clear evidence connecting the Hyksos to the Levites.

Was Moses of Hyksos Heritage?

Feinman uses a threefold criteria to identify the Levites (anachronistic?) that he seeks in Egypt. They need to be violent, Semitic resident aliens during the reign of Ramesses II. Only two groups pass his criterial screening: the Hyksos and the *n'rn*. Feinman dismisses the *n'rn* because of a lack of evidence of a literary output and settles on the Hyksos as the best candidate for his hypothetical Levites, who left Egypt without permission and later connected with other Semitic people who embraced a shared identity with their brothers.

Feinman devotes twelve hundred words to exploring Manetho's account of the Hyksos. In this section he reveals that his "Moses was Hyksos" connection, which is essential to his argument, rests entirely on the portion of Manetho preserved by Josephus in *Against Apion*. At various points, he cites *Ag. Ap.* 1.74–78 and 1.82–90. Most scholars accept that Josephus inaccurately conflates the Hyksos expulsion with the Israelite exodus. However, Manetho, an Egyptian priest writing in the mid-third century BC, clearly differentiates between the two events. Manetho provides a detailed description of the Hyksos expulsion from Egypt (*Ag. Ap.* 1.88–90) but then goes on to describe a second group of people, the Jews (*Ag. Ap.* 1.251), who wreaked havoc in Egypt under the leadership of Moses (*Ag. Ap.* 1.250). Eventually, Amenophis, the king of Egypt, and his army chased Moses and his people out of Egypt (*Ag. Ap.* 1.252). That Manetho clearly understood that the Hyksos and the Israelites were two distinct people groups is evident in the fact that he records correspondence between Moses and the Hyksos (*Ag. Ap.* 1.241).

In addition to Manetho's account, Josephus also cites Chemeron (*Ag. Ap.* 1.288–292) and Lysimachus (*Ag. Ap.* 1.304–311), whose accounts of the departure of the Israelites from Egypt are similar to that of Manetho. It was Josephus (who wrote his history in the first century AD), not Manetho, who equated the Israelite exodus with Manetho's description of the expulsion of the Hyksos. Manetho wrote his account four centuries prior to Josephus. Josephus vigorously refuted the earlier accounts of Manetho, Chemeron, and Lysimachus (*Ag. Ap.* 1.252, 293, 304).

Like Josephus, Feinman blends Manetho's description of the Hyksos expulsion with the Israelite's escape. He describes Manetho's account (*Ag. Ap.* 1.228–320) of the Israelites' escape as "an extensive description of the exodus departure itself" but then states that "it included all the Hyksos and only the Hyksos." A careful reading of the cited passage reveals that this account does not refer to the Hyksos at all except for mentioning them as a distinctly separate group of people (*Ag. Ap.* 1.241).

Feinman rests his case on Josephus's conflated account even though Manetho, Josephus's source, contradicts the basis of his account. Josephus's conclusion is at odds with the source from which he draws his information. While the Israelites and the Hyksos are both Semitic groups, there are stark differences between them. Most important, the Hyksos were rulers who were forced out of Egypt, and the Israelites were slaves who escaped Egypt. Of course, Feinman is unencumbered by the need to invest the same authority in the biblical account as he does in the first-century AD account of Josephus.

Did the Exodus Occur during the Reign of Ramesses II?

At the very beginning of his chapter, Feinman reveals his approach to interpreting historical documents by the quote "literature is politics / politics is literature." Apparently, Feinman believes that all literature, including the Bible, should be read as propaganda. If this is the case, the modern scholar can feel free to invent his or her own explanation for the significance of the events and people related in ancient (or modern) writings. Imagination is needed to interpret any writing and to uncover the true message behind the text, the author's real agenda. Feinman's text amply illustrates such creative imaginations.

Since the Bible's account of the exodus is at significant variance with biblical scholarship that denies it occurred, it is necessary to go to other sources in an effort to reconstruct the history of the time. Even if Feinman were correct regarding the propagandistic nature of the Bible, the original authors would not merely invent people and places that appear in their accounts. Particularly when writing about well-known events, they would aim to get the basic facts right, including personal and place names, in order to give their work some semblance of credibility.

The first such alternative source examined is the writings of Manetho, as preserved in part in Josephus's *Against Apion*. Manetho's treatment of the exodus reveals a conspicuous place, Avaris, and a conspicuous person, Amenophis. However much spin Manetho wanted to put on his interpretation of what happened when the "lepers and other impure people" (*Ag. Ap.* 1.233) left Egypt, he provides two interesting details—the people who left were abandoning a place called Avaris, and the pharaoh who was oppressing them was named Amenophis. There would have been no incentive to change the two names that Manetho found in his source documents, however much he may have distorted historical events to serve his propagandistic purposes. The naming of the place, Avaris, and the pharaoh, Amenophis, should be the two things given the most credibility in the sources Feinman has chosen to advance his contention that the exodus was a historical event. The two proper nouns, however, mitigate against his dating of the exodus to the time of Ramesses II, placing it instead in the time of a pharaoh named Amenophis. As I explained in my contribution, the findings of archaeologists working with the Austrian Academy in Egypt's delta have shown that a Semitic population abandoned Avaris in the mid-Eighteenth Dynasty, about the time of Amenhotep II. Further, the only pharaohs named Amenophis (Greek for Amenhotep) were in the Eighteenth Dynasty. This fact alone argues powerfully against Ramesses II as the pharaoh of the exodus.

Another ancient writing called upon by Feinman to establish there was a literal exodus and that it occurred in the time of Ramesses II instead of Manetho's Amenhophis/Amenhotep is the Quarrel of Seqenenre and Apophis. The author's analysis of the motive behind the writing of this story is certainly creative and appears very original. Most readers will find it difficult to infer that the audience was expected to identify Seqenenre as a type of Ramesses II and Apophis as representing Merenptah in order to properly understand the text. Did the original author intend to signify the biblical parting of the *yam sûp* when he placed hippopotami in the water? This all seems most unlikely.

Finally, Feinman appeals to Leiden Hymn 30, in which the god Amun-Re triumphs over the forces of chaos while "riding the waves unscathed." The reader is expected to interpret Amun-Re as Ramesses II, and the mention of water is supposed to refer to the parting of the *yam sûp*, even though the true pharaoh of the exodus (not Ramesses II) hardly rode the waves unscathed. In light of all these problems, it is difficult to accept the conclusion that "the Quarrel Story and Leiden Hymn 30 as interpreted here match the biblical account."

I agree that the general *motif* of Egyptian royal literature is to exalt the pharaoh as the upholder of *ma'at* and that various texts should be read with this propagandistic intent in mind. My problem is not with Feinman's observations; it is with his interpretation. He seems to favor an allegorical approach to the interpretation of ancient literature, regardless of its genre. Narrative literature should be read as historical prose unless the context requires a different approach.

Conclusion

I commend Dr. Feinman for accepting the historicity of the exodus and introducing readers to Josephus and Manetho, ancient historians who wrote about the exodus. However, after considering the evidence he has presented, I do not agree that Moses, a Levite, was of Hyksos descent. Likewise, I do not believe that Feinman has proven his case that the biblical exodus occurred during the reign of Ramesses II.

RESPONSE TO PETER FEINMAN
(THE THIRTEENTH-CENTURY EXODUS VIEW)

JAMES K. HOFFMEIER

I appreciate that Dr. Feinman identifies with a thirteenth-century exodus. He reaches this conclusion using a novel approach. Rather than isolating historical, cultural, and linguistic details in the Hebrew text that find corresponding Egyptian elements from a particular period, as scholars typically do, Feinman considers "three Egyptian texts which were produced directly as a result of the historical exodus" to make his case. These are the Quarrel of Seqenenre and Apophis, Leiden Hymn 30, and the 400-Year Stela of Ramesses II. As a fellow supporter of the thirteenth-century exodus date, naturally I welcome new data that supports my position.

The first document is a Late Egyptian literary tale from the thirteenth century that is set historically more than three hundred years earlier. This story has been typically interpreted as offering some kernel of historical memory of the initial hostilities between the Theban king (Seqenenre Tao II) and his northern counterpart, the Hyksos ruler of Avaris (Apophis). I agree with Feinman that the grisly remains of Seqenenre point to his brutal death, likely in battle with the Hyksos,[50] but he then veers off into speculation suggesting that the sixteenth-century event is spun into a literary tale for the thirteenth-century setting of the story in which Merenptah audaciously takes a swipe at his father, Ramesses II. Merenptah, in Feinman's words, "was declaring that his father Ramesses II had been . . . humiliated, defeated" by the events surrounding the exodus.

50. James E. Harris and Kent Weeks, *X-Raying the Pharaohs* (New York: Scribner's Sons, 1973), 29.

There are obvious problems with this proposal. First and foremost, if the biblical exodus story did not exist, this interpretation of the story would never come to mind. True, Josephus connects the exodus with the Hyksos expulsion as reported in Manetho. His agenda, however, is to argue for the antiquity of the Jewish people by integrating them into broader ancient Near Eastern history. Second, while the date of the Quarrel Story may fall into the reign of Merenptah, it is a stretch to believe it was intended to validate Merenptah. And third, it is inconceivable that Merenptah would criticize his legendary father. According to the Osiris myth, which every king sought to emulate, the role of the Horus (the king) is to defend *(nḏ)* his dead father (Osiris).

Behind Feinman's interpretation of the Quarrel Story lies an important question: what was the political, economic, and social impact of the plagues and exodus on Egypt? I concur with Kenneth Kitchen, who thinks Ramesses II was the pharaoh of the exodus, that "for imperial Egypt, the exodus was a fleeting, if unpleasant, incident; for the Hebrews, it was epochal, and for the spiritual history of the world, of incommensurable effect."[51] Consequently, I don't think there were long-term ramifications for the pharaoh, and if it was Ramesses II, it seems unlikely that about fifty years after the event, Merenptah felt the need to promote himself as upholder of *ma'at* who succeeded where his father had failed.

The second text comes from a segment of the Leiden Hymn to Amun-Re. Feinman thinks that it contains Ramesses II's self-serving perspective on the exodus by mythologizing those events to cast a positive picture: he triumphed over chaos (the Hebrews and the plagues) by defeating the mythological Apophis (same name as the Hyksos ruler). Feinman opines, "Ramesses II employs the mythical Apophis, a cosmological being of chaos, rather than the historical Hyksos Apophis of the Quarrel Story. I conjecture that Ramesses's use of Apophis is not simply another mythical hymn but his claim of restoring cosmos." Here too, without knowledge of the biblical story, one would never think of such an explanation.

The third text is the 400-Year Stela of Ramesses II that has been discussed in several of the chapters in this book. One might connect

51. Kenneth A. Kitchen, *Pharaoh Triumphant: The Life and Times of Ramesses II* (Warminster: Aris & Phillips, 1982), 71.

this figure with the 400 years Abraham's descendants would sojourn in a foreign land (Gen 15:13), which may be a rounded-off number for the more specific 430 years for the duration of Hebrew stay in Egypt (Exod 12:40–41). The 400-year figure in the stela is unique. It refers to the regnal year of Seth's kingship,[52] apparently commemorating the establishment of the Baal/Seth cult at Avaris by the Hyksos. Kitchen accepts this notion but adds, "The 400 years is perhaps best linked with the emergence of his [Ramesses II's] family to some kind of prominence in the East Delta, and with them their god Seth."[53] This understanding would be closer to the biblical idea of four centuries from the arrival of the Hebrews until their departure. Feinman puts a different twist on the event this stela commemorated. He asks, "Why did Ramesses II choose to erect this stela? I suggest he did so because after some Hyksos led people out of Egypt, he needed to reaffirm the loyalty of the Hyksos who remained. Manetho's statement of a total expulsion should not be treated as gospel. Even the Babylonian exile did not include all the peoples of the land. A more realistic view is that the leadership and its army were the ones who left the land when Ahmose triumphed. Other Hyksos remained."

I agree with Feinman that the Theban King Ahmose's expulsion of the Avaris-based Hyksos (ca. 1540 BC) was likely limited to the political and military elites and that "other Hyksos remained." Included in this would have been Hebrews and other Semitic-speaking peoples. What I find puzzling is that Feinman continues to apply the term "Hyksos" to Semites in Egypt throughout the New Kingdom, including the Hebrews. The term "Hyksos" derives from two Egyptian terms, *ḥqꜣ ḫꜣswt*, meaning "foreign ruler." The earliest writings applied to Nubian chieftains during the period 2300–2200 BC.[54] The leader of the band of Semites *(ꜥꜣmw)* depicted in the famous tomb of Khnumhotep II at Beni Hasan (1865 BC) is called a *ḥqꜣ ḫꜣswt*; so are the Levantine tribal chieftains encountered in Tale of Sinuhe (ca. 1925 BC).

52. Kenneth A. Kitchen, *Ramesside Inscriptions: Historical and Biographical*, 8 vols. (Oxford: Blackwell, 1976–1990), no. 288.6–7.

53. Kenneth Kitchen, *Ramesses II: Royal Inscriptions*, vol. 2 of *Ramesside Inscriptions: Translated and Annotated* (Oxford: Blackwell, 1999), 171.

54. Donald B. Redford, "Textual Sources for the Hyksos Period," in *The Hyksos: New Historical and Archaeological Perspectives*, ed. Eliezer D. Oren (Philadelphia: Univ. of Pennsylvania, 1997), 19.

Following the lead of the third-century Egyptian historian Manetho, whom Josephus quoted,[55] historians and archaeologists typically apply the term "Hyksos" to the foreign population that occupied and ruled the delta during the Second Intermediate period. Manetho wrongly parsed the word to mean "shepherd kings." Egyptians of the second millennium BC did not refer to the foreign population of the delta as Hyksos. Rather they were called *ꜥꜣmw* (as the group is in Khnumhotep II's tomb) or *sṯtyw/styw*. These terms are used interchangeably in the two Kamose Stelae to describe the residents of the northeastern delta.[56] When Hatshepsut refers to the foreign rulers from Avaris from fifty years earlier, she too calls them *ꜥꜣmw*. Using the term "Hyksos" for the Semitic population in Egypt after the beginning of the New Kingdom and including the Hebrews is confusing, misleading, and anachronistic. I believe, and perhaps Dr. Feinman would agree, that the change of fortunes for the Hebrews described in Exod 1 was the result of the Theban kings driving out the ruling Hyksos *(ꜥꜣmw)*, followed by the Egyptian authorities now seeking to control the foreign population by forced labor for state building efforts.

Feinman follows Richard Elliott Friedman[57] in his recent belief that the principal exodus group were Levites. This explanation is a revival of an old theory presented by Theophile Meek in *Hebrew Origins* (1936).[58] Owing to the religious nature of ancient peoples, Meek maintained that "the origin of priesthood is manifestly to be traced back to the earliest stage of social evolution and is doubtless to be found very close to the beginning of magical and religious practices."[59] For Meek, the preponderance of Egyptian personal names among the Levites is evidence for their presence in Egypt; he argued, "This would indicate that the Levites at least were once resident in Egypt, so long in fact that they must have intermarried to some degree with Egyptians and so have given Egyptian names to their children."[60]

---

55. H. St. J. Thackeray, *Josephus: The Life; Against Apion*, LCL 186 (Cambridge: Harvard Univ. Press, 1966), 195.

56. For recent translations of these texts, see Redford, "Textual Sources for the Hyksos Period," 17–18.

57. Richard Elliott Friedman, *The Exodus: How It Happened and Why It Matters* (New York: HarperOne, 2017).

58. Theophile J. Meek, *Hebrew Origins* (New York: Harper & Brothers, 1936), 31–33, 116–43.

59. Meek, *Hebrew Origins*, 116.

60. Meek, *Hebrew Origins*, 32.

I have argued in this volume that the "Egyptian" influence on the Levites stems from their serving as priests for the Hebrew community in Egypt, a priesthood steeped in Egyptian clerical tradition.[61] The problem of a Levites-only exodus is that you have a priestly guild or clan leaving Egypt without the faith community it served! If the Levites figured prominently in the exodus, there must have been a community of followers who accompanied them.

Feinman naturally seeks to explain the origins of the Levites. The Torah portrays the Levites as having violent tendencies. Levi is involved in killing the sons of Hamor in the Dinah story (Gen 34:25–31), and Moses slew the Egyptian taskmaster (Exod 2:11–15). Following Friedman and William Propp, Feinman agrees that the name Levite derives from a word meaning "attached" or "joined," hence the idea of a resident alien, suggesting that they were not a particular, identifiable ethnic group. This prompts Feinman to investigate who they were. Two candidates are put forward, a "Hyksos" group and a military unit known as *n'rn*. Starting from the militaristic aspects of the Levites, he finds a contender among a military wing of Ramesses II's forces at the battle of Qadesh in Syria in 1275 BC—the *n'rn*. Ramesses II admits that he was ambushed by the Hittites, and it was an elite but obscure military contingent called the *n'rn* that saved the day. Because the term *n'rn* is related to Hebrew *na'ar*, meaning "lad" or "young man," many think they were Canaanites or Syrians. I concur with Alan Schulman's persuasive arguments that the *n'rn* were actually Egyptian.[62] Because the Bible credits Levites with writing, a literate, fighting (and priestly?) class is essential for Feinman. He claims, "The *n'rn* did not have the writing, cultural, and leadership experience of the Hyksos who had once ruled Egypt (Fifteenth Dynasty, ca. 1650–1550 BC) and remained a more elite and educated group. One may speculate that the commanding officers of this Semitic division were Hyksos."

61. For a more detailed treatment of this, see James K. Hoffmeier, "Egyptian Religious Influences on the Early Hebrews," in *"Did I Not Bring Israel out of Egypt?" Biblical, Archaeological, and Egyptological Perspectives on the Exodus Narratives*, ed. James K. Hoffmeier, Alan R. Millard, and Gary A. Rendsburg, BBRSup 13 (Winona Lake, IN: Eisenbrauns, 2016), 3–36.

62. Alan R. Schulman, "The *N'rn* at the Battle of Kadesh," *Journal of the American Research Center in Egypt* 1 (1962): 47–52; idem, "The *N'rn* at Kadesh Once Again," *JSSEA* 11 (1981): 7–19.

This is all highly speculative, especially the claim that one group, the Hyksos (which technically do not exist at this point in history), was literate, whereas the *n'rn* were not. On what evidence does he make this claim? Nevertheless, Feinman considers the Levites to be Hyksos from whom the exodus party emerged. This brings us back to the 400-Year Stela. Feinman thinks Ramesses II had it erected at Pi-Ramesses "after the exodus when he sought to shore up his political support with the Hyksos who had not joined the 'resident alien' Hyksos in the exodus." While I am not convinced that the 400-Year Stela had anything to do with the exodus (except perhaps a similar usage of the number four hundred), I agree with Feinman that there was a Semitic population in the delta in the thirteenth century, including Levites and other Hebrews, and that they departed Egypt. If indeed the Levites were a priestly caste that served the Hebrew community before the emergence of the YHWH cult, this may explain why among them there were literate, Egyptianized priests.

Dr. Peter Feinman offers a creative interpretation of some Egyptian texts in support of the thirteenth-century exodus. While I find Ramesside era reconstruction makes best sense of the biblical and Egyptological data, I am not convinced that these particular Egyptian texts relate to the exodus tradition.

RESPONSE TO PETER FEINMAN
(THE TWELFTH-CENTURY EXODUS VIEW)

GARY A. RENDSBURG

Peter Feinman uses the approach of "literature as politics," a method of reading (certain) texts with which I am in full agreement. I myself have written a series of articles using this approach, with particular attention to the book of Genesis.[63] Feinman applies this method to the ancient Egyptian tale known to scholars as the Quarrel of Seqenenre and Apophis (or simply the Quarrel Story), known from a single incomplete manuscript (Papyrus Sallier 1) dated to the reign of Merenptah. The story is set during the time of the Hyksos, with reference to two kings: Apophis, the Fifteenth (Hyksos) Dynasty pharaoh, and Seqenenre, the Seventeenth Dynasty pharaoh.

The Hyksos, Asiatic invaders, had taken control of a large portion of northern Egypt and had established their capital in the eastern delta. The Seventeenth Dynasty, ruling from Thebes, is given credit for removing the Hyksos from Egypt, thereby paving the way for the powerful New Kingdom, initiated by the Eighteenth Dynasty and still thriving during the Nineteenth Dynasty, when the Quarrel Story was written.

As Feinman observes, the end of the Quarrel Story is missing. Any

63. The relevant studies are as follows: Gary A. Rendsburg, "Biblical Literature as Politics: The Case of Genesis," in *Religion and Politics in the Ancient Near East*, ed. Adele Berlin (Bethesda, MD: Univ. Press of Maryland, 1996), 47–70; idem, "Reading David in Genesis: How We Know the Torah Was Written in the Tenth Century B.C.E.," *BRev* 17, no. 1 (February 2001): 20–33, 46; idem, "The Genesis of the Bible," in *The Blanche and Irving Laurie Chair in Jewish History*, Separatum published by the Allen and Joan Bildner Center for the Study of Jewish Life, Rutgers, State Univ. of New Jersey (2005), 11–30. In addition, see ch. 21, "When Was All This Written?" in Gary A. Rendsburg, *How the Bible Is Written* (Peabody, MA: Hendrickson, 2019), 443–67.

attempt to create an ending constitutes pure speculation. Yet this is what Feinman does: based on the real-life head wounds observable in Seqenenre's mummy, Feinman posits that "literary Seqenenre suffered a humiliating death at the hands of the ignoble foreigner from the north, just as historical Seqenenre had." He then suggests that Seqenenre is a literary foil for Ramesses II, even though this most powerful of pharaohs was, well, powerful throughout. In Feinman's reconstruction Ramesses II's son Merenptah deserves the credit for restoring the true glory of Egypt, just as Seqenenre's son Kamose deserves the real credit for removing the Hyksos from the land—or at least he does according to the Quarrel Story, authored during Merenptah's reign as a political statement.[64]

The final step, moreover, is to see the exodus account in the Quarrel Story: "The Quarrel Story in its current form and its proposed conclusion resonates with the biblical account of the exodus." This is all a bit too much to bear. One teetering card is placed upon another, until the entire house collapses.

I might concur that the Quarrel Story bears a political message, but if so, it much more likely refers to the presence of numerous Asiatics in the delta more generally during the Nineteenth Dynasty, with the need for the current pharaoh to act in some regard. But given the fragmentary state of the papyrus, with the end of the tale wanting, caution should be advised before one accedes to even this level of interpretation. The bottom line is that we know very little about the purpose of the Quarrel Story; hence reading the Israelites into the tale, especially after creatively reconstructing its ending, is irresponsible.

Feinman believes that not only the Quarrel Story but also other Egyptian texts from the Ramesside period denote the struggle between the Egyptians and the Israelites. Thus Leiden Hymn 30, in which Amun-Re defeats Apophis, is understood as the Egyptian counterpoint to what the Bible narrates in Exod 14–15. The great god Amun-Re defeats Apophis, the embodiment of chaos, which thereby serves as a

64. Truth be told, even though our only manuscript dates to Merenptah's reign, the story itself may date to the reign of Ramesses II or even earlier. The prose is written in Late Egyptian, but beyond that, greater precision cannot be had. See Camilla Di Biase-Dyson, *Foreigners and Egyptians in the Late Egyptian Stories: Linguistic, Literary and Historical Perspectives*, Probleme der Ägyptologie 32 (Leiden: Brill, 2013), 194.

mythic parallel to how Pharaoh and his army emerged triumphant over the Israelites.

There is another angle to Feinman's essay. To his mind, the Hyksos (or their descendants) were still resident in Egypt during the Nineteenth Dynasty, and a portion of them (if I understand him correctly) emerged as the Levites of the Bible. Now, there's a leap! And then these Levites led the exodus from Egypt, in line with the theory put forth by Richard E. Friedman.[65]

Another group also makes an appearance in Feinman's essay—the *n'rn*. *N'rn*, a Semitic term for "soldiers," "warriors," appears in Late Egyptian texts dated to the New Kingdom.[66] Feinman asks the question, "Were the Levites of *n'rn* origin?" I am not sure that he ever answers the question in point-blank fashion, but apparently he believes this group should be added to the matrix. If so, it is rather curious that Feinman does not invoke Exod 2:6, where the three-month-old Moses is referred to as a *na'ar*. While I certainly would not read the usage in said manner—especially since the same word is applied to other newborns and toddlers in the Bible[67]—the passage could add support to Feinman's proposal. In the end, all of this brings Feinman to renew Manetho's (third-century BCE) proposal: the Hebrews who left Egypt were Hyksos!

In sum, the reader is urged to accept that the Hebrews and/or their Levite leaders are in some way connected to latter-day Hyksos and/or Semitic *n'rn*-warriors present in Egypt during the Nineteenth Dynasty. Literary texts from that epoch, especially the Quarrel Story but also Leiden Hymn 30, are then read as allegories for or representations of (in one way or another) the Israelite-Egyptian conflict during the period of Ramesses II and Merenptah. To paraphrase what I stated earlier on only one aspect of Feinman's article, all of this is too much to bear. At this point, even more teetering cards have been placed one upon the other, so that the edifice, constructed from a series of speculations, collapses to the ground.

---

65. Richard Elliott Friedman, *The Exodus* (New York: HarperOne, 2017).

66. James E. Hoch, *Semitic Words in Egyptian Texts of the New Kingdom and Third Intermediate Period* (Princeton: Princeton Univ. Press, 1994), 182–83.

67. *DCH* 5:708.

RESPONSE TO PETER FEINMAN
(THE EXODUS AS CULTURAL MEMORY VIEW)

RONALD HENDEL

Peter Feinman makes a vigorous case for the historicity of the exodus and its date. He says it happened at the end of the seventh year of the reign of Ramesses II, which would be May 1272 BCE, according to one of the standard chronologies. His case is very interesting, taking us on a tour of some Egyptian texts that are little known to outsiders. It is also, in my view, unconvincing. But the texts and topics he addresses are worth engaging with. I will give some of the reasons why I am dubious about the connective tissue of his argument. Feinman says he focuses on "three issues: the Levites, the Hyksos, and a proposed historical reconstruction." I will address these in order.

First, he argues that the Levites were "resident aliens" in Egypt. But there is no reason to think this. The word Levite comes from the root *lwy*, which means something like "to accompany, surround, be attached to." So a *liwyâ* is a "wreath." The Levites are a priestly tribe, who in some sense are "attached to" Yahweh and to the other tribes of Israel. In the latter sense they are analogous to resident aliens, but only because they are members of a tribe (Levi) who are dispersed among the other tribes. They are not actually resident aliens, and their name doesn't mean that. "Resident alien" is the meaning of another Hebrew word, *gēr*. To suggest that any West Semite in Egypt could qualify as a Levite because they were resident aliens in Egypt is to stretch the word beyond what it will bear.

Second, he says that at least some of the West Semites in Egypt during the time of Ramesses II were Hyksos. But this also stretches the word too far. The Hyksos were a dynasty of West Semitic rulers who reigned from 1638–1530 BCE, roughly three centuries before Ramesses II. The word Hyksos comes from their title, "rulers of foreign lands" *(ḥqꜣ ḫꜣswt)*. It is anachronistic to speak of Hyksos in the Ramesside period. There were many West Semites in Egypt then but no Hyksos. I don't think this is a linguistic quibble. There also were, as Feinman says, West Semites in the Egyptian army. The elite military battalion were called *naʿarīn* ("youths"). *Naʿarīn* is a West Semitic word[68] and may have included West Semitic warriors. Or it may, like the Navy SEALs, have included any elite warrior. But these were not Hyksos warriors, nor were they Levite warriors.

Third, Feinman creates an innovative historical reconstruction based on some fascinating Egyptian texts. He places the most weight on the first of these, the Quarrel of Seqenenre and Apophis, which was a school text in the Ramesside period. The only known copy was written in the era of Merenptah, the son and successor of Ramesses II. Feinman says that this story contains "Merenptah's spin on the exodus" and that it is "a smoking gun for the exodus, expressed in Egyptian terms." These are strong claims, which I don't think the story can support. The Quarrel Story, as Feinman relates, presents a quarrel between two Egyptian rulers during the Hyksos dynasty. The Hyksos king is Apophis, and the native Egyptian king, who rules in Thebes in Upper Egypt, is Seqenenre. These were real kings. Although the story is broken in the middle, we know that Seqenenre started the war of reunification against the Hyksos, but he died in battle. His successors Kamose and Ahmose continued the war to ultimate victory. So while Seqenenre lost the battle, his cause prevailed. But we don't know how the Quarrel Story ends.

Feinman argues that this story is a symbolic expression of the exodus, by speculating that the protagonists are cryptic symbols of Moses (= Apophis) and Ramesses II (= Seqenenre). I don't see any reason to think that this is so. The story makes good sense as a cultural memory of the traumatic rule of the Hyksos and their defeat by the heroic Theban kings. Since the story breaks off, we don't know how it ends, but it's pretty clear who the good guys and the bad guys are. There's nothing

---

68. Editor's note: See James E. Hoch, *Semitic Words in Egyptian Texts of the New Kingdom and Third Intermediate Period* (Princeton: Princeton Univ. Press, 1994), 182–83.

in the story to suggest that Moses or the Levites or the Hebrews are involved. The traumatic memory of Hyksos rule is sufficient to explain the persistence of the story and why it would have been included in the curriculum in the Ramesside period. The rest is sheer speculation.

The same type of criticism applies to Feinman's use of the other Egyptian texts. The hymn in Papyrus Leiden I 350 praises the sun god, Amun-Re, in his daily defeat of the Apophis-serpent. This is a different figure than the Hyksos king Apophis, but the king may have been regarded as a figure of chaos in the Ramesside period. In any case, as Feinman says, this hymn expresses the trope that the god (and by implication his chosen king) "harpoons the forces of chaos and restores *ma'at*." This is a normal Ramesside era hymn to the sun god.

Similarly, the 400-Year Stela has nothing to do with the exodus. Ramesses II erected it in Avaris to commemorate the four-hundred-year reign of the god Seth (Baal). This is probably connected with the Ramesside restoration of the worship of Seth, which is reflected in the name of Ramesses's father, Seti I. It is an intriguing text, but there's no reason to connect it to the events of the exodus. Four hundred years is a round number, and it's hard to imagine that this stela has anything to do with the biblical memory of the 400 or 430 years of Egyptian slavery (Gen 15:13; Exod 12:40). But even if it does indirectly, the stela is not about the exodus.

In another article on this topic, Feinman makes good use of a novel by the Nobel laureate Naguib Mahfouz, *Thebes at War*, about Egypt during the Hyksos era.[69] He calls it "a novel solution" to the end of the Quarrel Story. Feinman admits that his textual interpretations and historical reconstructions are speculative. I agree. In my view, they're too novel to count as history. But I think that they would make an excellent historical novel, perhaps a sequel to Mahfouz.

69. Naguib Mahfouz, *Thebes at War: A Novel of Ancient Egypt* (New York: Anchor, 2005).

REJOINDER

PETER FEINMAN

To begin with, I would like to thank editor Mark Janzen for the opportunity to participate in this book. The process has been an educational one for me, as I am sure it will be for readers as well. I've been able to get a better sense of who each of these contributors are, as I now have five examples of each of their writings about a focused topic.

First, I've noticed that we define the exodus differently. Stripling's exodus is a divine event with miracles. In his comments Stripling also suggests Amenhotep II's raid into Canaan was an attempt to replenish the slave stock lost because of the departure of Israel. Stripling had the opportunity to present a historical reconstruction as I did but based it on a Moses-led miraculous exodus in 1446 BCE instead. He even could have included the peoples Joseph-el and Jacob-el, whom Thutmose III listed as conquered. He did not do this. Instead he mostly relied on chronologies and genealogies from the Bible as a matter of faith. He is preaching to the choir, which limits his audience. Stripling and I differ on both date and methodology.

Rendsburg proposes a minor event that no one would notice amid the chaos. Furthermore, to make his proposal work, he has to relocate Merenptah's Israel from Canaan to Egypt. Hendel rightly critiques Rendsburg for proposing an example of one of Hendel's minor exodoi as THE EXODUS. By contrast, I suggest a major event that matches the spirit if not necessarily the letter of the biblical account and keeps Merenptah's Israel in Canaan, where it belongs.

Readers should be aware of these differences in the meaning of the term "exodus." These differences among the contributors are not just in date but in scope and type. No matter what, Stripling is not going to abandon his miracle exodus, Rendsburg is not going to abandon his trivial exodus, and I am not going to abandon my Moses-versus-Ramesses exodus. Hoffmeier offers no particular exodus. Hendel proposes multiple minor ones, but I think he could be persuaded to accept my Moses version. He could modify his "We were slaves in Canaan" exodus and explain the Israelite alliance with anti-Egyptian "Rahab Canaanites."

I turn now to the three Egyptian texts I used. They are what make my proposal "speculative," "creative," and "original." I begin with Leiden Hymn 30. Egypt had capital punishment. Egypt had ceremonial executions. Egypt had rituals associated with the actual killing of human beings. They were public events. One of the most egregious crimes a person could commit was to rebel. A rebel was a disrupter of *ma'at*. His violation of cosmic order was a capital crime. He was equated with Apophis, symbol of chaos. By no coincidence whatsoever these terms and themes are the exact ones expressed in Leiden Hymn 30.

Ramesses II wanted to execute Moses in accordance with Egyptian traditions for the crime of being a rebel, an Apophis. He was unable to do so because Moses had left the country. A destruction using an inanimate object, as execration texts mention, would not suffice as long as people knew Moses was alive. I presume at some point a Canaanite vassal king informed Ramesses that Moses was dead. Wouldn't it be nice to have the Nineteenth Dynasty equivalent of the Amarna letters, this time mentioning the Israelites instead of the Habiru? Ramesses still lived, so now he could ritually execute Moses in absentia in a traditional Egyptian setting. Only with the death of Moses could Ramesses successfully claim in the hymn that the rebels had been destroyed, chaos had been defeated, and cosmic order restored. I should have elaborated on ceremonial executions within the Egyptian culture in my original contribution. However, to do so would have required hundreds of words plus footnotes.

There is some confusion over the use of the term "Hyksos." It can be a common noun, a proper noun, or an ethnic term. I used it to mean the warriors from across the river Nile (aka "Hebrews") who originated in Retjenu *(Rṯnw)*, exact Levant location unknown, who eventually ruled Egypt. Technically, they did so not as a dynasty with father/son rule but as individuals. Not all of them left as a result of Ahmose's victory. Those who remained still can be called Hyksos. Stripling mentions Aper-el in his comments and identifies him as a captured Canaanite of significant prominence in the Amarna age. But he just as easily could have been an assimilated Hyksos. My interpretation is that Ramesses II would not have commemorated the Hyksos with the 400-Year Stela unless there still were Hyksos present in the land. The unique occurrence in Egyptian culture of observing a four-hundred-year anniversary, and for a people of foreign origin, did not occur when none of the people honored were in the audience.

Those Hyksos had remained in Egypt after other Hyksos led people out of Egypt in the exodus. Only afterward did these exodus leaders acquire the name Levites. They were not Levites in Egypt, and the exodus was not a Levite-only event, contra Stripling's comment. There is a story to be told of how this post-exodus name originated in Canaan. Here the comments of Hendel and Hoffmeier are of value; those of Rendsburg are not.

There are only two major stories of a Semite-Pharaoh confrontation in Egypt, excluding the battles against Apophis by Kamose and Ahmose—the biblical account of the exodus and the Quarrel Story. I claim they are connected. Rendsburg comments, "Any attempt to create an ending constitutes pure speculation. Yet this is what Feinman does." Egyptologists who speculate that the ending is "Pharaoh smites the enemy" also are engaging in pure speculation. I included some examples in my contribution, but Rendsburg doesn't challenge those speculations. Why not?

Upon closer examination, I don't buy into Ramesses II's propaganda that he was great. The Moses-led exodus cast a shadow over him. Leiden Hymn 30 fooled no one. Moses was dead but his people still lived. As a result, Merenptah fought Israel in Canaan and claimed to have restored *ma'at*. Everything fits together.

The exodus is part of a larger historical sequence. American historians know that the French and Indian War, the Revolution, and the War of 1812 are all connected. Sometimes the same sites were involved. Similarly, the exodus was not an isolated event. It was part of a series of encounters involving Egypt and Israel in the thirteenth and twelfth centuries until Egypt finally withdrew from Canaan. These interactions include Ramesses and Moses, Merneptah and Joshua, Ramesses III and Deborah, and Ramesses VI and Shiloh. To reconstruct that history and the related biblical passages exceeds the parameters of this book, but readers should be made aware of this extended story, which also includes the Canaanites. Thutmose III at Megiddo was part of the Canaanite and Israelite cultural memory and not just Egypt's. Hendel should expand his scope of cultural memory to include Seqenenre and Thutmose III. Any reconstruction of the exodus needs to extend forward and backward in time.

To create order out of chaos is a challenge. It is one worth undertaking. I invite readers to consider this scenario. Suppose all you had were

1. a biography of Benedict Arnold ending in 1775,
2. the Victory Monument at Saratoga,
3. Thomas Cole's painting *View of Fort Putnam.*

Would you be able to connect them? Would you conclude that Arnold was a traitor? Even if you already knew Arnold was a traitor, would you be able to connect them? There is a blank facade on the Victory Monument where Arnold, a hero at Saratoga, should be. How would you know he deliberately was excluded? How would you know Cole used light and shadow over the fort at West Point to symbolize George Washington and Arnold? The parallel is not exact, but it is suggestive of the creativity sometimes needed to connect the dots in a historical reconstruction.

Leiden Hymn 30, the Quarrel Story, and the 400-Year Stela are three unique texts in Egyptian history. Individually, each one is sufficient to prove the historicity of a Moses-led exodus in the time of Ramesses II if you accept my interpretation. They are not isolated but connected. Collectively, they cohere into a single story that provides insight into Egyptian and Israelite history. Here the contrast between Rendsburg and Hendel is strongly revealed. Rendsburg is unable to see the unity of the texts. Hendel, even though he disagrees with me, does. Yes, my historical reconstruction could become a novel as Hendel suggests, but I don't have the necessary skills to do it. However, since my contribution to this book tells a story that could become a novel or a movie, then I say, "Mission accomplished."

CHAPTER FOUR

THE TWELFTH-CENTURY EXODUS VIEW

GARY A. RENDSBURG

In an article published in 1992, titled "The Date of the Exodus and the Conquest/Settlement: The Case for the 1100s," I proposed that the exodus should be dated to the twelfth century BCE, specifically to the reign of Ramesses III (r. 1187–1156 BCE).[1] Three decades later I stand by that opinion. I welcome this opportunity to present the argument again, albeit in slightly different fashion.[2]

The Term "Exodus"

Let us begin with a consideration of the word exodus. In the very act of proposing a date for the exodus (as is the case with many scholars, including most contributors to this volume), I aver that there is some modicum of historicity to the biblical tradition. The exodus tradition is the single most repeated trope in all the Bible, appearing in all genres: narrative prose (Exod 1–14), poetic recollections (Pss 78; 105), historical

1. Gary A. Rendsburg, "The Date of the Exodus and the Conquest/Settlement: The Case for the 1100s," *VT* 42 (1992): 510–27.

2. All translations of biblical texts herein are mine. The dates for Egyptian pharaohs are borrowed from William J. Murnane, "The History of Ancient Egypt: An Overview," *CANE* 2 (1995): 691–717, esp. pp. 712–14. Note that Murnane places "ca." before all the dates, though I have dispensed with this usage, if only to streamline the presentation. Malcolm H. Wiener, "Dating the Emergence of Historical Israel in Light of Recent Developments in Egyptian Chronology," *TA* 41 (2014): 50–54, has proposed an upward shift of about one decade for Nineteenth and Twentieth Dynasty chronology, but such an adjustment would have little or no effect on the outline presented herein.

summations (Judg 6:8; 1 Sam 12:8), legal hortatory (Exod 20:2; 29:46; Lev 19:36; Deut 13:10), liturgical declarations (Deut 26:8), prophetic speeches (Amos 9:7; Hos 2:15; Jer 11:4), and more. This alone does not guarantee the historicity of the tradition, but the national collective memory so evident throughout the Bible must have stemmed from somewhere—even if that somewhere is but a historical kernel—especially when there exists sufficient historical and archaeological material to corroborate the biblical account.[3]

Early Israel

As I will argue anon, at some point during the twelfth century, a group of people of indeterminate size, identifiable as Israelites, who had been resident in the eastern Nile delta for several generations, left Egypt, traversed the Sinai, and eventually settled in the central hill country of Canaan. I will refer to this group as "core Israel," with reference to the people whose collective experience generated the foundational biblical narrative.

Undoubtedly, there were other elements of Israelites, or people who would later identify as Israelites, with similar or parallel experiences. Some may have left Egypt slightly earlier; some may have left slightly later; while some may never have been to Egypt at all but rather lived as pastoral nomads in the desert regions to the south of Israel and/or in Transjordan. Still others had totally different experiences, such as the tribe of Dan, which reached the land of Canaan by sea, and the tribe of Asher, which apparently was resident in the Galilee region throughout the period under discussion (see the following).[4] Regardless, the core

---

3. On the exodus as historical memory, see the programmatic essay by Ronald Hendel, "The Exodus in Biblical Memory," *JBL* 120 (2001): 601–22, as well as his contribution to the present volume. On historical and archaeological information relevant to the eisodus (for the term, see n. 7), slavery, and exodus traditions, see Gary A. Rendsburg, "The Early History of Israel," in *Crossing Boundaries and Linking Horizons: Studies in Honor of Michael C. Astour on His 80th Birthday*, ed. Gordon D. Young, Mark W. Chavalas, and Richard E. Averbeck (Bethesda, MD: CDL, 1997), 433–53; Gary A. Rendsburg, "Israelite Origins," in *"An Excellent Fortress for His Armies, a Refuge for the People": Egyptological, Archaeological, and Biblical Studies in Honor of James K. Hoffmeier*, ed. Richard E. Averbeck and K. Lawson Younger (University Park, PA: Eisenbrauns, 2020), 327–39. For the most detailed discussions, see James K. Hoffmeier, *Israel in Egypt: The Evidence for the Authenticity of the Exodus Tradition* (Oxford: Oxford Univ. Press, 1996); idem, *Ancient Israel in Sinai: The Evidence for the Authenticity of the Wilderness Tradition* (Oxford: Oxford Univ. Press, 2005).

4. For these stories, see Rendsburg, "Early History of Israel," 447–50. See also 1 Chr 7:20–24, which implies that Ephraim was resident in Canaan as well, for which see Sara Japhet, *I & II Chronicles*, OTL (Louisville: Westminster John Knox, 1993), 181–82.

exodus event (or process), which will be the main subject of this essay, came to define the later Israelite historical consciousness.

An American Analogy

It may help readers to consider an American analogy, one that has been used by others as well.[5] The *Mayflower* event was a singular journey, which (after some stops and starts) left Plymouth, England, on September 6, 1620, and arrived at present-day Cape Cod, Massachusetts, on November 9, 1620. This event was eventually integrated into the American national epic, but there were earlier journeys, including those which led to the establishments of the Roanoke Colony (1585) and the Jamestown settlement (1607), and of course numerous later voyages, including the arrival of others on a second ship named *Mayflower* in 1629, 1630, 1633, 1634, and 1639. Add to this the arrival of people from other European countries, most important the Dutch settlement of the Hudson Valley during the years 1609–1624, and we begin to see the emergence of the American nation. Naturally, the history of America is more complex, as it includes the diversity of Native Americans, Spanish colonization in Florida (starting already in 1565), Africans brought to these shores against their will (commencing in 1619),[6] French colonization in Louisiana (starting in 1699), and more. But of all the Atlantic crossings, the one remembered and still celebrated by the vast majority of Americans on Thanksgiving Day is the *Mayflower* event.

And such was likely true with early Israel as well. Diverse elements coalesced into the nation of Israel, but only one event or process was remembered and celebrated—*the* exodus from Egypt (as part of the Passover observance). This tradition created a unified national narrative with all twelve tribes engaged in the same eisodus,[7] slavery, and exodus (in addition to their descent from a single individual, Jacob/Israel). This

5. See William G. Dever, *Who Were the Early Israelites and Where Did They Come From?* (Grand Rapids: Eerdmans, 2003), 234.

6. To be more precise, in August 1619; hence I am keenly aware that as I write these words in August 2019, I do so on the four hundredth anniversary of the first ship of slaves to endure the Middle Passage. See the excellent collection of essays in "The 1619 Project," *New York Times* (August 18, 2019).

7. "Eisodus" is the term used to describe the journey to and entrance *into* Egypt, as detailed in the latter portion of the book of Genesis.

idealized story united the disparate elements which coalesced into the people of Israel, rendering the historian's task of reconstructing *wie es eigentlich gewesen* ("how it actually was") exceedingly difficult.

We will proceed, accordingly, with the assumption that beneath the unified idealized narrative—with its epic and theological overlays—lies a historical kernel. With this as background and with all due caution resulting from the methodological issues previously outlined, we turn now to the matter of demonstrating a twelfth-century date for the exodus.

The Emergence of Israel in Canaan

During the twelfth century BCE, a new people appeared in the central hill country of Canaan, extending from the Jezreel Valley in the north to the Beersheba Basin in the south. Almost undoubtedly, these newcomers were the Israelites as attested in the Bible. During the epoch immediately prior to the arrival of the newcomers in the land, known as the Late Bronze Age (1500–1175 BCE), the central hill country was relatively open terrain. Extensive archaeological surveys of the region have identified only ca. 30 settlements dating to this period. However, in the subsequent Iron Age I era (1175–1000 BCE), the number of settlements within the same geographical area rose dramatically to ca. 250.[8] This expansion cannot be because of natural population growth alone. Rather it indicates the arrival of a new people in the region.

Elliptical Sites

Yet it is not only the number of sites that is relevant but also the distinctive configuration of many of these settlements, especially the earlier and smaller ones. Beginning in the twelfth century, the landscape becomes dotted with settlements arranged in elliptical patterns: the houses are aligned solely along the perimeter of the ellipse, while the interior of the site remains open, thereby creating a central courtyard (see figs. 1–2).

---

8. Israel Finkelstein et al., "Reconstructing Ancient Israel: Integrating Macro- and Micro-Archaeology," *HBAI* 1, no. 1 (2012): 141. For the most sustained exposition, see Israel Finkelstein, *The Archaeology of the Israelite Settlement* (Jerusalem: Israel Exploration Society, 1988). Over the years, the author has retreated from some of his statements in the book, though I consider them valid still, especially as the evidence remains unchanged.

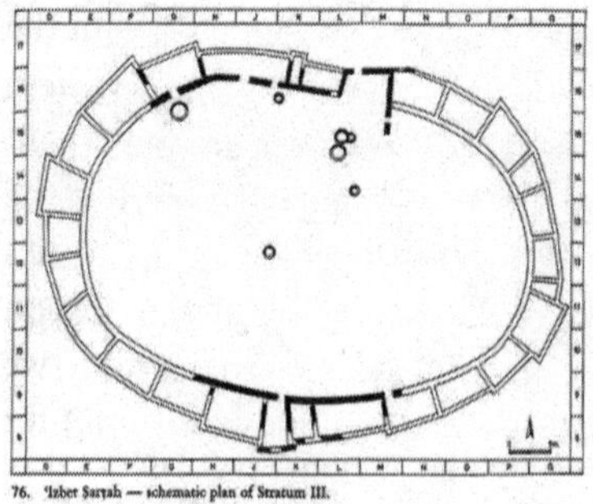

76. ʿIzbet Ṣarṭah — schematic plan of Stratum III.

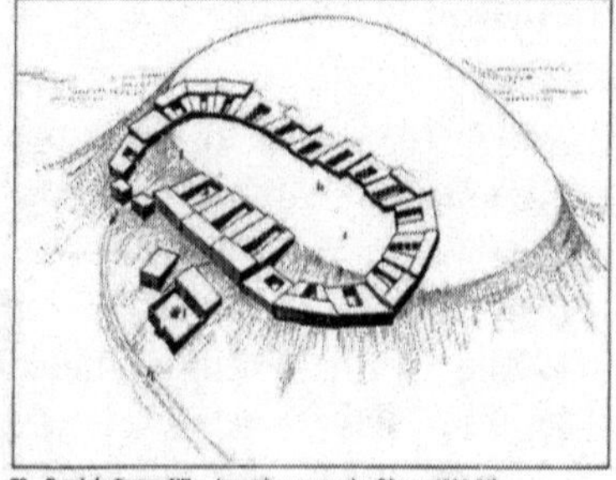

79. Beersheba Stratum VII — isometric reconstruction (Herzog 1984: 80).

Figure 1: Iron Age I elliptical courtyard sites

Source: Israel Finkelstein, *The Archaeology of the Israelite Settlement* (Jerusalem: Israel Exploration Society, 1988), 239, 243 (the latter based on an earlier source, as indicated)

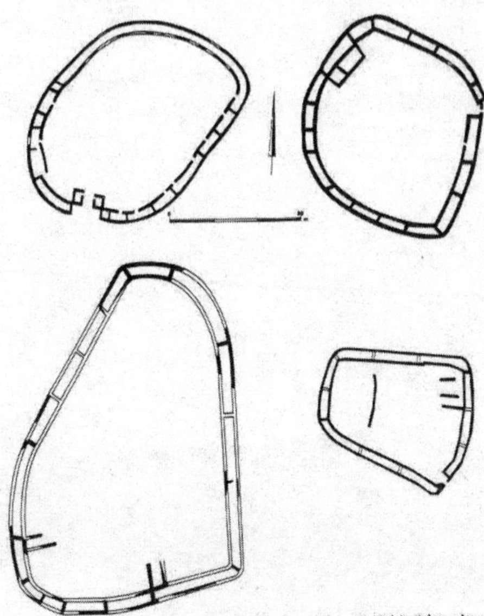

78. Iron Age Courtyard sites in the Negev Highlands: top left — Ein Qadeis; right — Atar Haroʾa; bottom left — Raḥba; right — Ketef Shivṭa (Cohen 1979: 64).

Figure 2: Iron Age I elliptical courtyard sites

Source: Israel Finkelstein, *The Archaeology of the Israelite Settlement* (Jerusalem: Israel Exploration Society, 1988), 241, based on an earlier source, as indicated

The Lifestyle of Desert Nomads

The layout of these settlements strikingly resembles the manner in which the desert-dwelling bedouin of our own era fashion their encampments—with the tents erected side by side along the perimeter, leaving the interior as an enclosed space for the sheep and goats. In the nighttime only a few shepherds on guard duty, along with their sheepdogs, are required to ensure the safety of the flocks; in the daytime the sheep and goats are led out of the enclosure to graze in the surrounding countryside (see figs. 3 and 4).

80. Tent encampment in Transjordan, after a picture published by Musil (1908: 131).

81. Tent encampment in the Judean Desert (Dalman 1939: Pl. 12).

Figure 3: Bedouin tent encampments from the first half of the twentieth century

Source: Israel Finkelstein, *The Archaeology of the Israelite Settlement* (Jerusalem: Israel Exploration Society, 1988), 246, based on earlier sources, as indicated

Photo © Gary A. Rendsburg

Figure 4: Bedouin tent encampment in the Judean Desert, 1978

Based on this parallel, we can posit that the people responsible for the Iron Age I courtyard or elliptical sites were former pastoral nomads—or better, seminomads—who over time became more sedentary. As they transitioned from their former nomadic ways to a more settled way of life, they did not leapfrog from bedouin-style encampments to full-fledged villages. Instead when they began to construct more permanent domiciles, these newcomers to the central hill country organized their structures according to their customary elliptical site plan. These early Iron Age I settlements served the same practical purpose—protection of livestock—but the dwellings changed from portable tents made of animal skins to simple yet permanent houses constructed of stone.[9]

This process accords with the biblical record, which portrays the Israelites as pastoralists, traversing the wilderness region to the south of Israel, then entering the sown (arable land) and settling in the central hill country. Moreover, since this process is not attested in this region until the twelfth century BCE, we also should look to the twelfth century for the background of the exodus. To be sure, a fifteenth-century

9. For a wide-ranging survey on sedentarization, with modern parallels, see Thomas E. Levy and Augustin F. C. Holl, "Migrations, Ethnogenesis, and Settlement Dynamics: Israelites in Iron Age Canaan and Shuwa-Arabs in the Chad Basin," *Journal of Anthropological Archaeology* 21 (2002): 83–118.

date is out of the question, for such a dating raises the question, where were the Israelites for several centuries before they emerged in the land of Canaan? True, a thirteenth-century date still might be possible, since the chronological bridge between the exodus and the emergence of Israel in Canaan is not as great. As we shall see, however, there are additional reasons for us to focus on the twelfth century BCE as the date for the exodus from Egypt.

In general, the Israelites simply settled the open terrain of the central hill country, building settlements on previously unoccupied sites or on sites which long had been deserted. The best known and/or best excavated ones are Ai, Giloh, Shiloh, 'Izbet Ṣarṭah, and Khirbet Raddana, all located in the core area of the central hill country, and Tel Masos and Tell es-Seba' in the Negev region.[10]

The Occasional Battle

Occasionally, as was necessary, the newcomers to the land may have fought a battle to conquer a city or defeat a people in the area. Where such evidence exists, the archaeological data point to the twelfth century BCE. The archaeological evidence at Ḥesban, the location of biblical Heshbon, reveals that the earliest level of occupation, Stratum XIX, began ca. 1200 BCE.[11] According to Num 21:25, the Israelites engaged the Amorites at Heshbon, defeated them, and captured the city. If we are to accept any historicity behind the biblical account, one must date this encounter to the twelfth century BCE.

Lachish provides another example. Stratum VI, dated to the twelfth century, was still governed by the Egyptians, as confirmed by two small finds, one bearing the name of Ramesses III (1187–1156 BCE) and one bearing the name of Ramesses IV (1156–1150 BCE). Stratum VI then was destroyed by fire, ca. 1140 BCE, after which the site was abandoned.[12] While the archaeological data do not (and typically cannot)

10. For general discussion, see Amihai Mazar, *Archaeology of the Land of the Bible*, ABRL (New York: Doubleday, 1992), 334–38 (and for the location of these sites, see the map on p. 309).

11. Lawrence T. Geraty, "Heshbon," *NEAEHL* 2:626–30; and in greater detail the collection of essays in David Merling and Lawrence T. Geraty, eds., *Hesban After 25 Years* (Berrien Springs, MI: Andrews Univ., 1994).

12. David Ussishkin, "Lachish," *NEAEHL* 3:900–4. For further details, see David Ussishkin, "Levels VII and VI at Tel Lachish and the End of the Late Bronze Age in Canaan,"

inform us *who* was responsible for the destruction, given the geography, the chronology, and the account in Josh 10:31–32, the Israelites are a prime candidate. It is true that Josh 10 does not mention the burning of Lachish by the Israelites (see esp. v. 32), but the other elements fit well. Again, if there is any historical validity to the biblical account, the Israelite attack on Lachish could not have occurred until *after* the Egyptian presence at the city had receded, ca. 1150 BCE.[13] In sum, the picture that emerges from the archaeological record compels us to focus on the twelfth century for the emergence of Israel in the land of Canaan, and by extension for the exodus from Egypt as well.

Ramesses III

To my mind, the best candidate for the pharaoh of the exodus is Ramesses III (r. 1187–1156 BCE). This king had more important problems to worry about during his reign—the attack of the Sea Peoples coalition (which included the Philistines). This time would have been propitious for the Israelites to consider leaving. With the very independence of Egypt at stake—Ramesses III's own records attest to what extent the nation's forces were needed to defend against the invasion[14]—the exodus of the Israelites would not have been difficult at this time.

By contrast, those who argue for a thirteenth-century date for the exodus typically assign the event to the reign of either Ramesses II (r. 1279–1213 BCE) or Merenptah (r. 1213–1203 BCE). Yet both of these pharaohs were quite powerful, and Egypt was stable during this period, making it difficult to imagine the exodus occurring with either of these kings on the throne.[15]

---

in *Palestine in the Bronze and Iron Ages: Papers in Honour of Olga Tufnell*, ed. Jonathan N. Tubb (London: Univ. College London Institute of Archaeology, 1985), 213–30. On the Egyptian objects, see Eric H. Cline, *1177 B.C.: The Year Civilization Collapsed* (Princeton: Princeton Univ. Press, 2014), 120–21.

13. See the classic article by James M. Weinstein, "The Egyptian Empire in Palestine: A Reassessment," *BASOR* 241 (1981): 1–28, with its treatment (per the title) of the general picture, including the evidence regarding Lachish. Even at a distance of forty years, with new data forthcoming from new excavations, the picture described by Weinstein remains more or less valid.

14. See W. F. Edgerton and J. A. Wilson, *Historical Records of Ramses III*, SAOC 12 (Chicago: Univ. of Chicago Press, 1936), 35–58. For a recent survey of the material, see Eric H. Cline and David O'Connor, "The Sea Peoples," in *Ramesses III: The Life and Times of Egypt's Last Hero*, ed. Eric H. Cline and David O'Connor (Ann Arbor: Univ. of Michigan Press, 2012), 180–208.

15. True, there also was a Sea Peoples invasion during the reign of Merenptah, but this attack appears to have been readily repulsed by the Egyptian forces (see the following).

Merenptah Stela

In proposing Ramesses III as the pharaoh of the exodus, I argue for a different interpretation of the Merenptah Stela than the one typically offered by scholars.[16] The relevant lines from the stela read as follows:

> Canaan is plundered,
> Ashkelon is carried off,
> and Gezer is captured.
> Yenoam is made into non-existence;
> Israel is wasted, its seed is not;
> and Hurru is become a widow because of Egypt.[17]

I understand the line about Israel as a reference to the slavery period. This explains the use of the people-determinative; they are not a foreign location (as is indicated for the other entities mentioned) but rather a people living in Egypt.[18] The hymn's author knew that Israel had originated in Canaan, and therefore included mention of them between Canaan and Hurru. If the Merenptah Stela refers to an Egyptian victory over the Israelites after the exodus, as the fifteenth-century dating presupposes and as many varieties of the thirteenth-century dating assume, one would expect some mention of this encounter in the Bible, especially since the biblical writers did not shy away from including material about Israel's defeats (see further on). Since no such encounter is mentioned

16. The most detailed study of the Merenptah Stela remains Helmut Engel, "Die Siegesstele des Merenptah," *Bib* 60 (1979): 373–99. For more recent thorough surveys of these relevant lines in the inscription, see Michael G. Hasel, "*Israel* in the Merneptah Stela," *BASOR* 296 (1994): 45–61; idem, "The Structure of the Final Hymnic-Poetic Unit on the Merenptah Stela," *ZAW* 116 (2004): 75–81—even if I disagree with the author's interpretation of *prt*, translated by Hoffmeier (see next note) and others as "seed" (in the sense of "people," "offspring") though which Hasel prefers to understand literally as "grain."

17. "The (Israel) Stela of Merneptah," trans. James K. Hoffmeier (*COS* 2.6:41).

18. Although he ultimately rejected this view, it is worth noting that the same position was put forward as one of several options for the interpretation of "Israel" in the Merenptah Stela by W. M. Flinders Petrie immediately upon his discovery of the stela. See his essay "Egypt and Israel," *The Contemporary Review* 69 (May 1896): 617–27, esp. p. 624, and the summary thereof in his book *Six Temples at Thebes, 1896* (London: Quaritch, 1897), 30. Others opined similarly, by dating the exodus to the reigns of various pharaohs at the end of the Nineteenth Dynasty, i.e., who followed Merenptah; for a summary of such views, which tended to be rather idiosyncratic, see Engel, "Die Siegesstele des Merenptah," 396–97.

in the Bible, the reference to Israel in the Merenptah Stela most likely denotes the Israelites while they were still in Egypt.[19]

Alternatively, "Israel" in the Merenptah Stela could refer to Israelite elements in Canaan who never experienced the eisodus, slavery, and exodus (see above). During his campaign in Canaan, it is quite possible that Merenptah encountered some segment of the population which identified as Israelite. These may have been seminomadic Shasu-type people, of the type portrayed on the outer western wall of the Cour de la Cachette at the Karnak Temple, as analyzed by Anson Rainey.[20] Alternatively, they may have been Israelite elements in Canaan proper, such as the tribe of Asher, referred to in Papyrus Anastasi I (the so-called Satirical Letter), column 23, line 6, in the region of Megiddo.[21]

Regardless of how we interpret the mention of Israel in the Merenptah Stela, this singular reference does not imply—as most scholars have argued—that the core group of Israel who had been enslaved in Egypt had already left Egypt prior to ca. 1210 BCE and were ensconced in the land of Canaan at this date.

The Spring of Merenptah

Additionally, we should take note of the little-known fact that the name Merenptah appears in the Bible. Among the hundreds of toponyms mentioned in Josh 13–22, listed within the tribal allotments we read *maʿyan mê neptôaḥ*, "the spring of Me-Neptoaḥ" (Josh 15:9; 18:15), located on the boundary between Judah and Benjamin. Because the Hebrew word *mê* means "waters of," readers of the Bible have often interpreted this toponym as "the spring of the waters of Neptoaḥ," with only the last element as a pure proper noun. I believe the term is better understood as "the spring of Merenptah," especially because the

19. I do not mean to imply that it was Merenptah who instituted the slavery. I believe that this was accomplished by Ramesses II and that the slavery continued under Merenptah. In any case, this point has no direct effect on the main issue under discussion.

20. Anson F. Rainey, "Rainey's Challenge," *BAR* 17, no. 6 (November/December 1991): 58–60, 93; idem, "Israel in Merenptah's Inscription and Reliefs," *IEJ* 51 (2001): 57–75.

21. For the original publication, see Alan H. Gardiner, *Egyptian Hieratic Texts* (Leipzig, 1911), 25*. There are, of course, numerous alternative interpretations of *ỉsr* in this passage, for which see H. W. Fischer-Elfert, *Die satirische Streitschrift des Papyrus Anastasi I* (Wiesbaden: Harrassowitz, 1986), 199–200. To my mind, though, the connection between *ỉsr* and Asher remains secure.

final /r/ was lost in Late Egyptian.[22] So while the pharaoh's name may have been written with the hieroglyphs *Mr-n-ptḥ* (meaning "beloved of Ptaḥ"), the pronunciation of the first element would have been closer to what is preserved in Josh 15:9; 18:15. The location of "the spring of Merenptah," moreover, is known, since its name lives on as modern Lifta (with further apocopation of the original name and phonological adjustments), five kilometers northwest of Jerusalem, precisely where one would expect to find it, according to the information conveyed in the Joshua passages.[23]

While some have doubted the historicity of Merenptah's claim that he campaigned in Canaan (even after considering the Amada Stela, in which Merenptah gains the epithet *ḫfʿ Qḏr*, "seizer of Gezer"[24]), the presence of a toponym called the "spring of Merneptah" in the Judean hills named for him seals the argument. There can be no doubt that Merenptah's troops campaigned in the land of Canaan, including, it would appear, in close proximity to Jerusalem.[25]

---

22. See Antonio Loprieno, *Ancient Egyptian: A Linguistic Introduction* (Cambridge: Cambridge Univ. Press, 1995), 38. For the original proposal, see Franz Calice, "König Menephthes im Buche Josua?" *OLZ* 6 (1903): 224. For a more recent treatment, see Gary A. Rendsburg, "Merneptah in Canaan," *JSSEA* 11 (1981): 171–72 (with Corrigenda printed as supplement to *JSSEA* 12 [1982]).

23. On the identification of "the spring of the waters of Neptoaḥ" ("the spring of Merenptah") with modern-day Lifta, see, e.g., Yohanan Aharoni, *The Land of the Bible: A Historical Geography*, 2nd ed., trans. Anson F. Rainey (Philadelphia: Westminster, 1979), 255; Richard S. Hess, *Joshua* (Leicester: Inter-Varsity, 1996), 244; Cyrus H. Gordon and Gary A. Rendsburg, *The Bible and the Ancient Near East* (New York: W. W. Norton, 1997), 175.

24. Original publication: Urbain Bouriant, "Notes de Voyage," *Recueil de travaux relatifs à la philologie et à l'archéologie égyptiennes et assyriennes: pour servir de bullletin à la Mission Française du Caire* 18 (1896): 159. Standard edition: Jarsolav Černý, *Le temple d'Amada, Cahier V: Les inscriptions historiques* (Cairo: Centre de documentation et d'études sur l'ancienne Égypte, 1967), 1–3 (i.e., pp. 1–3 of the Merenptah text, since the volume is a collection of unbound individual pages). My thanks to Edward Bleiberg, Brooklyn Museum, for providing me with a scan of the relevant pages from this hard-to-obtain volume. See also Kenneth A. Kitchen, *Ramesside Inscriptions: Historical and Biographical*, 8 vols. (Oxford: Blackwell, 1976–1990), 4:1 (repeated on p. 33).

25. For a thorough review of all the evidence, see Michael G. Hasel, *Domination and Resistance: Egyptian Military Activity in the Southern Levant, ca. 1300–1185 B.C.*, Probleme der Ägyptologie 11 (Leiden: Brill, 1998), 178–89. Though I hasten to add that Hasel did not discuss "the spring of Merenptah" on the Judahite-Benjaminite border. As an example of a scholar who denies Merenptah's campaign in Canaan, see Hourig Sourouzian, *Les monuments du roi Merenptah*, Deutsches Archäologisches Institut, Abteilung Kairo, Sonderschrift 22 (Mainz: von Zabern, 1989), 169.

Egyptian Presence in Canaan

All of this background is relevant as we seek to determine the date of the exodus. To expand on the point made previously: if the Israelites had left Egypt at some point in the thirteenth century and were resident in the central hill country by the end of the thirteenth century (per the standard approach), the following question arises. Why do the books of Joshua and Judges nowhere mention an encounter between the Egyptians and the Israelites? We also could ask this question for the narrative portions of the book of Numbers. According to the biblical account, once the Israelites crossed the Sea of Reeds (Exod 14–15), they never again encountered Egyptian troops.

Historical documentation clearly reveals an ongoing Egyptian presence in the land of Canaan during the reign of Ramesses III. Egyptian officials were stationed at Gaza and Deir el-Balaḥ in the southern coastal plain; at Lachish,[26] Tel Sera' (perhaps Ziklag), Tell el-Far'ah (South), and perhaps Beth-Shemesh in the south southern inland area (in addition to centers nearer the coast, such as Gaza and Deir el-Balaḥ); and at Megiddo and most prominently Beit Shean in the north.[27] In addition, Egyptian mining in the Timna' Valley continued throughout the Nineteenth Dynasty and into the reign of Ramesses III during the Twentieth Dynasty (though perhaps with a brief interruption during the transition between the two dynasties).[28]

Given the clear presence of Egyptians in Canaan at this time, can one envision the Israelites traveling through the general region of the Timna' Valley (as they did, regardless of how one reconstructs the wilderness itineraries of the book of Numbers) and then settling in the region of Lachish during the latter part of the thirteenth century or the early decades of the twelfth century (as a thirteenth-century exodus would imply) *without ever* encountering the Egyptian presence in the land? This defies all manner of probability, in my opinion.

It is far better to assume that the Israelites left Egypt during the reign of Ramesses III, during the turmoil generated by the Sea Peoples invasion (ca. 1180 BCE), thereby bringing them to the land of Canaan

---

26. For the evidence concerning Lachish, see above, p. 000.

27. For a survey, see James M. Weinstein, "Egypt and the Levant in the Reign of Ramesses III," in Cline and O'Connor, *Ramesses III*, 164–71.

28. Weinstein, "Egypt and the Levant," 171.

about twenty-five years later, at the very point when there was no longer a strong Egyptian presence in the land. This would explain why the Bible never mentions the Egyptians beyond Exod 14–15. Again, people of all sorts are encountered—Amalekites, Edomites, Moabites, Ammonites, and Canaanites—but not Egyptians.[29]

Exodus 13:17 and the Sea Peoples Invasion

A further clue to the date of the exodus is provided by Exod 13:17: "And it was, when Pharaoh sent-forth the people, and God did not lead them by way of the land of the Philistines, though it was closer, for God said, 'Lest the people reconsider when they see war and return to Egypt.'" If we take this verse at face value, it tells us that at the very time the Israelites left Egypt, there was military conflict along the coastal route, referred to here as the "way of the land of the Philistines." Could there be any greater clue as to the date of the exodus?[30]

We know that the Sea Peoples attacked Egypt during the reign of Merenptah, as described in the Great Karnak Inscription, but three points should be noted. First, the invasion (and even that word may be too strong) did not cause undue woe to Egypt. Second, the events seem to have occurred to the west of the Egyptian delta, given the alliance between the Sea Peoples and the Libyans. And third, the Philistines were not included among the Sea Peoples at this time.[31] I make these points to say that should anyone wish to associate Exod 13:17 with the invasion of the Sea Peoples during the reign of Merenptah, such a connection would be tenuous at best.

By contrast, the Egyptian documents which describe the invasion of the Sea Peoples ca. 1180 BCE during the reign of Ramesses III testify to the great turmoil that consumed the country. They also imply that the action took place to the east of the delta and perhaps along the Sinai coast. In addition, the Medinet Habu inscriptions place the Philistines

---

29. The mention of the Egyptians in Judg 10:11, in the mouth of God, must refer back to the exodus narrative.

30. For an adumbration of this argument, though with (to my mind) too much specificity in the overall approach, see M. B. Rowton, "The Problem of the Exodus," *PEQ* 85 (1953): 45–60, esp. p. 58.

31. For discussion, see Colleen Manassa, *The Great Karnak Inscription of Merneptah: Grand Strategy in the 13th Century BC*, Yale Egyptological Studies 5 (New Haven: Yale Egyptological Seminar, 2003), 77–82.

at the head of the coalition (though admittedly this is not the case in Papyrus Harris I).[32]

Thus, if there is any historical reality to the biblical tradition recorded in Exod 13:17, everything points to the Sea Peoples invasion during the reign of Ramesses III ca. 1180 BCE as the probable background for the statement. Furthermore, while I would not push the argument too far (though David Noel Freedman has done this[33]), the mention of Philistia alongside Edom, Moab, and Canaan in Exod 15:14–15 implies that the Philistines were present in Canaan at the time of the Israelites' approach. Granted, the mention of Philistia here could be an anachronism (as perforce it must be for the thirteenth-century and fifteenth-century datings of the exodus), but its presence in the Song of the Sea is notable nonetheless.

It also may be possible to incorporate Amos 9:7 into this discussion. The verse reads as follows: "Did I not bring Israel up from the land of Egypt, and the Philistines from Caphtor, and Aram from Qir?" Might this verse imply that all three movements were more or less coeval? Unfortunately, since we do not know where Qir is located,[34] and thus cannot say more about Aramean origins, including when the Aramean migration may have occurred, the question cannot be answered. Yet the posited contemporaneity of the named movements is suggestive. To be sure, the Philistines' migration from Caphtor (Crete specifically or the Aegean more generally) and the Israelites' migration from Egypt were more or less contemporary, at least according to the reconstruction presented here.

As an aside, albeit an important one, note the following: those scholars who deny the Israelite experience in Egypt altogether but accept the fact (demonstrable through archaeological evidence) that the Philistines migrated from Caphtor to the southern coastal plain of Canaan would have us believe that the Israelites knew more about the history of their neighbors than they knew about their own history!

---

32. For detailed discussion and translation of the relevant texts, see Cline and O'Connor, "The Sea Peoples," 180–208.

33. David Noel Freedman, "Early Israelite Poetry and Historical Reconstructions," in *Symposia Celebrating the Seventy-Fifth Anniversary of the Founding of the American Schools of Oriental Research (1900–1975)*, ed. Frank Moore Cross (Cambridge: American Schools of Oriental Research, 1979), 95 (reprinted in David Noel Freedman, *Pottery, Poetry, and Prophecy: Studies in Early Hebrew Poetry* [Winona Lake, IN: Eisenbrauns, 1980], 177).

34. For the most recent treatment, with a new suggestion, see Yoel Elitzur, "Qīr of the Aramaeans: A New Approach" (in Hebrew), *Shnaton* 21 (2012): 141–52, with English abstract on pp. ix–x.

Biblical Genealogies and Other Chronological Clues

We now turn to evidence of a different sort—the genealogies and other chronological clues recorded in the Bible.

1 Kings 6:1

An oft-cited verse for fixing the date of the exodus is 1 Kgs 6:1: "And it was, in the four hundred and eightieth year of the Israelites' going-out from the land of Egypt, in the fourth year, in the month of Ziv, that is, the second month, in the reign of Solomon over Israel; and he built the House to the LORD." This seems to give us a clear chronology. If we can fix the date of Solomon's construction of the temple, or more generally of his reign, and work back 480 years, we have the date of the exodus.

Of course, the calculus is not that simple. We are able to date Solomon's reign with confidence to ca. 965–930 BCE. We also note the reference to Shishak, king of Egypt, as a contemporary of Solomon in 1 Kgs 11:40. Shishak = Shoshenq, founder of the Twenty-Second Dynasty, who ruled 945–924 BCE.[35] Since the construction of the temple was begun during the fourth year of Solomon's reign and was completed seven years later (1 Kgs 6:38), we can date the construction project to the years 961–954 BCE. Let's keep the math simple and use the year 960 BCE as a fixed point for the purposes of our calculations. If the exodus from Egypt transpired 480 years earlier per 1 Kgs 6:1, the date of the exodus can be assigned to ca. 1440 BCE (see the position argued by Scott Stripling in this volume.)

The Use of Years in the Biblical Narrative and Ancient Near East Traditions

However, the problems with this approach are twofold. First, as argued previously, a fifteenth-century date for the exodus leads to the question, where were the Israelites before they first emerged in the historical and archaeological record? Second, one cannot take at face value the years

35. I accept the standard teaching and reject the disassociation of the two figures, as posited by (most of) the contributors to Peter James and Peter G. van der Veen, eds., *Solomon and Shishak: Current Perspectives from Archaeology, Epigraphy, History and Chronology: Proceedings of the Third BICANE Colloquium Held at Sidney Sussex College, Cambridge 26–27 March, 2011*, BAR International Series 2732 (Oxford: Archaeopress, 2015). For a detailed review see Ronald Wallenfels, "Shishak and Shoshenq: A Disambiguation," *JAOS* 139 (2019): 487–500.

presented in the early biblical books. The numbers used are always greatly exaggerated, and at times they are imbued with symbolism (even if the exact nature of that symbolism eludes us).

For example, the life spans of Joseph (representing the generation that moved from Canaan to Egypt) and Joshua (representing the generation that returned from Egypt to Canaan) are both 110 (Gen 50:26; Josh 24:29), a figure which represents the ideal life span of an ancient Egyptian.[36] In addition, while not directly related to our present task, note the pattern present in the following set of life spans.[37]

Abraham:	$175 = 5^2 \times 7$ (Gen 25:7)
Isaac:	$180 = 6^2 \times 5$ (Gen 35:28)
Jacob:	$147 = 7^2 \times 3$ (Gen 47:28)

The exact significance of these numbers may escape us, but presumably they meant something to the author and to the informed portion of his reading audience.

The use of round numbers, especially multiples of forty, and exaggerated ones, is characteristic of the epic tradition. Examples include God's words to Abram that his ancestors would be strangers in a foreign land for four hundred years (Gen 15:13), the forty years of wandering (Deut 29:5), Moses' age of 80 at his first appearance before Pharaoh (Exod 7:7), his death at the age of 120 (Deut 34:7), the various instances of forty and eighty in the book of Judges (3:11, 30; 5:31), and the forty-year reigns of both David and Solomon (2 Sam 5:4; 1 Kgs 11:42).[38]

This same use of exaggerated numbers using multiples of forty is attested in both Egyptian and Akkadian literature. For the former, note the 400-Year Stela found at Tanis, dated to ca. 1300 BCE, even if we cannot be sure about the specific anniversary commemorated.[39] For the

---

36. J. M. A. Janssen, "On the Ideal Lifetime of the Egyptians," *Oudheidkundige Mededelingen uit het Rijksmuseum van Oudheden* 31 (1950): 33–44.

37. Nahum M. Sarna, *Understanding Genesis* (New York: Schocken, 1966), 84.

38. For an additional round number, though not one which is a multiple of forty, see Jephthah's use of "three hundred years" in Judg 11:26.

39. For discussion see Hans Goedicke, "Some Remarks on the 400-Year Stela," *ChrEg* 41, no. 81 (1966): 23–39; idem, "The 400-Year Stela Reconsidered," *Bulletin of the Egyptological Seminar* 3 (1981): 25–42. For more recent treatments see Manfred Bietak, "On the Historicity of the Exodus: What Egyptology Today Can Contribute to Assessing the Biblical Account of the Sojourn in Egypt," in *Israel's Exodus in Transdisciplinary Perspective: Text, Archaeology,*

latter, note that Nabonidus, king of Babylon (r. 556–539 BCE), asserted that Naram-Sin, king of Akkad (r. ca. 2254–ca. 2218 BCE) ruled 3,200 years earlier,[40] when we know that the distance separating the two rulers is actually ca. 1,700 years.

All of this is simply to say that no historical reconstruction should be based on the 480-year time span mentioned in 1 Kgs 6:1. Over time, and especially during the period of the kingdoms of Israel and Judah, accurate records were kept by royal chancelleries, so that the years provided in the canonical book of Kings (at least from 1 Kgs 12 onward), which in turn derive from the annals of the kings of Israel (1 Kgs 14:19, etc.) and the annals of the kings of Judah (1 Kgs 14:29, etc.), are most reliable. However, this same accuracy does not apply to the round, exaggerated numbers used in the early biblical tradition.[41]

In recognition of the nonhistorical nature of the 480-year figure in 1 Kgs 6:1, some scholars have attempted to interpret the number as symbolic of 12 generations × 40 years (per generation). Yet this too fails, for there are neither 480 years nor twelve generations separating the exodus from the construction of the temple. Instead a new approach is warranted.

Genealogies in the Bible

When attempting to reconstruct estimated dates for the early biblical period, a better guide is the approximate span of time that can be calculated based on the genealogies in the Bible.[42] Our reliance on the genealogies is based on the contemporary sociological-anthropological

---

Culture and Geoscience, ed. Thomas E. Levy, Thomas Schneider, and William H. C. Propp, Quantitative Methods in the Humanities and Social Sciences (New York: Springer, 2015), 31–32; James K. Hoffmeier, "Egyptian Religious Influences on the Early Hebrews," in *"Did I Not Bring Israel out of Egypt?" Biblical, Archaeological, and Egyptological Perspectives on the Exodus Narratives*, ed. James K. Hoffmeier, Alan Millard, and Gary A. Rendsburg, BBRSup 13 (Winona Lake, IN: Eisenbrauns, 2016), 14. Admittedly, in this case, there may be some approximate mathematical reality to the span of four hundred years.

40. Nabonidus, Sippar Cylinder Inscription, col. 2, line 58, for which see "The Sippar Cylinder of Nabonidus," trans. Paul-Alain Beaulieu (*COS* 2. 123A::312).

41. On the shift from the epic storytelling tradition (mainly Genesis through Samuel) to the style of the book of Kings and elsewhere, Gary A. Rendsburg, "The Epic Tradition in Ancient Israel—And What Happened to It?" in Isaac Kalimi, ed., *Writing and Rewriting History in Ancient Israel and Near Eastern Cultures* (Wiesbaden: Harrassowitz, 2020), 17–30.

42. See Gary A. Rendsburg, "The Internal Consistency and Historical Reliability of the Biblical Genealogies," *VT* 40 (1990): 185–206; idem, "Date of the Exodus and the Conquest/Settlement."

parallel afforded by bedouin culture, where one may observe very accurate genealogical reckoning reaching back seven or even ten generations.[43]

A Twentieth-Century Anecdote

I once asked my teacher, Cyrus Gordon, if he had an opinion about the exaggerated years in the early books of the Bible and the repeated use of forty. Professor Gordon told me that in 1931 he was excavating (with E. A. Speiser) at Tepe Gawra, and on the team were a local father-and-son pair. Gordon was struck by the diligent and industrious young lad, and so one day he complimented the father on his fine son. The father thanked him, and Gordon asked him, "How old is your son?" The father responded, "By Allah, I do not know. He may be twenty, he may be thirty, he may be forty; by Allah I do not know. But you can figure out how old he is; he was born one year after the British occupied Iraq." Well, the British occupied Iraq during World War I, defeating the Ottomans, in 1917, which means that the boy was born in 1918, so that in 1931 he was thirteen years old—to which Gordon added that this seemed about right, as the lad looked like a young teenager. But when asked to produce his son's age, the Iraqi villager father could not provide a precise response but defaulted to inflated round numbers, culminating in forty. This anecdote, I submit, goes a long way to explaining the repeated use of the numeral 40 in the Bible, in addition to multiples thereof.[44]

The Genealogy of King David

Fortunately, the Bible provides us with a key genealogy that bridges the exodus and the tenth century BCE, the time of the united monarchy. I refer to the lineage of King David, which appears as a simple list at the end of the book of Ruth (4:18–22) and in more extended fashion in 1 Chr 2:5–15.[45] The key component of the genealogy is the line of Nahshon-Salmon-Boaz-Obed-Jesse-David, thereby informing us that

---

43. On reflections of modern bedouin culture in the Bible, see Clinton Bailey, "How Desert Culture Helps Us Understand the Bible," *BRev* 7, no. 4 (August 1991): 14–21, 38; idem, *Bedouin Culture in the Bible* (New Haven: Yale Univ. Press, 2018), with genealogies discussed on pp. 169–72.

44. For Gordon's recollections of his years in Iraq, including the excavation at Tepe Gawra, though without this anecdote, see Cyrus H. Gordon, *A Scholar's Odyssey* (Atlanta: Society of Biblical Literature, 2000), 31–37.

45. The author of the gospel of Matthew (see 1:3–6) then utilized this material to open his account of the life of Jesus.

David comes five generations after Nahshon. David, as most scholars agree, reigned ca. 1000–965 BCE (one generation before Solomon). His ancestor Nahshon is mentioned in two places in the larger exodus and wilderness account—in Exod 6:23 as the brother-in-law of Aaron and in Num 1:7 as the tribal leader of Judah. Thus we can situate Nahshon as living at the time of the exodus.

How Long Is a Generation?

To calculate the time span separating David from Nahshon, we need to estimate the number of years per generation. Scholars of the Bible and the ancient Near East have usually worked with rather low figures such as twenty to twenty-five years per generation.[46] But this range is incorrect. Instead the average generation should be calculated at thirty years.[47] In a moment I will justify my use of this number, but let me first define what I mean by an "average generation."

I use this term to mean the average age at which a man fathers all his children. A true average would be reached by calculating the ages of all men at the birth of all their children. Obviously, the data available to us from ancient Israel or from other places in the ancient world do not allow for an exact calculation. But I believe a figure of thirty years per generation can be substantiated via several approaches.

---

46. For the figure of twenty years per generation, see K. L. Noll, *Canaan and Israel in Antiquity: A Textbook on History and Religion*, 2nd ed. (London: Bloomsbury T&T Clark, 2013), 99. For the figure of twenty-two years per generation, see Bernhard Grdseloff, "Edom, d'après les sources égyptiennes," *Bulletin des études historiques juives* 1 (1946): 71. For the range of twenty to twenty-five years per generation, see M. L. Bierbrier, *The Late New Kingdom in Egypt (c. 1300–664 B.C.): A Genealogical and Chronological Investigation*, Liverpool Monographs in Archaeology and Oriental Studies (Warminster: Aris & Phillips, 1975), xvi, 112–13. The most commonly used figure is twenty-five years per generation, as posited by the following scholars: H. H. Rowley, *From Joseph to Joshua* (London: British Academy, 1950), 79; G. Ernest Wright, *Biblical Archaeology*, 2nd ed. (Philadelphia: Westminster, 1962), 84; Jacob M. Myers, *1 Chronicles*, AB 12 (Garden City, NY: Doubleday, 1965), 20; John J. Bimson, *Redating the Exodus and Conquest*, JSOTSUp 5 (Sheffield: Almond, 1978), 88; Hoffmeier, *Israel in Egypt*, 125.

47. In my survey of standard works by biblical scholars, I have found only one individual who uses the figure of thirty years—Kenneth Kitchen (Kenneth A. Kitchen, *Ancient Orient and Old Testament* [London: Tyndale, 1966], 72). Though even this author has retreated from said number, for in a later publication, Kitchen used the figure of "roughly 22/25 years" per generation (idem, *On the Reliability of the Old Testament* [Grand Rapids: Eerdmans, 2003], 307, reference courtesy of Mark Janzen).

The first is to calculate the average generation of known lineages (which are in the main royal lineages) from the ancient Near East. I have made a preliminary study based on eighteen royal lineages of at least four generations, and I have arrived at the figure of 28.8 years per generation. Examples include those shown in the dynasty chart.[48]

The figure of 28.8 years per generation is very close to the average generational span of ca. 30 years calculated by David P. Henige after an exhaustive study of more than seven hundred royal genealogies worldwide.[49] Moreover, if we assume, as most scholars do, that filial succession normally passed to the firstborn son,[50] then the figure of 28.8 years per generation arrived at solely through the use of royal lineages is likely below the actual average. To compensate for this factor, I have raised the figure to a slightly higher number and propose 30 years per generation for the purposes of historical reconstruction. In all likelihood, it probably should be raised even higher.[51]

---

48. The cumulative average of the seven examples presented here is 28.3 years per generation. I hope to return to this subject, with full documentation and with a more sustained treatment, at some point in the future.

49. David P. Henige, *The Chronology of Oral Tradition: Quest for a Chimera* (Oxford: Clarendon, 1974), 121–44. Much of this research is summarized in concise form in idem, "Generation-Counting and Late New Kingdom Chronology," *JEA* 67 (1981): 182–84. To mention just one royal lineage of more recent vintage, but which has some resonance in the field of biblical studies, note the so-called Solomonic dynasty of Ethiopia, which includes seventeen generations spanning the years 1270–1851 (from Yekuno Amlak through Yohannes III), or 582 years, for an average of 34.2 years per generation.

50. Firstborn royal succession is assumed in the story of Adonijah and Solomon in 1 Kgs 1–2 (see esp. 1:5–6 and 2:15). From Egypt we have a specific reference to Amenhotep II as the eldest son of Thutmose III (in the Great Sphinx Stela, for which see George Steindorff and Keith C. Seele, *When Egypt Ruled the East*, 2nd ed. [Chicago: Univ. of Chicago Press, 1957], 68; "Egyptian Historical Texts," trans. John A. Wilson, in *ANET*, 244). That said, Aidan Dodson and Dyan Hilton (*The Complete Royal Families of Ancient Egypt* [London: Thames & Hudson, 2004], 132–33) apparently ignore the statement and reconstruct the family tree of this portion of the Eighteenth Dynasty differently. In a well-known case of non-firstborn succession to the throne, documents from the Nineteenth Dynasty reveal that Merenptah was but the thirteenth of Ramesses II's many sons, though one also must consider that Ramesses II lived an exceedingly long life, so presumably he outlived many of his sons. On this issue, see Dodson and Hilton, *The Complete Royal Families of Ancient Egypt*, 160–61 (family tree), 171 (brief entry on Merenptah).

51. According to Mayer Gruber ("Breast-Feeding Practices in Biblical Israel and in Old Babylonian Mesopotamia," *JANESCU* 19 [1989]: 61–83), birth interval was about three to four years in antiquity.

Dynasty Chart

Name of dynasty	Number of generations	Span of years (all BCE)	Span of kings	Number of years	Average age per generation
Akkad	4	2334–2193	Sargon through Shar-kali-sharri	142	35.5
Ur III	4	2111–2004	Ur-Nammu through Ibi-Suen*	109	27.3
First dynasty of Babylon	8	1817–1583	Sumu-la-El through Ammi-ditana†	286	29.4
Egyptian Twelfth Dynasty	7	1938–1759	Amenemhet I through Sobekneferu	180	25.7
Assyrian dynasty	19	1114–612	Tiglath-pileser I through Sin-shar-ishkun‡	503	26.5
Judah	18	1000–586	David through Zedekiah§	415	23.1
Achaemenid	6	522–338	Darius through Artaxerxes III	185	30.8

*Admittedly, caution is advised, since some doubts remain concerning the precise relationships (filiation, etc.) of some of the rulers: http://cdli.ox.ac.uk/wiki/doku.php?id=ur_iii_royal_family.

†The first dynasty of Babylon lasted longer than this span, but filiation can be established only for these eight generations.

‡This calculation assumes that Tiglath-pileser III was the son of Adad-nirari III (and thus was the fourth of his sons to reign as king). For discussion, see Hayim Tadmor and Shigeo Yamada, *The Royal Inscriptions of Tiglath-pileser III (744–727 BC) and Shalmaneser V (726–722 BC), Kings of Assyria*, The Royal Inscriptions of the Neo-Assyrian Period 1 (Winona Lake, IN: Eisenbrauns, 2011), 12, 147. My thanks to Peter Machinist (personal communication, August 19, 2019) for discussing the issue with me and for this reference.

§Note, incidentally, that the Davidic dynasty is the second longest attested royal family in the ancient Near East (surpassed only by the Assyrian dynasty, no. 5 here), a testimony to the constancy and durability of the Judahite monarchy. This feature may have played a role in the biblical ideology which held that the Davidic dynasty would remain on the throne forever (2 Sam 7:13; 22:51; Ps 18:50). At the same time, though, the lineage from David through Zedekiah has the lowest number of years per generation in our sampling.

This figure accords nicely with the results of Martha Roth's study of age at marriage, based on documentation available from the Neo-Assyrian and Neo-Babylonian periods.[52] She concluded that the average age at marriage for males was 30 years old. By extension, the average age of fathering children, or the average generation as I have defined it, must be even higher than 30; perhaps 35 would be a good estimate. I recognize that Roth based her research on Mesopotamian society, not on Israelite society, but in lieu of any other material, I am inclined to accept her conclusions as equally valid for ancient Israel.

The Genealogy of King David and the Date of the Exodus

But what do all these calculations have to do with fixing the date of the exodus? Let us return to the genealogy from Ruth 4:18–22 and 1 Chr 2:5–15: Nahshon-Salmon-Boaz-Obed-Jesse-David. Since, per scholarly consensus (based especially on the Solomon-Shoshenq synchrony previously noted), David can be dated to ca. 1000 BCE and Nahshon lived five generations earlier, all we need to do is determine the proper coefficient to be multiplied by these five generations.

If we allow for 30 years per generation, then Nahshon lived 150 years before David, or ca. 1150 BCE. Any figure higher than 30 years per generation will, of course, place Nahshon slightly earlier in the first half of the twelfth century. Thus, if we allow for 32 years per generation, Nahshon lived ca. 1160 BCE. If we allow for 35 years per generation, then Nahshon lived ca. 1175 BCE. However we calculate the time span between David and Nahshon, we arrive at the reign of Ramesses III for the time period of a figure who is a member of the exodus-wilderness generation.

Others may claim that the genealogy of David has been telescoped, that one or two or even more generations are missing from the lineage, and thereby dismiss this evidence and still argue for a thirteenth-century or even a fifteenth-century exodus. As anthropological studies have shown, however, lineage lengthening (the insertion of links in the genealogical chain) is far more common than lineage telescoping (the removal of links in the chain).[53]

---

52. Martha T. Roth, "Age at Marriage and the Household: A Study of Neo-Babylonian and Neo-Assyrian Forms," *Comparative Studies in Society and History* 29 (1987): 715–47.

53. Henige, *The Chronology of Oral Tradition*, 38. See the following for examples of the genealogies of Samuel and Zadok in the book of Chronicles.

Unfortunately, the genealogy of David is the only one in the Bible that can be used for the purposes of dating the exodus. In theory, we would benefit from similar genealogies from others in David's circle or from the approximate era, but no others are available. The lineage of Saul presented in 1 Sam 9:1—Aphiah-Becorath-Zeror-Abiel-Kish-Saul—is promising, but each of his ancestors listed there is mentioned only there and not earlier in the Bible. It would be helpful if Aphiah or Becorath appeared in the exodus-wilderness narratives, but they do not.

Of all the characters alive ca. 1000 BCE, David and Saul are the only two figures with genealogies reaching back multiple generations. The explanation for this was put forward some years ago by Abraham Malamat, based on comparative sociological information, including African tribal lineages: "Dominant tribal lineages (e.g., Judah), and royal or aristocratic pedigrees, have normally been transmitted with greater care and are thus deeper than their less important counterparts."[54] David's lineage, of course, can be traced farther back, all the way to his tribal father Judah (again, see Ruth 4:18–22, in combination with Gen 38:29; 46:12) and thus by extension to Abraham. No doubt, especially in light of Malamat's observation, the Israelite scribes preserved and transmitted such information carefully. More relevant to our present purposes, David's lineage links up with a known personage from the exodus-wilderness narratives, which is not the case with Saul's lineage.

Jonathan, Grandson of Moses, and Phinehas, Grandson of Aaron

The dating of the exodus to the twelfth century BCE also helps explain a conundrum in the Bible, one not often addressed by scholars. In Judg 18:30 we learn that Jonathan the son of Gershom the son of Moses is yet alive,[55] while in Judg 20:28 we read that Phinehas son of Eleazar son of Aaron is still active. How is it possible for grandsons of Moses and Aaron to be present in accounts at the end of the book of Judges, just a few pages before Samuel appears on the scene (at the beginning of the book of Samuel)? One explanation is that the various accounts in the book of Judges may not be presented in chronological order. Moreover,

54. Abraham Malamat, "Tribal Societies: Biblical Genealogies and African Lineage Systems," *European Journal of Sociology* 14 (1973): 126–36, esp. p. 136.

55. Reading "Moses," of course, and not "Manasseh," a scribal adjustment introduced at a later time to exonerate the Mosaic lineage from any hint of idolatry.

the stories of Jonathan and Phinehas are in the so-called appendix to the book of Judges, so it is even less clear where they might fit in the overall timeline.

Nevertheless, it is rather striking that these two grandsons of the leaders of the exodus-wilderness generation are present in the narratives concerning the migration of the Danites (Judg 18) and the war against Benjamin (Judg 20). This makes a fifteenth-century date for the exodus entirely impossible and makes a thirteenth-century date for the exodus almost impossible. Why? Because these two stories indicate that the time span from the exodus-wilderness-settlement events/processes to the appointment of King Saul ca. 1020 BCE was much less than most people have posited. All is clarified and resolved, however, if one dates the exodus to the twelfth century BCE.

The Genealogies of Samuel and Zadok in the Book of Chronicles

Previously I noted that the genealogy of David is the only one in the Bible that may be used for the purpose of dating the exodus. Yet I must retreat ever so slightly from said statement, for there are two other genealogies we could consider, though only in theory. I refer here to the genealogies of Samuel and Zadok in the book of Chronicles, but they are not serviceable for our present enterprise, as each of them has undergone artificial lengthening, and for the same basic purpose.

The registry in 1 Chr 6:18–23 places Samuel nineteen generations removed from his tribal father Levi, while the parallel lineage in 1 Chr 6:7–13 is garbled and too difficult to reconstruct.[56] The genealogy of Zadok also occurs twice in Chronicles (1 Chr 5:30–34; 6:35–38),[57] though without variation, with David's priest appearing thirteen generations from the same tribal father Levi.[58]

Lineage lengthening is patently evident in the Samuel genealogy. Ebiasaph and Assir appear as father and son in 1 Chr 6:22,[59] while in

56. In English Bibles, these verses are sometimes numbered 1 Chr 6:33–38 and 1 Chr 6:22–28, respectively.

57. In English Bibles, these verses are sometimes numbered 1 Chr 6:4–8 and 1 Chr 6:50–53, respectively.

58. The genealogy in Ezra 7:2–5 adds another link (Azariah, between Meraioth and Amariah), making Zadok fourteen generations removed from Levi. For further variation in the Zadok genealogy, see Neh 11:11; 1 Chr 9:11.

59. In English Bibles, this verse is sometimes numbered 1 Chr 6:37.

Exod 6:24 they are brothers, sons of Korah. In addition, the repeated presence of the name Elkanah (three times) raises an eyebrow.

The solution to the problem at hand is the following: neither Samuel nor Zadok was a true Levite. Samuel was from the tribe of Ephraim (1 Sam 1), yet he functioned as a priest in the book of Samuel (as apprentice to Eli at the tabernacle in Shiloh; see also 1 Sam 7:9; 9:12–13; 16:1–5); Zadok was the former Jebusite king-priest in Jerusalem, who was allowed to retain his sacerdotal duties after David conquered the city and established it as the capital and religious center of Israel.[60]

During the period of the Judges and at the beginning of the monarchy, individuals such as Samuel and Zadok could operate as priests within Israel (for other examples, see Judg 17:5; 2 Sam 8:18; 20:26). By the postexilic period (if not sometime earlier), the ideal of the Levite monopoly on the priesthood had taken hold, so that when Chronicles was compiled in the fourth century BCE, there was a need to provide Samuel and Zadok with invented Levite genealogies.[61] Accordingly, neither of these genealogies bears any value for the issue at hand. As such, my earlier statement remains: the genealogy of David is the only one in the Bible that may be used for the purposes of dating the exodus.

Conclusion

Three main arguments converge to posit a twelfth-century date for the Israelite exodus from Egypt. First, archaeological data inform us that the Israelites emerged in the land of Canaan during the twelfth century BCE (not in the thirteenth century, and certainly not in the fifteenth century). Second, during the first half of the twelfth century BCE, Egypt needed to contend with new geopolitical realities—the invasion of the Sea Peoples, ca. 1180 BCE, and the end of Egyptian rule in Canaan, ca. 1150 BCE. The exodus should be situated within this context, and more specific, during the reign of Ramesses III (1187–1156 BCE). Third, the genealogy of King David indicates a

60. See, most importantly, H. H. Rowley, "Zadok and Nehushtan," *JBL* 58 (1939): 123–32; Christian E. Hauer, "Who Was Zadok?" *JBL* 82 (1963): 89–94. For my most recent statement on the matter, see Gary A. Rendsburg, *How the Bible Is Written* (Peabody, MA: Hendrickson, 2019), 446–47.

61. For further details, see Rendsburg, "Internal Consistency and Historical Reliability," 195–98.

twelfth-century date for his ancestor Nahshon, a member of the exodus-and-wilderness generation. Additional references, such as the presence of Jonathan and Phinehas, grandsons of Moses and Aaron, respectively, in the latter chapters of the book of Judges, also point to the relatively short time span between the events narrated in the Torah and the rise of the monarchy. As we conclude, I will repeat the belief I voiced almost thirty years ago: however we envision the exodus of the Israelites from Egypt, the best historical setting for that event/process is the twelfth century BCE.

RESPONSE TO GARY A. RENDSBURG
(THE FIFTEENTH-CENTURY EXODUS VIEW)

SCOTT STRIPLING

Professor Rendsburg has long advocated for an exodus of "core Israel" from Egypt in the twelfth century BC, and in his chapter he presents three primary reasons for his view. I respect that he allows for the historicity of this watershed event and at points attempts to argue his case from biblical texts. Rendsburg correctly notes that the exodus narrative occurs, or at least allusions to it are mentioned, in seven different biblical genres. He presents a well-researched paradigm to which most readers probably have not been exposed. Along with the new paradigm, he presents new terminology such as "eisodus," the protracted process by which the Israelites (composed of diverse elements) came to populate the eastern Nile delta.

Archaeological Data

Archaeological data inform us that the Israelites emerged in the land of Canaan during the twelfth century BCE (not in the thirteenth century, and certainly not in the fifteenth century).

Rendsburg informs readers that Canaan boasted a meager population in the Late Bronze Age but experienced significant demographic growth in Iron Age I.[62] While this is generally true, Rendsburg's footnote muddies the water for his argument. He cites two sources by

62. Rendsburg's Late Bronze Age dates are 1500–1175 BC, and his Iron Age I dates are 1175–1000 BC. I prefer 1483–1177 for the Late Bronze Age and 1177–980 for Iron Age I. Standard dates are 1550–1200 for the Late Bronze Age and 1200–1000 for Iron Age I.

Israel Finkelstein, a renowned minimalist, followed by an explanatory note that Finkelstein no longer fully supports the positions for which he advocated in the cited sources.[63] Surely, there are scholars to cite who currently support the points Rendsburg seeks to make regarding population densities in various time periods.

There is an explanation for the sparse population in Canaan in Late Bronze II (ca. 1200–1000 BC). In my chapter I argue for a small number of Israelites involved in the exodus. My estimate was forty thousand people, but it could be as low as twelve thousand. Professor Hoffmeier, in his chapter, suggests similar numbers. When the Israelites arrived around 1400 BC, they remained largely nomadic, and when they did live in houses, they were Canaanite houses that previously existed (Deut 6:11; Josh 24:13). A few thousand seminomads spread from Arad to Mount Hermon, on both sides of the Jordan River, would not leave a significant imprint on the archaeological record. After all, the large Middle Bronze Age (ca. 1950–1550 BC) cities housed only a fraction of the people in the Late Bronze Age as they did in the prosperous Middle Bronze Age.[64] The existing cities which the Israelites inherited had plenty of room in them for demographic growth. By Iron Age I, population growth and normal anthropological patterns led to the establishment of more than two hundred new sites, concentrated in the central highlands. I have excavated two of these sites, Khirbet el-Maqatir and Shiloh, and I am very familiar with the material culture in this region.

Rendsburg's section on the elliptical courtyard style of urban planning in Iron Age I and modern bedouin encampments does not prove that seminomadic Israelites were not already in Canaan for several generations prior to Iron Age I. Numerous Iron Age I sites were not elliptical (e.g., Khirbet el-Maqatir), and numerous modern bedouin sites are not circular. These examples are purely anecdotal.

Rendsburg focuses on two sites, Heshbon and Lachish, as evidence of a twelfth-century BC conquest. Heshbon may be located at Tall Jalul

63. Minimalism is the view that biblical texts do not reflect actual history unless archaeology corroborates the accounts.

64. Shlomo Bunimovitz, "On the Edge of Empires—Late Bronze Age (1500–1200 BCE)," in *The Archaeology of Society in the Holy Land*, ed. Thomas E. Levy (London: Leicester Univ. Press, 1995), 326–27.

or Tall al-'Umayri, not Ḥesban,[65] and Rendsburg admits that Lachish is not even mentioned in the conquest narratives in the book of Joshua.[66] By contrast, in my chapter I offer abundant archaeological evidence supporting the conquest at the end of the fifteenth century BC.

The Merenptah Stela poses another problem for Rendsburg's argument that the exodus occurred in the twelfth century BC. After all, how could Israel be conquered around 1210 BC if they were still in slavery in Egypt? To get around this, Rendsburg generates an alternate reading in which Merenptah lists among his vanquished foes the slaves over whom he and his predecessors have ruled in Egypt for many generations, and over whom they continued to rule. He acknowledges that his view does not find support among scholars. To counter this opposition, Rendsburg argues that if the exodus had occurred prior to Merenptah, his conquest would have been mentioned in the Bible. However, I can offer countless examples of historical events that directly impacted ancient Israel which are not mentioned in the Hebrew Bible. An Israelite cultic site operated on Mount Ebal when the Bible indicates the tabernacle was operating at Shiloh, but the Bible is silent on this important point.

Geopolitical Data

> *During the first half of the twelfth century BCE, Egypt needed to contend with new geopolitical realities—the invasion of the Sea Peoples, ca 1180 BCE, and the end of Egyptian rule in Canaan, ca. 1150 BCE.*

Rendsburg reminds readers that a coalition of seafaring tribes, one of which was later known as the Philistines, attempted but failed to invade Egypt in the first decades of the twelfth century BC. They did, however, succeed in establishing a strong presence in the southern Canaanite coastal plain. With this backdrop, he introduces Exod 13:17, which states that "God did not lead them [Israelites] by way of the land of the Philistines." This, along with the genealogies discussed in the next section, serves as Rendsburg's biblical proof. He writes, "Could there be any greater clue as to the date of the exodus?" In other words,

65. Lawrence T. Geraty, "Heshbon," *NEAHL* 3:626.

66. Thomas E. Levy, *Crossing Jordan: North American Contributions to the Archaeology of Jordan* (London: Equinox, 2007), 129.

how could Philistines be a threat to Israel in a fifteenth- or thirteenth-century BC exodus? As I demonstrate in my contribution, the Philistine reference is an anachronistic editorial update for later readers. I find it ironic that Rendsburg reads the biblical text authoritatively here but not in other places, where it appears to contradict his views.

To be sure, if a scholar could detach himself or herself from the biblical text and search for cultural realia in which the exodus might fit, the twelfth century BC would be a good candidate. The attempted invasion by the Sea Peoples certainly weakened Egypt, but in my view we cannot ignore the five biblical passages which point to the exodus in the mid-fifteenth century BC (see my contribution). Likewise, we cannot ignore the Soleb Hieroglyph, the Berlin Pedestal, or the plain reading of the Merenptah Stela.

Genealogical Data

The genealogy of King David indicates a twelfth-century date for his ancestor Nahshon, a member of the exodus-and-wilderness generation.

Before attempting to synchronize the genealogies in Ruth 4 and 1 Chr 2 with a twelfth-century BC exodus, Rendsburg attempts to undermine the plain reading of 1 Kgs 6:1. This approach is required, since it is impossible to take this verse at face value and contend for an exodus outside the fifteenth century BC. Even Rendsburg admits that 1 Kgs 6:1 "seems to give us a clear chronology." His first objection to this seemingly clear chronology is the paucity of proof to support a population increase in Canaan in the Late Bronze II period. I have already addressed this. Next, Rendsburg claims that "one cannot take at face value the years presented in the early biblical books. The numbers used are always greatly exaggerated."

I find Rendsburg's argument to lack substance. He informs readers that Jacob and Joseph both lived to 110 years of age, an ideal lifetime for an Egyptian. I cannot say with certainty that the biblical writers were unaware of the "ideal lifetime" connection, but the writers did believe that 110 years closely described the life span of their venerable progenitors. Whether one lived to be 108 and the other 112 is not worth quibbling about. I sometimes say that my great-great-grandfather Chowning lived to the age of 100, but in fact it might be slightly more or slightly less. I am not positive. If I said that my father, who died at age 51, lived to 100, because I wanted to hyperbolize his influence and stature, I would be guilty of lying. The latter example illustrates what Rendsburg believes the biblical writers were doing in Gen 50:26 and Josh 24:29.

Rendsburg makes the same case for the number forty, or rather, multiples of the number forty. I concede that Moses could have been forty-one when he fled Egypt and seventy-nine when he stood before Pharaoh upon his return, rather than forty and eighty. If this were the case—and I am not saying that it is—the integrity of the biblical chronology derived from these numbers would remain intact. Rendsburg has a problem with the Bible's use of large, round numbers such as the four-hundred-year Egyptian sojourn alluded to in Gen 15:13. He sees hyperbolic rounding as a common literary device in Egyptian and Akkadian literature. As an example, he cites "the 400-Year Stela found at Tanis, dated to ca. 1300 BCE." In the accompanying footnote, Rendsburg admits that the stela may have "some approximate mathematical reality to the span of four hundred years." He would have us take the four hundred years mentioned in Gen 15:13 as hyperbole while accepting the four hundred years on the stela from Tanis at approximate face value. I see no reason to value the accuracy of the biblical text less than that of an Egyptian inscription.

Rendsburg's point in undermining the biblical math is to erode confidence in 1 Kgs 6:1, which he calls "nonhistorical." However, 1 Kgs 6:1 is very specific: "In the four hundred and eightieth year after the Israelites came out of Egypt, in the fourth year of Solomon's reign over Israel, in the month of Ziv, the second month, he began to build the temple of the LORD" (NIV). This passage is clear that 479 years passed between the exodus and initiation of the building of Solomon's Temple. The number 479 has nothing to do with rounding to a multiple of 40. By supplying the month, the author makes it clear that the time span was not 480 years. If the biblical writer knew when the exodus occurred, and he certainly claims to know, how else would he have communicated it to his readers than with straightforward language? If my reasoning prevails, Rendsburg's case is untenable.

This brings us to Rendsburg's attempt to use biblical genealogies to establish the exodus in the twelfth century BC. He argues that since

Ruth 4:18–22 and 1 Chr 2:5–15 offer only five generations from David to Nahshon, who lived at the time of the exodus, then the event must have occurred in the twelfth century BC, during the reign of Ramesses III. Like many genealogies in the Bible, these two are truncated, or telescoped. Fortunately, the Chronicler does provide a complete genealogy shortly after he offers the truncated version. First Chronicles 6:33–37 lists eighteen generations from David to the time of the exodus. Though Rendsburg presents some interesting modern, anecdotal, and sociological data, common sense requires that the more complete genealogy take precedence over the truncated versions. I cover 1 Chr 6:33–37 in my chapter as well.

Rendsburg also argues that when biblical writers referred to a generation, this covered a span of thirty to thirty-five years. He acknowledges that conventional scholarship uses twenty-five years as the norm for a generation's length. By making this shift and allowing only five generations between David and the exodus, Rendsburg is able to place the exodus during the reign of Ramesses III.

Conclusion

I commend Professor Rendsburg for advancing his ideas in this chapter. Though I disagree with most of his points, I was able to reexamine my own paradigm by juxtaposing it with an alternate view. This is never a bad thing. In the end, however, I was not convinced.

RESPONSE TO GARY A. RENDSBURG
(THE THIRTEENTH-CENTURY EXODUS VIEW)

JAMES K. HOFFMEIER

Few Hebrew Bible scholars have the skills and training to work competently with ancient Near Eastern texts and to take on the task of examining the cultural and historical backgrounds of the exodus narratives. Gary A. Rendsburg is one of them, so I take seriously his advocacy for a twelfth-century exodus, and specifically one during the reign of Ramesses III (1184–1153 BC). Rendsburg is in good company, as Manfred Bietak, the longtime excavator of Tell el-Dab'a (Avaris) and an authority on the northeastern delta's paleoenvironmental history, thinks a Twentieth Dynasty exodus date makes best sense of the Egyptian evidence and how it accords with the Bible.

While I disagree with this twelfth-century dating and see a number of problems with this interpretation, I do not think Rendsburg's reconstruction should be summarily dismissed. The stature of Rendsburg and Bietak demand that this date be taken seriously.[67] The difference between the thirteenth-century time frame (ca. 1270–1250 BC) I am advocating and Rendsburg's date (1180 BC or slightly later) is only seventy to ninety years.

The Merenptah Stela

The major stumbling block for a twelfth-century date is the occurrence of "Israel" in the Merenptah Stela of 1208 BC. For a century,

67. In 2019, independent researcher Larry Bruce argued that the reference to Israel in the Merenptah Stela could mean that the Israelites were in Egypt; like Rendsburg, he posits a Twentieth Dynasty exodus. Bruce draws heavily on Rendsburg's earlier works and that of Manfred Bietak. See Larry Bruce, "The Merneptah Stele and the Biblical Origins of Israel," *JETS* 62 (2019): 463–93.

Egyptologists have consistently interpreted this reference to signal that a people named Israel, regardless of when they arrived, were present in Canaan before the end of the thirteenth century. In his classic work from 1905, *A History of Egypt*, James Henry Breasted wrote, "They were sufficiently amalgamated to be referred to as 'Israel,' and they here make their first appearance in history as a people."[68] Nearly fifty years later another University of Chicago Egyptologist, John Wilson, maintained that the Egyptian "scribe was conscious of a people known as Israel somewhere in Palestine or Transjordan" and that, consequently, "we do have a *terminus ante quem* for the Exodus of the Children of Israel from Egypt."[69] Fifty years after Wilson, Joyce Tyldesley explained that the reference to Israel confirms that "whatever the nature of the biblical exodus, the Hebrews were a genuine socio-political entity dwelling in Palestine before Year 5 of Mernepath's reign."[70]

It is fair to say that most Egyptologists concur with these three statements, and there is some reason to believe that a general geographical location within Canaan is discernible. Kenneth Kitchen, the foremost Ramesside scholar of our era, argues that because Ashkelon, Gezer, and Yenoam occur on the stela, it "leaves limited leeway for siting a people-group 'Israel,' most likely in the central hills of western Palestine."[71] On the other hand, Anson Rainey located the Israelites of Merenptah "somewhere in Transjordan."[72]

To get around the dilemma of Israel's presence in the southern Levant before 1208 BC, Rendsburg is forced to interpret Israel's inclusion on the stela as signifying its servitude in Egypt or to argue that it is pointing us to other Israelites who were not in Egypt at that time. If the writing "Israel" was in a toponym list on a gateway with the familiar scene of Pharaoh smiting his enemies, then one might make the case that these toponyms represent all foreign lands and peoples under Egypt's hegemony. But the mention by Merenptah is associated with a

68. James Henry Breasted, *A History of Egypt* (New York: Scribner's Sons, 1905), 466.

69. John A. Wilson, *The Culture of Egypt* (Chicago: Univ. of Chicago, 1951), 255.

70. Joyce Tyldesley, *Ramesses: Egypt's Greatest Pharaoh* (New York: Penguin, 2001), 187.

71. Kenneth A. Kitchen, "The Physical Text of Merneptah's Victory Hymn (The 'Israel Stela')," *JSSEA* 24 (1994): 74.

72. Anson Rainey and R. Steven Notley, *The Sacred Bridge: Carta's Atlas of the Biblical World* (Jerusalem: Carta, 2006), 99.

specific military campaign in Canaan.[73] No one would argue that the inclusion of Ashkelon, Gezer, and Yenoam indicates that these city-states were enslaved *in* Egypt. So why should Israel be?

Larry Bruce recently suggested that since the Bible places the Hebrews in the frontier zones like the northeastern delta and Wadi Tumilat (Goshen), they were in land considered foreign and not technically in Egypt.[74] Consequently, the reference to Israel could point to Hebrews in these "foreign" zones. These two areas border Sinai, which is foreign or hilly land, as indicated by the use of the sign 𓈉. Yet this interpretation is untenable, as these frontier zones were not considered foreign and constitute Egypt's fourteenth Lower Egyptian nome, or province, while the Wadi Tumilat was the eighth nome that extended out to the Lake Timsah and Bitter Lakes area.[75] Neither of these eastern regions are foreign turf! Both were defended by sizable *khetem*-forts at Tjaru (Hebua I and II) and Pithom (Tell el-Rataba), respectively, which served as official access points to Egypt and functioned as provincial capitals.[76] There is no justification for thinking that the northeastern frontier zone and the Wadi Tumilat are outside of Egypt, thus allowing Israelites located there to be considered to be in a foreign land.

Alternatively, Rendsburg suggests that the reference to Israelites in Merenptah's day represent those not in Egypt. This is not a new proposal, as Petrie speculated about this possibility in the early twentieth century.[77] Rendsburg points to the possible mention of Asher in Papyrus Anastasi I to support these proposals, but this equation is largely rejected. Indeed, Shmuel Aḥituv emphatically says that "it cannot allude to the Israelite tribe of Asher, but to a place name," as suggested by the foreign

73. Frank J. Yurco, "Merneptah's Canaanite Campaign," *JARCE* 23 (1986): 189–215; idem, "Merneptah's Canaanite Campaign and Israel's Origins," in *Exodus: The Egyptian Evidence*, ed. Ernest S. Frerichs and Leonard H. Lesko (Winona Lake, IN: Eisenbrauns, 1997), 27–55.

74. Bruce, "The Merneptah Stele and the Biblical Origins of Israel," 467–59.

75. John Baines and Jaromír Málek, *Cultural Atlas of Ancient Egypt* (New York: Facts on File, 1980), 15.

76. On the function of the *khetem*-fort, see Ellen Morris, *The Architecture of Imperialism: Military Bases and the Evolution of Foreign Policy in Egypt's New Kingdom*, Probleme der Ägyptologie 22 (Leiden: Brill, 2005), 804–9.

77. W. M. Flinders Petrie, *From the XIXth to the XXXth Dynasties*, vol. 3 of *A History of Egypt*, 6 vols. (London: Methuen, 1905), 114.

land determinative (𓈈) written with the name.[78] Furthermore, the Bible knows nothing of any Israelite tribe in Canaan who joined the Egypt group after their arrival to the land. There is a lack of both biblical and extrabiblical textual and archaeological evidence for Israelite tribes in Canaan during the sojourn in Egypt. "Israel" in the Merenptah Stela was, as has long been recognized, a people group, not a territory (no land or city sign with the name). This suggests that some sort of tribal confederation called Israel already existed in Canaan by the end of the thirteenth century and that this unification had taken place previously.

Given this reality, one wonders why there is no reference to a clash between Israel's militia and Merenptah's forces in the books of Joshua and Judges. Dr. Rendsburg draws attention to this silence as evidence they were not in Canaan. I agree that this omission is enigmatic, but two plausible explanations come to mind.

1. Could it be that this encounter occurred after the military activity described in the book of Joshua and before clashes with enemy states that were led by judges?
2. If the conflict with Egyptian troops occurred during the early period of the book of Judges, could it have been a single battle and not a prolonged struggle and occupation that allowed time for a judge-leader to rise to the occasion and respond to the crisis?

The book of Judges tends to report on oppressions in which a judge united the tribes and liberated Israel. There were apparently other clashes that did not rise to a level resulting in the need for a judge-leader. Judges 10:11–12 records a list of seven oppressing peoples, including Egyptians, Amorites, Sidonians, and Maonites. As Lawson Younger has observed, the book of Judges contains no corresponding narratives for these four opponents.[79] It could well be that this reference to Egypt is an allusion to the Merenptah campaign. A further testimony to Merenptah's campaign in Canaan is the name of the spring near Jerusalem, found in Josh 15:9 and 18:15. "The spring of the waters of Neptoaḥ" is a mistranslation

78. Shmuel Aḥituv, *Canaanite Toponyms in Ancient Egyptian Documents* (Leiden: Brill, 1984), 73.

79. K. Lawson Younger, *Judges and Ruth*, NIV Application Commentary (Grand Rapids: Zondervan, 2002), 243.

of Hebrew *ma'yan mênep̱tôaḥ*. I agree with Rendsburg that this should be read "the spring of Me(r)neptah."[80] It appears to be the one mentioned in Papyrus Anastasi III, called "the well/spring of Me(r)neptah" in the hills of Canaan, which Ricardo Caminos identified with the toponym of Josh 15:9 and 18:15.[81] The ancient name of this spring survives in the present-day Lifta, located about five kilometers (three miles) east of Jerusalem in Benjamin's tribal territory.[82] Perhaps Merenptah's troops encountered Israelites in the area of Benjamin near the spring after attacking Gezer and on their way to Yenoam.[83] These Hebrews could have been in the area only a decade or two at most.

Ramesses III: Pharaoh of the Exodus?

The reign of Ramesses III (1184–1153 BC), as Rendsburg rightly notes, was a tumultuous time for Egypt and its last great pharaoh. But the problems began earlier during the dynastic transition, with the death of the last Nineteenth Dynasty ruler, a woman named Tausert. Clashes occurred over who would succeed her, and Setnakht ultimately won out. He reigned just two years and was succeeded by his son Ramesses III, who faced major foreign invasions and was assassinated in a coup.[84] Two incursions of Libyan tribes came from the west in the fifth and eleventh regnal years of Ramesses III, and in between, in regnal year 8 (1176 BC), there were major land and sea battles. The Sea Peoples swept in from the east after dealing repeated blows to Anatolia, the Levant, and Cyprus before striking Egypt. The Philistines may have been the largest confederacy, and their role in later biblical history is well known. Egypt's well-fortified eastern frontier held off the onslaught, but there

80. The Egyptian name *Mr-n-ptḥ* means "Beloved of Ptah," and in Late Egyptian, final *r* quiesces, i.e., is not vocalized, as any good New Englander would do (Englanda!).

81. Ricardo A. Caminos, *Late-Egyptian Miscellanies* (London: Oxford Univ. Press, 1954), 108–11.

82. Rainey and Notley, *The Sacred Bridge*, 181–83.

83. The route taken by the Egyptian army is the subject of debate, especially as locations for Yenoam are proposed on either side of the Jordan River. Merenptah's army may have traveled from Gezer across the hill country to the Jordan Valley and then north on the ridge road via Bethel and Shechem. Either way, it seems that the Egyptian force would want to link up with troops and supplies at the Egyptian fort at Beit Shean before attacking Yenoam.

84. Jacobus van Dijk, "The Amarna Period and the Later New Kingdom (c. 1352–1069 B.C.)," in *OHAE*, 296–97.

must have been significant losses of personnel and military material.[85] It is generally believed that from this point onward Egypt's imperial power began to decline.

With all the calamities that struck Egypt during the first third of the reign of Ramesses III, it is difficult to believe that the troubles associated with the plagues of Exod 7–11 (even if they were limited and included some sort of Egyptian military setback as described in Exod 14) would not have led to the complete collapse of Egypt midway through his reign. Surely, the departure of a group of disgruntled Semitic slave laborers would hardly have been a source of great anxiety for this war-weary king. Therefore I find an exodus at this time problematic.

In the end, I believe Rendsburg makes as good a case as possible for a twelfth-century exodus date. Yet while it is plausible, major hurdles abound (only a few of which I have treated), making it an improbable context for the exodus.

---

85. On the location and nature of these battles, see James K. Hoffmeier, "A Possible Location in Northwest Sinai for the Sea and Land Battles between the Sea Peoples and Ramesses III," *BASOR* 380 (2018): 1–25.

RESPONSE TO GARY A. RENDSBURG
(THE THIRTEENTH-CENTURY HYKSOS/LEVITE-LED EXODUS VIEW)

PETER FEINMAN

Rendsburg offers a third date for a historic exodus, the twelfth century BCE. He dates it not to the reign of Ramesses II in the thirteenth century but to Ramesses III (1187–1156 BCE). In his opinion, as with Hoffmeier, the event is simply mentioned too often throughout the Bible for it not to have "stemmed from somewhere." There has to be a "historical kernel."

Rendsburg gives us a Thanksgiving analogy. He uses the example of the *Mayflower* arriving in 1620 (in what becomes Massachusetts) and notes that this voyage was but one of many to reach America in colonial times, in multiple locations, involving multiple peoples by race, ethnicity, and religion. Rendsburg then observes, "But of all the Atlantic crossings, the one remembered and still celebrated by the vast majority of Americans on Thanksgiving Day is the *Mayflower* event. . . . Diverse elements coalesced into the nation of Israel, but only one event or process was remembered and celebrated—*the* exodus from Egypt."

True enough, but there is more to the story than Rendsburg notes. The arrival of the Pilgrims and their first Thanksgiving were two different events, one occurring in 1620 and the other in 1621. In addition, there are multiple Thanksgiving stories. There is the historic kernel, and then there is the national holiday created by Lincoln, observed on the fourth Thursday of November. There is the Norman Rockwell Thanksgiving that for decades has been a staple of elementary school assemblies, and now there is the politically correct Thanksgiving. In 2020, for the four-hundred-year-anniversary celebration of the arrival of the Pilgrims, the organizing committee is shining the light on the Wampanoag people who greeted them, rather than on the Pilgrims. There is a Thanksgiving of cultural memory, a concept consistent with the approach taken by Hendel in his contribution to this book.

The first section of Rendsburg's contribution is devoted to the emergence of Israel in the twelfth century BCE. In particular, he focuses on the settlements in the central hill country of Canaan. The settlements expand dramatically in number and are to be attributed to Israel, given their elliptical design. Rendsburg posits that the people responsible for them were "former pastoral nomads—or better, seminomads." He compares this description with the biblical record of "Israelites as pastoralists, traversing the wilderness region to the south of Israel." Rendsburg doesn't cite specific biblical verses, and my first reaction was to think of patriarchal era pastoralists rather than exodus era pastoralists. He apparently means the latter, judging by his comment that such settlement didn't commence until the twelfth century BCE, and he dismisses the fifteenth century as "out of the question" on the basis of a lack of evidence for Israel between the purported fifteenth-century exodus and twelfth-century settlement. He acknowledges the possibility of a thirteenth-century exodus but prefers the twelfth century.

The settlement wasn't entirely peaceful. Rendsburg cites the biblical battle in Num 21:25 against the Amorites at Heshbon as an example. The verses related to this battle have generated debate within biblical scholarship as to whether they originated within Israel or were incorporated into Israel. Since Rendsburg mentioned the "diverse elements" which became Israel, he has an obligation here to discuss whether one of those diverse elements from the Transjordan brought this tradition or cultural memory with them when they became part of Israel. It is not enough to simply note the archaeological evidence and the text, unless the text can be ascribed to both Israel and the twelfth century BCE.

Similarly, his reference to the destruction of Lachish in 1140 BCE deserves scrutiny. He acknowledges that archaeology cannot identify who was responsible for the destruction. Was Egypt responsible as it withdrew from the land? Was it the Philistines as they entered the land? Was it Israel, according to Josh 10:31–32? The biblical verses surrounding these verses mention a number of cities destroyed by "the edge of the sword" (ESV), as if the destruction happened in one campaign.

As Rendsburg notes, the biblical verses do not mention fire, and Rendsburg does not indicate whether these other locations were destroyed around 1140 BCE as well. He hasn't made the case that it was Israel that destroyed Lachish.

In his next section Rendsburg turns to the reign of Ramesses III, "the best candidate for the pharaoh of the exodus." He chooses this period as propitious because of the invasion of the Sea Peoples. Pharaoh was too busy staving off an attack to bother with the departing Israelites.

He then redefines the meaning of the Merenptah Stela. Rendsburg knows that the reference to Israel in the thirteenth century BCE, only thirty years before Ramesses III, is a potential Achilles' heel for his interpretation. He solves that problem by asserting that the stela refers to Israel as a people in Egypt and not in Canaan. He knows this is not the typical explanation, but it is essential if he is to maintain his twelfth-century date. To put it bluntly, this explanation doesn't work. Pharaohs compiled many lists of peoples they had destroyed throughout the Eighteenth and Nineteenth Dynasties. These lists always refer to locations outside of Egypt, save when pharaohs were battling the Hyksos in Egypt or rebuffing invasions from Sea Peoples and others. This redefinition of the Merenptah Stela invalidates the twelfth-century proposal entirely.

Strangely, Rendsburg places Merenptah in Canaan anyway, according to the biblical texts. He refers to the references in Josh 15:9 and 18:15 to the "spring of Me-Neptoaḥ," and he locates this spring near Jerusalem and declares it is right where one would expect it to be, according to the Joshua passages. Here there is widespread agreement. Merenptah was in Canaan, and there is a biblical memory of it. But according to Rendsburg, the Merenptah Stela does not refer to Israel in Canaan but to Israel in Egypt! No. There was a thirteenth-century BCE exodus in the time of Ramesses II, and his son and successor Merenptah campaigned in the land of Canaan, where he claimed to have destroyed the seed of Israel, which his father had failed to do. Merenptah is boasting here of having surpassed his predecessors. This explanation is far more straightforward than the one proposed by Rendsburg.

There are several important historical issues to be addressed here. Rendsburg is correct to ask where the biblical record of the encounter with Merenptah is found. He is correct to ask about its omission in the books of Joshua and Judges. He is correct to ask about other related peoples, his diverse elements like the Shasu or the tribe of Asher located near Megiddo. He is correct to mention that Egypt remained present in the land of Canaan during the reign of Ramesses III. To address these concerns, I wish to expand on my own contribution, detailing an exodus in the reign of Ramesses II and extending my historical reconstruction to events in the reign of Ramesses III.

Rendsburg and I agree that in human terms, an exodus during a time of Egyptian vulnerability makes the most sense. I date this event after Ramesses II's failure at Qadesh; Rendsburg dates it "during the turmoil generated by the Sea Peoples invasion." Rendsburg and I both agree that the Israelite settlement in the land of Canaan was delayed. I claim it was because of the absence of a successful Canaanite spring, a rebellion against Egyptian rule; Rendsburg claims it was because of delayed departure of a "strong Egyptian presence in the land." But Egypt remained in the land until Ramesses VI in 1139 BCE, based on the fragmented bronze statue of him discovered at Megiddo. This also means that Egypt was able to travel deep into Canaan for decades after the reign of Ramesses III. By Rendsburg's reasoning, settlement should have occurred after Ramesses VI withdrew from Canaan.

Like Seti, Ramesses II, and Merenptah, Ramesses III also campaigned in Canaan. True, Ramesses III does not mention Israel, but he tended to copy from Ramesses II, his hero, role model, and namesake, and there was no Israel in Canaan then. Egyptologist Donald Redford notes that *ssy* is a standard Egyptian shortened form for Ramesses, and he derives the biblical Sisera from the Song of Deborah from Ramesses.[86] My hypothesis is that Israel led a NATO coalition of like-minded anti-Egyptian Canaanites against Ramesses III. Deborah's army demonstrates that Rendsburg's diverse elements had decided to ally with Israel the people. They later became part of Israel the political entity when they went to Hebron and accepted David as their king, possibly as part of an anti-Philistine action.

Rendsburg also cites the Philistines in Exod 13:17, asking, "Could there be any greater clue as to the date of the exodus?" He dates their

86. Donald B. Redford, *Egypt, Canaan, and Israel in Ancient Times* (Princeton: Princeton Univ. Press, 1992), 257–58, n. 2.

arrival to 1180 BCE (meaning during the reign of Ramesses III). Another explanation is that the "way of the land of the Philistines" was the name known by the author of that verse and to his audience (see my response to Hoffmeier). Again, the dating of a text is crucial to determining its relevance to the date of the exodus.

Rendsburg also cites Amos 9:7 on Israel remembering the Philistine arrival from Caphtor. He asks how the Israelites could remember the Philistine history better than their own, but Rendsburg does not address the presence of the Philistines in the patriarchal narratives, given this 1180 BCE arrival. Those narratives undermine Rendsburg's claim of an excellent Israelite memory. To further substantiate his point, Rendsburg mentions the presence of the Philistines in Exod 15:14–15. The explanation for the Song of the Sea example directly relates to the challenge Rendsburg raises about the absence of Egypt in Joshua and Judges. Consider this proposed scenario from a thirteenth-century BCE exodus:

1. Ramesses II—the exodus occurs (Moses)
2. Merenptah—claims to have destroyed the seed of Israel in the land of Canaan (Joshua)
3. Ramesses III—campaigns in Canaan (Deborah)
4. Ramesses VI—withdraws from Canaan

This scenario provides a four-step process from the exodus to Shiloh celebrating the deliverance from Egypt. It is consistent with the cultural memory approach of Hendel, since each iteration of the Israel-Egypt relationship became part of the celebrated cultural memory of Israel. I suggest that instead of viewing the Song of the Sea as a single composition, one should see each stanza as an expression of another encounter with Egypt. At this point in the thirteenth–twelfth centuries BCE, Israel was not writing the prose narratives of Joshua and Judges; it was composing songs and poetry written in a book of the wars against Egypt that eventually served as source documents for the prose narratives. This proposal raises the larger question of the writing of the Hebrew Bible, a topic which is beyond the scope of these contributions, although relevant to them.

The remainder of Rendsburg's contribution is devoted to genealogical concerns. Some of this was addressed in my response to Stripling, so I will not repeat it here. I am fascinated by Rendsburg's hypothesis of a thirty-year generation. He may wish to consider the Sed festival in Egypt, whereby the king is "reborn" after having reigned for thirty years.

Rendsburg uses the genealogies of Ruth 4:18–22 and 1 Chr 2:5–15 to substantiate his claim for a twelfth-century BCE exodus. The use of such genealogies is really a matter of faith, based on one's view of how the Hebrew Bible was written. The family connections he draws on involving David, Samuel, Zadok, and the grandsons of Moses and Aaron are expressions of the political situation at the time they were written and shed no light on the historical exodus. They should be understood as part of the cultural memory of Israel and the constant updating of traditions to reflect current needs. Returning to his Thanksgiving example, doesn't Rendsburg want to know why and how the Pilgrims left? The implicit assumption that the biblical text provides the explanation for the human motivations is an assumption that should be made explicit and justified. The issue of "where is the man Moses?" arises with other contributors as well and will be elaborated on in my final comments.

RESPONSE TO GARY A. RENDSBURG (THE EXODUS AS CULTURAL MEMORY VIEW)

RONALD HENDEL

I always learn a great deal from Gary A. Rendsburg's scholarship, and his work on the exodus is no exception. There are a few places where I disagree with his arguments, but this is natural in an area that has so many gaps and problems. I agree with his general approach to the exodus. He says that this "national collective memory so evident throughout the Bible must have stemmed from somewhere—even if that somewhere is but a historical kernel." I also agree that the exodus story would have appealed to many who had memories of Egyptian oppression. As he says, "There were other elements of Israelites, or people who would later identify as Israelites, with similar or parallel experiences. Some may have left Egypt slightly earlier; some may have left slightly later; while some may never have been to Egypt at all." Despite this variability of experiences, Rendsburg argues, there was one major exodus, even though its features are not specified, that he dates to the reign of Ramesses III (1187–1156 BCE).

This date is certainly possible. But if we think that the exodus may have been a process rather than a particular event, as Rendsburg allows, then a broader time period may be preferable. I am fond of Abraham Malamat's idea (cited in my chapter) that there may have been many exodoi, some involving a few people, and others more. A possible instance of a small one is in an officer's report in the Papyrus Anastasi V (end of the thirteenth century BCE), where the officer reports following after two slaves who had bypassed the Egyptian border fortress and fled into the eastern desert (see more about this letter in my chapter). The officer followed the slaves to the border wall at Tjeku (Sukkot), where he was told that they had passed the walls near Migdol. Both of these are places on the exodus route (Num 33:5–7). We gather that this was one of the many instances when slaves may have successfully escaped from Egypt. If we use our historical imagination, it is possible that this was one of the many small exodoi that contributed, collectively and over time, to the crystallization of the biblical memory of the exodus. In any case, this text suggests that some Canaanite slaves escaped from Egypt in the thirteenth century.

If we consider this possibility to indicate exodoi, then at least a part of the process occurred in the thirteenth century. It probably continued, as Rendsburg argues, in the twelfth century, when the Egyptian Empire was in the process of collapse (its end is dated to around 1125 BCE). The story would have woven together and reimagined the experience of all who escaped from Egypt during this period, including—as I suggest in my chapter—those who lived in Canaan under Egyptian domination. As Rendsburg says, "This idealized story united the disparate elements which coalesced into the people of Israel."

Rendsburg includes the archaeology of the Israelite settlement and biblical genealogies into his argument for a twelfth-century date for the exodus. His presentation of the archaeological evidence is well informed and important. (Although I would suggest that an oval settlement pattern might be a good adaptive strategy for a village without walls, not necessarily a clue of nomadic origins.) But I disagree with parts of his discussion about the reliability of biblical genealogies, particularly King David's genealogy, which is found only in 1 Chr 2:1–15 and Ruth 4:18–22. These are late texts, probably written more than five hundred years after the era of King David.

The earliest account of David's rise to kingship mentions only his father, Jesse of Bethlehem (1 Sam 16:1). The later genealogy is arguably a historical reconstruction by a biblical historian, drawing on earlier genealogies to create a continuous line from Judah to David. Some inconsistencies in the genealogical links indicate the secondary nature of the full Davidic genealogy in Chronicles and Ruth. Salma (also called Salmon) is the son of Nahshon and father of Boaz in Chronicles and Ruth. But in the same chapter of Chronicles, Salma is the son of Hur and father of Bethehem (1 Chr 2:51–54). Scholars have argued that this is from an earlier genealogy. Perhaps because of his association with Bethlehem, Jesse's home, Salma was taken into David's genealogy to serve as an intermediate link with the earlier segment from Judah to Nahshon. A chart may help to clarify these different genealogical strands.

Judah → Perez → Hezron (Gen 46:12)
Hezron → Jerahmeel → Ram (1 Chr 2:25–27)
Amminadab → Nahshon (Exod 6:23; Num 1:7)
Hur → Salma → Bethlehem (1 Chr 2:50–54)
Jesse → David (1 Sam 16:1)

This yields:

Judah → Perez → Hezron → Ram → Amminadab →
Nahshon → Salmon → Boaz → Obed → Jesse → David
(1 Chr 2:4–15; Ruth 4:18–22)

As Sara Japhet comments, these segments were probably combined creatively to fill out David's genealogy: "Whether these additions were made by the Chronicler himself or preceded him cannot be determined. The result is, all the same, a direct line leading from Judah to David."[87]

My point is that the genealogy from Judah to David may be, in part, a late creation and should not be relied on for historical chronology. We should grant the possibility that this genealogy is itself a historical reconstruction by the Chronicler or one of his sources. Genealogies are often fluid in their links and segments, with potential embedded claims. Particularly the middle parts are often fluid; anthropologists call these "floating gaps."

This genealogical example may seem a quibble, but it shows the complexity of the biblical evidence. As Rendsburg knows, it's not easy to make a compelling case about the historical framework of the exodus. By attending to these small details, we may hope to open the questions further, even if we cannot answer them all.

---

87. Sara Japhet, *I & II Chronicles: A Commentary*, OTL (Louisville: Westminster John Knox, 1993), 71.

REJOINDER

GARY A. RENDSBURG

Scott Stripling

1. Stripling appears to give me credit for introducing the term "eisodus," but in truth the word has been used for the story of the Israelites' migration to Egypt for about one century. The earliest reference that I could find is the article by H. H. Rowley titled "The Eisodus to Exodus," published in the *Expository Times* (1939).[88] Though the term was used already in nineteenth-century scholarship, albeit with reference to the Israelites' entering the land of Canaan (under Joshua).

2. I do not see the value in labeling people, in the present instance, for example, "Israel Finkelstein, a renowned minimalist." I prefer to deal with facts, whatever their source may be. But as long as the door has been opened, I am obliged to point out that Finkelstein describes himself as a centrist. More important, Finkelstein's retreat from his 1988 thesis does not eradicate the evidence. As I indicated in my essay, the data remain.

3. Stripling misrepresents me when he writes, "Rendsburg admits that Lachish is not even mentioned in the conquest narratives in the book of Joshua." I did not state this, for Lachish patently is mentioned (see Josh 10, esp. vv. 31–32).

4. I am at a loss to understand this statement: "An Israelite cultic site operated on Mount Ebal when the Bible indicates the tabernacle was operating at Shiloh, but the Bible is silent on this [former] important point." Naturally, this is incorrect; see Josh 8:30–35.

88. H. H. Rowley, "The Eisodus and the Exodus," *ExpTim* 50 (1939): 503–8.

5. Stripling mischaracterizes the nature of the biblical genealogies. "Common sense" (his term) does not require "that the more complete genealogy take precedence over the truncated versions." Real data indicate the opposite. In the words of David Henige, "The incidence of the artificial lengthening of king lists and genealogies and the concomitant development of an exaggerated notion of the length of the past are much more common than telescoping."

James K. Hoffmeier

1. As Hoffmeier points out, another proponent of a twelfth-century exodus is Manfred Bietak, and I regret that I did not cite him and incorporate some of his findings. See especially his article "On the Historicity of the Exodus" (shortened title), which in fact I cited in note 39 of my treatment, though in a more limited context.

2. Hoffmeier writes, "The Bible knows nothing of any Israelite tribe in Canaan who joined the Egypt group after their arrival to the land." Actually, it does: the tribe of Dan (as I mention in passing in my contribution). For further details, see the groundbreaking work by Cyrus Gordon and Yigael Yadin, with attention to such passages as Gen 49:16 and Judg 5:17.[89]

Peter Feinman

1. Feinman builds on a very tenuous proposal by Donald Redford, to argue that the biblical author transmogrified *ssy-rʿ*, supposedly a sobriquet of Ramesses II, into Sisera (Judg 4) = Ramesses III. Does this term actually exist? It is not among the five names of Ramesses II inscribed on his sphinx at the Penn Museum, and I do not find it recorded in such standard works as Erman's *Wörterbuch*, Ranke's *Personennamen*, and Kitchen's *Pharaoh Triumphant*. If it does exist, one must reckon with the shift of /ʿ/ to /ʾ/, which Redford simply dismisses, and then the transfer of the name to Ramesses III, per Feinman's proposal. All of this represents a very thin strand on which to build a hypothesis concerning a key story in the book of Judges.

---

89. Cyrus H. Gordon, "The Mediterranean Factor in the Old Testament," in *Congress Volume Bonn 1962* (Supplements to Vetus Testamentum 9; Leiden: E. J. Brill, 1963), 19–31, esp. p. 21; Yigael Yadin, "And Dan, Why Did He Remain in Ships," *Australian Journal of Biblical Archaeology* 1 (1968): 9–23.

2. The Philistines in the book of Genesis must represent an earlier wave of Mediterranean people who made their way to the land of Canaan. Note that they are governed by kings (Gen 20:2; 26:1), and not *sərānîm*, and that they live in Gerar (ibid.) and are active in Beersheba (Gen 21:31–32), and not the five cities of the Pentapolis. All of this was treated years ago by Yehoshua Grintz.[90] They have only a minimal connection to the main wave of Philistines who settled in Canaan in the wake of the Sea Peoples invasion and migration.

Ronald Hendel

1. Hendel makes some good points about the genealogy of King David, which in truth is known to us only from Ruth 4:18–22 and 1 Chr 2:4–15. I note, however, that he focuses mainly on the Chronicles version, with a nod to Sara Japhet. Since Chronicles is a late work, any information therein needs to be judged cautiously. I prefer to focus on the genealogy which closes the book of Ruth, accordingly.

Now, to be sure, the date of the book of Ruth is subject to great debate and a wide range of opinions. To the best of my knowledge, however, no one has subjected the book of Ruth to the most objective criterion available to scholars—the Noun-Verb ratio, based on the pathfinding methodology developed by Frank Polak.[91] A preliminary study indicates that the Noun-to-Nominal-Verb (NV) ratio in Ruth equals 0.571, while the Noun-to-Finite-Verb (NF) ratio equals 0.140, placing the book squarely in the classical (earliest) stratum of Biblical Hebrew prose.[92] True, many scholars believe that the genealogy in Ruth 4:18–22 is a later addition, but the burden of proof is on them, especially in light of Adele Berlin's analysis regarding the function of these verses as coda to the story.[93]

90. Yehoshua M. Grintz, "The Philistines of Gerar and the Philistines of the Seacoast," in *Studies in Memory of Moses Schorr, 1874–1941*, ed. Louis Ginzberg and Abraham Weiss (New York: Professor Moses Schorr Memorial Committee, 1944), 96–112 (in Hebrew); idem, "The Immigration of the First Philistines in the Inscriptions," *Tarbiẓ* 17 (1945–46): 32–42 (with an additional note in *Tarbiẓ* 19 [1947–48]: 64) (in Hebrew).

91. For the basic statement, see Frank H. Polak, "The Oral and the Written: Syntax, Stylistics and the Development of Biblical Prose Narrative," *JANES* 26 (1998): 59–105, with the summary statement on p. 70.

92. My thanks to Charles Loder (MA, Rutgers) for his assistance on this matter, as part of our current research into the date of the book of Ruth, to be presented in a coauthored article.

93. Adele Berlin, *Poetics and Interpretation of Biblical Narrative* (Sheffield: Almond Press, 1983), 109–10.

In addition, if the Chronicler wished to construct a single extended genealogy of David, according to the information present in the book, why did he not include individuals such as Jerahmeel, son of Hezron and father of Ram (1 Chr 2:25), and Bethlehem, son of Salma/Salmon (1 Chr 2:51)? (Though, naturally, this latter "individual" is nothing more than the name of the village.) That he did not include these people in his main genealogy of David (earlier in ch. 2) points to lineage lengthening in these specific cases. One will assume, accordingly, that the genealogy of David in 1 Chr 2:4–15 is inherited from an earlier source, either Ruth 4:18–22 or another independent text.

2. Hendel calls attention to the possibility or probability of multiple exodoi, as proposed by Abraham Malamat. While I did not emphasize the point sufficiently in my own chapter, I certainly agree with Hendel and Malamat on this point. As I stated, "Some may have left Egypt slightly earlier; some may have left slightly later"—though only one such journey was remembered, idealized into a grand exodus, and commemorated by later generations.

In addition to the time period of the Sea Peoples invasion during the reign of Ramesses III, another series of events which would have created a propitious time for Israelites to leave Egypt occurs during the transition between the end of the Nineteenth Dynasty and the start of the Twentieth Dynasty (as indicated by Hoffmeier as well), ca. 1200 BCE. Both the Elephantine Stela and Papyrus Harris I speak to the turmoil during this period, until Setnakht was able to create a stable monarchy and thereby found the Twentieth Dynasty. Further discussion of these texts, however, will need to wait for another occasion.

CHAPTER FIVE THE EXODUS AS CULTURAL MEMORY VIEW

RONALD HENDEL

My contribution to this discussion pivots on a seemingly simple question: what kind of picture of the past do we find in the book of Exodus? Is it an inerrant account of historical facts, guaranteed by the Holy Spirit? Is it an eyewitness account backed by the testimony of Moses? Or is it a collection of cultural memories in which historical events and social changes have been transformed into legend, theology, and literature? This question has a complicated history in modern biblical scholarship. The present volume is a case study in the complexity of the question.

I will make the case for the third response, the exodus as cultural memory.[1] A cultural memory is a representation of the past with present relevance, transmitted by the authoritative texts and interpreters of a particular group. To make the past relevant for the present, cultural memory distorts, omits, and fictionalizes aspects of the past. Furthermore, since the interests of various groups in the present are always changing, cultural memory is never stable. While the past itself

1. I have developed this model in several publications, including Ronald Hendel, "The Exodus in Biblical Memory," *JBL* 120 (2001): 601–22; idem, *Remembering Abraham: Culture, Memory, and History in the Hebrew Bible* (Oxford: Oxford Univ. Press, 2005); idem, "The Exodus as Cultural Memory: Egyptian Bondage and the Song of the Sea," in *Israel's Exodus in Transdisciplinary Perspective: Text, Archaeology, Culture, and Geoscience*, ed. Thomas E. Levy, Thomas Schneider, and William H. C. Propp, Quantitative Methods in the Humanities and Social Sciences (New York: Springer, 2015), 65–77.

does not change, memories of the past are dynamic, changing according to the fluctuating claims of the present.

A familiar example of cultural memory that is comparable to the biblical exodus is the story of the Pilgrims, who experienced their own exodus and journey to a new land. According to the account that children are taught in school, the Pilgrims journeyed to this country to escape from religious oppression in Europe, and they created in the New World a society dedicated to freedom and liberty. This is a mixture of history and legend. It is true that the Pilgrims saw their own exodus as a recurrence of the biblical exodus, and the New World was their promised land. But the Pilgrims were not the icons of liberty that our civic memory maintains. The Pilgrims were Puritans who rejected the religious tolerance that they found in England and Holland, and they sought to create in the New World a sectarian theocracy.[2] Their antagonism to liberty and religious freedom has been airbrushed out of the conventional account, and they are cast in the popular imagination as founders of liberty, like Jefferson and Washington.

The American story of the Pilgrim Fathers, like other cultural memories of national origins, enshrines ideals that are central to the nation's identity. The story conveys in dramatic form the origins of that identity and serves to actualize and revitalize that identity in the civic ritual of Thanksgiving. Since the story anchors and justifies contemporary American identity, it inevitably changes to accommodate new wrinkles in that identity. The Pilgrims' mistreatment of Native Americans has recently become a part of the story, and nowadays there are public ceremonies on Thanksgiving morning that commemorate the Native American memory of these events. The story becomes complicated and changes, in part because of the counter-memories of other groups. Conflicting claims on the past in the present keep cultural memory ever in motion.

This model of cultural memory also pertains to the biblical exodus. The memory of Israel's oppression and escape from Egyptian bondage exemplifies ideals that were central to ancient Israelite identity, including both a social ethic that protected the stranger and a religious

---

2. See Nick Bunker, *Making Haste from Babylon: The Mayflower Pilgrims and Their World: A New History* (New York: Vintage, 2010); Nathaniel Philbrick, *Mayflower: A Story of Courage, Community, and War* (New York: Viking, 2006).

commitment to the God who redeemed them. This religious bond is emphasized in God's introduction to the Decalogue: "I am the Lord your God, who brought you out of Egypt, out of the land of slavery" (Exod 20:2 NIV). The collective memory of the exodus from Egypt anchored ancient Israel's religious, ethical, and political identity, just as the exodus from the Old World anchors American identity.

I will try to show how the exodus story merges aspects of history, traditional lore, and narrative imagination into a powerful cultural memory. First, I emphasize that the concept of cultural memory is found in the exodus account itself, as Moses instructs the people to remember and recount the exodus story in future generations. In the midst of the story, Moses instructs the people to "commemorate this day, the day you came out of Egypt, out of the land of slavery, because the Lord brought you out of it with a mighty hand" (Exod 13:3 NIV), and he gives them instructions for commemorating the exodus in the Passover ceremony. The command to remember the exodus resounds in the Bible. In the Passover meal the participants recall the story as if it were their own. As the Passover haggadah says (quoting m. Pesaḥ. 10:5), "In every generation it is a person's duty to see him/herself as if he/she had come forth from Egypt." The celebrants are, in an experiential sense, there at the exodus.

The memory of the exodus revitalized Israelite identity and continues to do so for Jewish identity to the present day. It creates a circle of time between the salvific past and the lived present. This is what cultural memory accomplishes, and what the exodus exemplifies. It is a memory that seals the bond between the remembered past and the moral orientation of the present.

Inerrancy, Chronology, and Plagues

Now I will point out some of the differences and advantages of this approach to others in this volume. The model of cultural memory was developed in the intellectual context of modern sociology, anthropology, and historiography.[3] There is a rift between these kinds of inquiries and

3. See Maurice Halbwachs, *On Collective Memory*, ed. and trans. Lewis A. Coser (Chicago: Univ. of Chicago Press, 1992); for the ancient world, see Jan Assmann, *Cultural Memory and Early Civilization: Writing, Remembrance, and Political Imagination*, trans. David H. Wilson (Cambridge: Cambridge Univ. Press, 2011).

those that are rooted in a commitment to biblical inerrancy. The doctrine of inerrancy, as for instance formulated by the Chicago Statement on Biblical Inerrancy (1978), limits the kinds of inquiries that evangelical and orthodox scholars can pursue. Such boundaries for scholarship make a difference in how one approaches the biblical exodus.

Perhaps in response to such limitations, the dominant evangelical approach to the exodus takes liberties with the traditional doctrine of inerrancy. It reinterprets the biblical events and "corrects" the Bible's picture of the past. According to this approach, the Bible errs in its understanding of past events, but faithful scholars can restore the true picture. In terms of cultural memory, I would describe this approach as a particular kind of revision of cultural memory, which updates the biblical memory by replacing many of its miracles with natural events.

My first example of swerving from inerrancy is the chronology of the exodus, which others in this volume address. First Kings 6:1 states, "In the four hundred and eightieth year after the Israelites came out of Egypt, in the fourth year of Solomon's reign over Israel, in the month of Ziv, the second month, he began to build the temple of the Lord" (NIV). Based on this statement, a simple calculation, starting with a plausible date for Solomon's enthronement (ca. 970 BC), yields a date of ca. 1446 BC for the exodus. This is unambiguous biblical testimony for the date of the exodus. Yet distinguished evangelical scholars will fiddle with this date, since it does not correspond with what archaeological and historical evidence tells us about the time of Israel's emergence. Kenneth Kitchen argues for a date of the exodus in the middle of the 1200s and uses comparative evidence to explain why 1 Kgs 6:1 is incorrect. He argues, "Mesopotamian monarchs sometimes give long-range dates (like . . .. 1 Kgs 6:1, 480 years) which are invariably too long in absolute years."[4] The biblical chronology is wrong, but the faithful scholar can correct it.

This approach is adopted in much evangelical scholarship of the exodus, including in this volume. In my view, this concession to historical and archaeological evidence is admirable. But it is also a departure from the plain sense of the Bible. While I agree with Kitchen's general time frame for the origins of the exodus memory, he is certainly

4. Kenneth A. Kitchen, *Ancient Orient and Old Testament* (London: InterVarsity Press, 1966), 74–75; see also idem, *On the Reliability of the Old Testament* (Grand Rapids: Eerdmans, 2003), 202–3, 307–9.

departing from the biblical testimony. Identifying the Bible's errors and replacing them with historically plausible reconstructions is a curious strategy for evangelical scholars. It clearly departs from the traditional doctrine of inerrancy.[5]

Another case of stretching inerrancy is the standard evangelical approach to the exodus plagues. Following—perhaps unknowingly—an approach established by the Enlightenment deists, these scholars rationalize miracles into natural events, producing a residual account that is historically plausible. An early deist example is Nehemiah Grew's *Cosmologia Sacra* (1701), in which he argued that the plagues had "sundry Natural Causes," which gives them "Marks of Credibility."[6] He conjectured that the reddening of the Nile was caused by dysentery in the Nile's creatures—fish, hippopotami, crocodiles—which caused them to void blood in their excrement "as was sufficient to discolour and corrupt the Water." This is why the Nile turned red. The goal of this explanation was to show the reasonableness of the Bible. This approach eliminates most or all of the miracles in order to accommodate the Bible to a modern scientific worldview. This strategy of radical revision is a characteristic impulse of modern evangelical and orthodox scholars. It makes the past relevant in the present. But it also departs from the clear sense of the Bible.

According to the current version of this approach, the first nine plagues were a series of natural events. Only the last—the slaying of the firstborn son—was a miracle. The Bible, in a sense, misrepresents or misunderstands the plagues, an error which the modern scholar can correct. Here is Kitchen's explanation of the plagues as natural events following an inundation of the Nile.

> The narrative of Exodus 7 to 10 makes excellent sense as it stands and shows evidence of first-hand observation, thus enabling us to understand the course of events with greater clarity. Thus, the excessive inundation may have brought with it microcosms

---

5. On the development of this doctrine, see Ronald Hendel, "The Dream of a Perfect Text: Textual Criticism and Theology in Early Modern Europe," in *Steps to a New Edition of the Hebrew Bible*, Text-Critical Studies 10 (Atlanta: Society of Biblical Literature, 2016), 271–95.

6. Nehemiah Grew, *Cosmologia Sacra, or A Discourse of the Universe as It Is the Creature and Kingdom of God* (London: Rogers, Smith, & Walford, 1701), 196–99.

> known as *flagellates* which would redden the river and also cause conditions that would kill the fish. Decomposing fish floating inshore would drive the frogs ashore, having also infected them with *Bacillus anthracis*. The third plague would be mosquitoes, and the fourth a fly, *Stomoxys calcitrans*, both encouraged to breed freely in the conditions produced by a high inundation. The cattle-disease of the fifth plague would be anthrax contracted from the dead frogs, and the "blains" on man and beast (sixth plague), a skin anthrax from the *Stomoxys* fly of the fourth plague. Hail and thunderstorms in February would destroy flax and barley, but leave the wheat and spelt for the locusts whose swarming would be favoured by the same Abyssinian rains which had ultimately caused the high inundation. The "thick darkness" would be the masses of fine dust, *Roterde* (from mud deposited by the inundation), caught up by the *khamsin* wind in March.[7]

The plagues are a series of natural disasters. Kitchen adds that only "the death of the firstborn, the tenth of the plagues that afflicted Egypt on the eve of the Exodus, is avowedly in the realm of miracle."[8] This rationalizing interpretation of the plagues has been adopted by other evangelical scholars, including James Hoffmeier, who writes, "The first nine plagues are natural occurrences known to Egypt, albeit magnified and occurring in close proximity."[9] In this model, supernatural events are replaced by natural ones.

This description clearly conflicts with the Bible, according to which each plague was a miracle sent by God. In the Bible God does not inundate the Nile with flagellates to make it seem reddish. God turns the Nile into blood. In Exod 7:19 he says to Moses, "Tell Aaron, 'Take your staff and stretch out your hand over the waters of Egypt—over the streams and canals, over the ponds and all the reservoirs—and they will turn to blood.' Blood will be everywhere in Egypt, even in vessels of wood and stone" (NIV).

---

7. Kitchen, *Ancient Orient*, 157–58; see also idem, *On the Reliability of the Old Testament*, 249–52.

8. Kitchen, *Ancient Orient*, 157.

9. James K. Hoffmeier, *Israel in Egypt: The Evidence for the Authenticity of the Exodus Tradition* (Oxford: Oxford Univ. Press, 1996), 149.

The miraculous transformation of water into blood—even in bowls and barrels on land—is airbrushed away by these scholars. Hoffmeier writes, "Mythic language was a tool in ancient Israel's historiography,"[10] so he omits it in order that the events be made reasonable. But this distorts the biblical record.

James Barr has bitingly criticized this view: "In the Bible God turned the water of all Egypt into blood; according to Kitchen he did nothing of the sort."[11] This approach to the plagues fiddles with the doctrine of inerrancy. Barr continues: "Conservative scholarship, as we see it here, reduces the miraculous to a vanishing point in order to obtain a 'true' narrative, which hangs together by a series of scientifically plausible connections totally absent in the biblical story." The resulting explanation maintains "that the biblical version of the incident is false." These are strong words but an apt criticism.

This approach is rooted in the rationalizing mentality of the Enlightenment. The point is to establish, as Hoffmeier states, "that the main points of the Israel in Egypt and exodus narratives are indeed plausible."[12] But plausibility comes at a high price. The biblical events are largely emptied of their supernatural character. These scholars are using deist arguments about the reasonableness of the Bible without realizing that it undermines their commitment to the perspicacity of the Bible and its inerrancy.[13] They are revising the biblical representation of the past to make it conform to a modern scientific sensibility.

In contrast to the tangled logic of this approach to the exodus, the approach to the exodus as cultural memory embraces the miraculous quality of the events. This whole point of the plagues is that they are miracles, as God proclaims to Moses: "I will stretch out my hand and strike the Egyptians with all the wonders that I will perform among them" (Exod 3:20 NIV). God calls the plagues his "wonders" *(niplāʾôt)*;

---

10. Hoffmeier, *Israel in Egypt*, 213.

11. James Barr, *Fundamentalism* (Philadelphia: Westminster, 1978), 242.

12. Hoffmeier, *Israel in Egypt*, 226.

13. Compare the evangelical position of Iain Provan, V. Philips Long, and Tremper Longman III (*A Biblical History of Israel* [Louisville: Westminster John Knox, 2003], 128), who seem to want to have it both ways: "Such connections of cause-and-effect did likely at least partially exist at the heart of the ecological disaster that is said to have engulfed Egypt at this time. At the same time, however, these effects do not interest the authors of Exodus. . . . No reading of the past that takes the testimony of the biblical texts seriously can reduce that testimony to naturalistic terms."

they are marvelous supernatural events with which he defeats Pharaoh and rescues Israel. The miraculous quality of the plagues is emphasized by the repeated comment—in the hail mixed with fire, the locusts, and the slaying of the firstborn—that such a thing had never happened before (Exod 9:18, 24) and will never happen again (Exod 10:14; 11:6). The same emphasis on the miraculous nature of the event occurs in Josh 10:14, when God makes the sun stand still.[14]

The Plagues as Cultural Memory

The concept of the plagues as cultural memory is, perhaps surprisingly, supported by God's explanation of his larger purpose in sending them. In Exod 10:1–2 God says to Moses, "Go to Pharaoh, for I have hardened his heart and the hearts of his officials so that I may perform these signs of mine among them that you may tell your children and grandchildren how I dealt harshly with the Egyptians and how I performed my signs among them, and that you may know that I am the Lord" (NIV).

Here the plagues are called "signs" *('ōtôt)*, manifestations of God's power that have a communicative force. God's explanation begins with his reason for hardening the hearts of Pharaoh and his officials: "so that I may perform these signs of mine among them" (v. 1 NIV). This answers the knotty problem of why God would make Pharaoh *not* let his people go. He did so in order to multiply the plagues, to make them a great spectacle, worthy of commemoration. God also tells the deeper purpose of these signs and wonders: "that you may tell your children and grandchildren how I dealt harshly with the Egyptians and how I performed my signs among them" (v. 2 NIV). The purpose of the plagues is to make a great story, which the Israelites will tell their children and grandchildren. The signs and wonders are to be a cultural memory, passed down among future generations. God gives a third and final reason: "that you may know that I am the Lord" (v. 2 NIV). The point of this future cultural memory is that Israel will know God, and correspondingly, they will know that they are God's people. The reason for the story of God's salvific signs and wonders—which includes

14. See Yair Zakovitch, *The Concept of the Miracle in the Bible*, trans. Shmuel Himelstein (Tel Aviv: MOD, 1991), 40–41.

crossing the Red Sea—is so that Israel will know itself and its God. This is a powerful purpose for God's signs and wonders.

Notice that God's anticipation of the future recitation of the exodus story comes in the midst of the exodus story. The miraculous signs and wonders are not over yet. God's plan is to create a marvelous and durable cultural memory that each generation of Israel will celebrate. The exodus memory, God states, will inform the collective identity of Israel in each generation. The plagues, as God explains them, are the very stuff of cultural memory.

This is the meaning of the plagues, both in the story and in the annual commemoration in the Passover ritual. If we turn to explore the historical background of the plagues, the most obvious context is not animal diseases but, as scholars have long observed, ancient Near Eastern treaty curses and descriptions of divine punishment.[15] This is the conceptual field of the plagues, since they are God's punishment of Egypt. Seven of the exodus plagues have parallels in the curse section of Esarhaddon's Succession Treaty, which was composed and distributed to Assyrian vassals in 672 BCE.[16] In the curses, Assyrian gods are invoked to punish rebellion by, among other disasters, skin disease, darkness (from blindness), locusts, lice and other insects, plague, and death of one's children. The only biblical plagues that lack parallels in Esarhaddon's treaty are blood, frogs, and hail.

Many of the exodus plagues have close parallels in other Mesopotamian, Egyptian, and Northwest Semitic texts—from narratives, prophecies, treaties, and other genres—that describe curses, punishment, or earthly chaos. Here is a sample.

Blood

> She [Inanna] filled the wells of the land with blood, so it was blood that the irrigated orchards of the land yielded, it was blood that the slave who went to collect firewood drank, it was blood

15. See recently William H. C. Propp, *Exodus 1–18*, AB 2 (New York: Doubleday, 1999), 347–52; Gary A. Rendsburg, "Moses the Magician," in Levy, Schneider, and Propp, *Israel's Exodus in Transdisciplinary Perspective*, 243–58; and Rendsburg's essay in this volume.

16. The text of Esarhaddon's Succession Treaty is available at *The Open Richly Annotated Cuneiform Corpus*: http://oracc.museum.upenn.edu/saao/saa02/Q009186/html.

> that the slave girl who went out to draw water drew, and it was blood that the black-headed [Sumerian] people drank.
>
> —Sumerian narrative[17]

> The river [Nile] is blood, yet one drinks from it,
> Men shrink from people and thirst after water.
>
> —Egyptian wisdom text[18]

Darkness

> The sun is covered and does not shine for the people to see.
>
> —Egyptian prophecy[19]

> Sew up, close up the heavens with dense cloud,
> That darkness exist there, not brilliance . . .
> So that you instill dread in dense darkness.
>
> —Northwest Semitic prophetic narrative[20]

Plague

> May plague, the rod of Nergal, not be cut off from his land.
>
> —Old Aramaic treaty[21]

Hail and Locusts

> [May Ha]dad [pour out] every sort of evil on earth and in heaven and every sort of trouble. May he shower upon Arpad [h]ail-[stones]. For seven years may the locust devour.
>
> —Old Aramaic treaty[22]

From these examples, we can see that curses and other descriptions of divine punishment were commonplace in ancient Near Eastern

---

17. "Inanna and Šu-kale-tuda," *Electronic Text Corpus of Sumerian Literature*, http://etcsl.orinst.ox.ac.uk/cgi-bin/etcsl.cgi?text=t.1.3.3#.

18. "The Admonitions of an Egyptian Sage: The Admonitions of Ipuwer," trans. Nili Shupak (*COS* 1.42:94).

19. "The Prophecies of Neferti," trans. Nili Shupak (*COS* 1.45:108).

20. "The Deir 'Alla Plaster Inscriptions," trans. Baruch A. Levine (*COS* 2.27:143).

21. "Hadad-Yith'i," trans. Alan R. Millard (*COS* 2.34:154).

22. Joseph A. Fitzmyer, *The Aramaic Inscriptions of Sefire*, 2nd ed., BibOr 19 (Rome: Pontifical Biblical Institute, 1995), 45.

literature. As biblical scholars have surmised, such traditional material was drawn into the exodus memory as instances of God's punishing plagues against Egypt. The historical background of the plagues lies in ancient Near Eastern motifs of divine destruction, which become God's signs and wonders in the exodus, which Israel will remember in story.

Mnemohistory of the Exodus

To approach the exodus as cultural memory involves what Jan Assmann calls "mnemohistory," an inquiry into the winding paths by which historical memories and traditional motifs merged into an authoritative representation of the past. Having looked at some of this traditional lore in the background of the plagues, let us turn to the historical events and circumstances that arguably lie in the background of the exodus. Here we find that individual events are not as significant as the broad sweep of events in the period leading up to the rise of ancient Israel. This is the era of the Egyptian Empire in Canaan, which lasted for roughly 325 years (ca. 1450–1125 BC). Since the earliest textual evidence of Israel is from 1207 (the Merenptah Stela, which refers to Israel), and the archaeology of Israel's emergence points to the same period (ca. late thirteenth–twelfth century BC), this is the era when we would expect a nascent Israelite identity to crystallize, and with it a story of its foundational past.

There are two interrelated parts to our model of the mnemohistory of the exodus: the circumstances that lie behind Israel's memory of Egyptian slavery, and the circumstances that lie behind the escape from Egyptian slavery. The first part takes us into the colonial practices and ideology of the Egyptian Empire, and the second takes us into the era of the fall of the empire and the rise of Israel. There are other historical circumstances from earlier periods (e.g., the earlier Hyksos rule and expulsion from Egypt) and later periods (e.g., direct Egyptian rule over Israel in ca. 620–609 BC) that may have reflexes in the exodus account, but the broad picture of Israel's emergence as a result of escape from Egyptian slavery is best comprehended by the circumstances of Israel's origins in the Late Bronze Age–Iron Age transition, which the exodus story purports to describe.

Egyptian Slavery in Egypt and Canaan

During the Egyptian Empire in Canaan, thousands of Canaanites were taken into Egypt as slaves. There were three main mechanisms for the acquisition of Canaanite slaves in Egypt: (1) military campaigns, in which pharaohs would seek to pacify the northern territory and gain glory and booty, including slaves; (2) annual taxes levied on Canaanite cities, which included slaves; and (3) the large slave market, in which traders bought slaves in Canaan and sold them in Egypt. Let us consider briefly each source of Canaanite slaves.

Military Campaigns

It was the obligation of each pharaoh during the imperial period to subdue the restless colonial territories and extract their resources, including captives taken as slaves. The founder of the empire, Thutmose III, took 2,503 Canaanite captives after his victory at Megiddo, according to his list of booty.[23] His successor, Amenhotep II, claims to have taken more than 100,000 captives after his second campaign in Canaan.[24] This number is too high, leading Mario Liverani to conjecture that this was an estimate of "the entire population conquered and left in their land as Egyptian subjects."[25] According to this implication, all the people of Canaan were counted as captive slaves of Pharaoh. Later pharaohs continued this custom of taking slaves in their campaigns in Canaan.

The transport of Canaanite captives is vividly described in Ramesses III's account: "I have brought back in great numbers those that my sword has spared, with their hands tied behind their backs before my horses, and their wives and children in tens of thousands, and their livestock in hundreds of thousands. I have imprisoned their leaders in fortresses bearing my name, and I have added to them chief archers and tribal chiefs, branded and enslaved, tattooed with my name, and their wives and children have been treated in the same way."[26]

Even if the numbers here are inflated, the description is revealing. The captives were "branded and enslaved, tattooed with my name." Most of the Canaanite slaves were placed in workhouses in royal estates or temple properties.

---

23. Anthony J. Spalinger, *War in Ancient Egypt: The New Kingdom* (Oxford: Blackwell, 2005), 95.

24. Spalinger, *War in Ancient Egypt*, 144–45.

25. Mario Liverani, *The Ancient Near East: History, Society and Economy* (London: Routledge, 2011), 327.

26. Antonio Loprieno, trans., "Slaves," in *The Egyptians*, ed. Sergio Donadoni (Chicago: Univ. of Chicago Press, 1997), 204–5.

A satire of the soldier's life from the Ramesside period provides another glimpse of the capture and transport of Canaanite captives: "Come, [let me tell] you the woes of the soldier. . . . He is called up to Canaan. He may not rest. There are no clothes, no sandals. . . . His body is weak, his legs fail him. When victory is won, the captives are handed over to his majesty, to be taken to Egypt. The foreign woman faints on the march; she hangs herself [on] the soldier's neck. His knapsack drops, another grabs it while he is burdened with the woman."[27]

While this description focuses on the soldier's woes, the treatment of the captive Canaanite woman is tragic. One can imagine that a description written from the Canaanite perspective would expand on her tragedy and that of other captives taken into Egyptian slavery.

Annual Taxes

The annual taxes levied on Canaanite cities also included slaves. This is a recurring topic in the Amarna letters, as in a letter sent to the pharaoh by Abdi-Heba, king of Jerusalem: "Behold, I am a friend of the king and a tribute bearer of the king . . . [c]ame to me; I gave over [to his char]ge 10 slaves. Šuta, the commissioner of the king ca[me t]o me; I gave over to Šuta's charge 21 girls, [8]0 prisoners, as a gift for the king, my lord."[28]

In the diplomatic language of the time, "friend" and "gift" are circumlocutions for vassal and tribute. The regular tribute of Canaanites to be taken into Egypt as captive slaves was a harsh feature of imperial rule. As Ellen Morris comments, "The regular loss of hundreds of male and female 'slaves' that Egypt requisitioned on an annual basis would also have had a profound impact on Canaan's labor supply and on its social fabric."[29] Many Canaanite families and towns were affected by these cruel exactions.

The Slave Trade

There was also a brisk trade in Canaanite slaves during the imperial period. Letters and legal documents tell of boatloads of Canaanites transported to Egypt to be sold as slaves. Canaanite parents sold their

---

27. "Papyrus Lansing: A Schoolbook," in Miriam Lichtheim, *Ancient Egyptian Literature* (Berkeley: Univ. of California Press, 1976), 2:172.

28. EA 288, trans. William L. Moran, *The Amarna Letters* (Baltimore: Johns Hopkins Univ. Press, 1992), 331.

29. Ellen Morris, *Ancient Egyptian Imperialism* (Hoboken, NJ: Wiley Blackwell, 2018), 166.

children into slavery because of famine, and sometimes a person was sold into slavery because of malice, as in the following report: "His porters sold him to the Egyptians and they seized him and took his goods."[30] This episode is reminiscent of the Joseph story, whose brothers sell him into Egyptian slavery through the medium of Ishmaelite traders. As Antonio Loprieno writes, "During the Late Bronze Age in the Near East, Egypt was the main purchaser of slaves in a market that was probably controlled by Asiatic Bedouin."[31] A consequence was "the development of a legal system that codified the ownership of slaves, who could now be bought and sold by individuals."[32] Canaanite slaves became a commodity in Egypt, bought and sold in a thriving market.

All this evidence—of military campaigns, annual taxes, and the slave trade—gives us a sense of the large number of Canaanite slaves that were taken to Egypt.

As I have indicated, the transfer of Canaanites into Egyptian slavery had a weighty effect on life in Canaan. Many families were affected, and the economy and social fabric suffered. Moreover—and this is a key point—according to the imperial ideology, all the Canaanites were Egyptian slaves, not just those transported to Egypt. All of those living in Canaan—from kings to peasants—were slaves to Pharaoh. The language of slavery permeates the letters from local Canaanite kings to Pharaoh, as in a letter from Biridiya, king of Megiddo: "Say [to the ki]ng, my lord and my [Su]n: Message of Biridiya, the loyal slave of the king. I fall at the feet of the king, my lord and my Sun, seven times and seven times. May the king, my lord, take cognizance of his slave and his city."[33]

The king is the slave of Pharaoh, and so is the city and all its inhabitants. As Raymond Westbrook comments, "A vassal king . . . and his household, that is, the population of his country, were all slaves of the emperor."[34]

In many of the empire's colonial practices, the Canaanites were

---

30. Donald B. Redford, trans., *Egypt, Canaan, and Israel in Ancient Times* (Princeton: Princeton Univ. Press, 1992), 221, n. 30.

31. Loprieno, "Slaves," 202.

32. Loprieno, "Slaves," 205–6.

33. EA 365, trans. Moran, *The Amarna Letters*, 363.

34. Raymond Westbrook, "International Law in the Amarna Age," in *Amarna Diplomacy: The Beginnings of International Relations*, ed. Raymond Cohen and Raymond Westbrook (Baltimore: Johns Hopkins Univ. Press, 2000), 29.

treated as Egyptian slaves. Local Canaanites were subject to forced labor (corvée) in Pharaoh's fields and military installations in Canaan, as we learn in the continuation of Biridiya's letter: "In fact, only I am cultivating in Shunama, and only I am furnishing corvée workers. But consider the mayors that are near me. They do not act as I do. They do not cultivate in Shunama, and they do not furnish corvée workers. Only I (by myself) furnish corvée workers. From Jaffa they come, from [my] resources here, (and) from Nuribta."[35]

This letter refers to agricultural fields in the Jezreel Valley that were now the property of Pharaoh. The local king is providing forced laborers from Megiddo, Jaffa, and Nuribta to work the fields, and complains that the other local rulers are not providing laborers. Local Canaanites were conscripted into forced labor, cultivating Pharaoh's fields. In the eyes of Pharaoh and in their own eyes, the Canaanites living in Canaan were slaves to Egypt. They were all—from king to commoner—living under Egyptian bondage.

This view that all the Canaanites were slaves not only expresses the Egyptian imperial ideology but also may reflect the Canaanites' self-perception during this era. For the mnemohistory of the exodus, we may infer that the memory of Egyptian slavery belonged not only to those Canaanites who had been transported as slaves to Egypt but also to those who had never been to Egypt. All Canaanites living in the land of Canaan were, in theory and practice, slaves to Egypt. This is why a shared memory of Egyptian slavery was probably a bonding agent in the formation of a new people in the Canaanite highlands. All of the early Israelites—whether escaped slaves from Egypt, peasants from the Canaanite lowlands, or settling nomads—could share a memory of Egyptian oppression. This is arguably the historical context of this connective memory.

I emphasize that there were many Canaanite slaves in Egypt, some of whom would have fled back home during the collapse of the Egyptian Empire (see the following). But most Canaanites had never been to Egypt; Egypt came to them. The important point is that despite their different histories, the people who settled early Israel—most of whom were previously Canaanites[36]—shared a common memory of Egyptian bondage.

---

35. EA 365, trans. Moran, *The Amarna Letters*, 363.

36. On the archaeological and historical evidence, see Israel Finkelstein and Neil Asher Silberman, *The Bible Unearthed* (New York: Free Press, 2001), 96–117; Lawrence E. Stager, "Forging an Identity: The Emergence of Ancient Israel," in *The Oxford History of the Biblical*

Escape from Egyptian Slavery

The exodus story is a miraculous liberation from Egyptian slavery and domination, in which God defeats Pharaoh through his mighty signs and wonders and rescues his people from Egypt. There is a range of historical circumstances that could have caused or contributed to this cultural memory. First, we know that some slaves did escape from Egypt. A letter—used as a model in scribal schools—tells of an officer who pursued two escaped slaves who had bypassed the Egyptian border fortress and fled into the eastern desert: "I was sent forth from the broad-halls of the palace . . . following after these two slaves . . . When [I] reached the fortress, they told me that the scout had come from the desert [saying that] they had passed the walled place north of the Fortress of Seti Merneptah . . . When my letter reaches you, write to me about all that has happened to [them]. Who found their tracks? Which watch found their tracks? What people are after them? Write to me about all that has happened to them and how many people you send out after them."[37]

We do not know anything more about the two slaves in the letter. But we can imagine that many Canaanite slaves escaped from Egypt, particularly at the empire's end, when the border fortresses were abandoned. Many Canaanites stayed in Egypt after generations of acculturation. But many could have escaped with the decline of the border forts and police. As Abraham Malamat surmises, there were likely many small exodoi from Egypt during the imperial era and after.[38]

The major circumstance of this period was the collapse of the Egyptian Empire in Canaan. The decades-long decline changed the lives of the Canaanite imperial subjects. Although we lack direct testimony for the Canaanites' response to imperial collapse, the archaeological evidence of destroyed Egyptian fortresses and administrative bases in Canaan tells a tale. As Ellen Morris observes,

---

World, ed. Michael D. Coogan (Oxford: Oxford Univ. Press, 1998), 123–75; and the essays in Ernest S. Frerichs and Leonard H. Lesko, eds., *Exodus: The Egyptian Evidence* (Winona Lake, IN: Eisenbrauns, 1997).

37. "The Pursuit of Runaway Slaves," trans. John A. Wilson, in *ANET*, 259. This letter comes from Papyrus Anastasi V.

38. Abraham Malamat, "The Exodus: Egyptian Analogies," in *Exodus: The Egyptian Evidence*, ed. Ernest S. Frerichs and Leonard H. Lesko (Winona Lake, IN: Eisenbrauns, 1997), 16.

> While the feelings of local communities subjected to Egyptian rule remains a source of speculation, the fate that many of these bases suffered at the end of the Nineteenth Dynasty is quite clear. Four of the bases located in the heart of Egypt's empire (Ashdod, Tel Mor, Aphek, and Tell el-Hesi) came under attack and were put to flame in the turbulent decades between c. 1213 and 1190, when the instability and chaos that marked the end of the Late Bronze Age was first felt in earnest. During this time Merneptah apparently faced rebellions from Ashkelon, Gezer, Yeno'am, and even a tribe by the name of Israel, making its debut in extra-biblical historical sources. Whether the damage to Egyptian bases at roughly this period resulted from this or other insurrections is not known. A fierce burning event in an administrative building at Beth-Shean, however, may indicate that the disturbance even reached this stalwart bastion of Egyptian power.[39]

The violent destruction of Egyptian bases in Canaan seems to indicate what Aaron Burke calls "patterns of resistance to Egyptian domination" during the latter part of the empire.[40] This is the period when Canaanites had the experience of escape from Egyptian bondage *within* the land of Canaan.

If all the Canaanites were slaves to Egypt during the imperial period, the demise of the empire brought them freedom from Egyptian bondage. In this respect, a story of miraculous escape from Egypt would be a unifying catalyst for a new cultural identity. Such a story may have been formulated by slaves who had escaped from Egypt (the exodoi of small groups addressed previously) or may have featured them as protagonists. For our inquiry, it is important to emphasize that this story could pertain to *all* Canaanites who were former subjects of the empire and who had joined the new tribal polity of Israel. The passage from Egypt to Israel was a passage of identity and a passage to a new land, the Canaanite highlands, where Merenptah found Israel.

Israel's rise was historically a consequence of the decline and fall of

---

39. Morris, *Ancient Egyptian Imperialism*, 210.

40. Aaron A. Burke et al., "Excavations of the New Kingdom Fortress in Jaffa, 2011–2014: Traces of Resistance to Egyptian Rule in Canaan," *AJA* 121 (2017): 128.

the Egyptian Empire in Canaan. On this all historians and archaeologists agree. What I am adding is that the exodus story transformed these historical events, facilitated by the shared memory of Egyptian bondage, into God's miraculous rescue of Israel from Egyptian slavery. This story of the birth of a people follows the general pattern of a symbolic rite of passage: separation (from Egypt), liminal period (in Sinai), and reincorporation into a new identity (in Israel). The journey from Egypt to Israel is part of this narrative framework, but the journey was a transformation of identity as much as a physical journey. The story celebrates the transformation of Egyptian slaves into a free people, whom God delivered from Egypt on the wings of eagles (Exod 19:4).

Conclusions

I suggest that the exodus story can be fruitfully approached as a cultural memory. This means that it is not plain history, nor is it pure fiction. It is a mixture of reminiscences of historical events and circumstances, traditional motifs, and narrative imagination. It recalls and revises the past, forgetting some aspects while foregrounding others, with the aim to make the past usable in the present, to anchor ancient Israel's identity and ideals.

This approach is compatible with the archaeological and historical evidence that indicates that the biblical account is historically problematic. The approach emphasizes that the exodus did not happen as a sequence of punctual events, as the Bible presents it. It accepts the impossibility that some three million people—along with their animals—crossed the Red Sea (Exod 12:37) and wandered in the Sinai for forty years yet left no trace in the archaeological record.[41] But it emphasizes that the exodus did happen as a transformation—both historical and symbolic—from Egyptian bondage to the birth of the people of Israel. The exodus story is a mixture of history and fiction, which through the alchemy of cultural memory produced a durable past.

As we have seen, the mnemohistory of the exodus suggests that plagues are largely drawn from the repertoire of divine curses and punishments that we see in treaties, narratives, and prophecies from the

---

41. Archaeological estimates of the population of early Israel in the Iron I period range from 45,000 to 150,000 people; see Finkelstein and Silberman, *The Bible Unearthed*, 109; Stager, "Forging an Identity," 100.

ancient Near East. The Bible lists many of these plagues in its covenant curses. Deuteronomy 28 includes several of them, directed against Israel: "The LORD will afflict you with the boils of Egypt and with tumors, festering sores and the itch, from which you cannot be cured. . . . Swarms of locusts will take over all your trees and the crops of your land. . . . All these curses . . . will be a sign and a wonder to you and your descendants forever. . . . He will bring on you all the diseases of Egypt that you dreaded, and they will cling to you" (vv. 27, 42, 45–46, 60 NIV).

These plagues, called "a sign and a wonder," allude to the exodus plagues and fit easily into the covenant curses. Such disasters wander among the genres of law, narrative, and prophecy as the awesome punishments of God, wielded against enemies and rebels by his mighty hand and outstretched arm.

The mnemohistory of the exodus also arguably includes the centuries-long experience of Egyptian bondage during the Egyptian Empire, in which thousands of Canaanites became slaves in Egypt and many thousands more were Egyptian slaves in Canaan. This collective memory of Egyptian bondage allows us to understand why a story of miraculous rescue from Egyptian slavery could have served as a connective memory in early Israel, unifying former slaves who escaped from Egypt with the majority of early Israelites who had never been to Egypt but also had memories of Egyptian oppression. The rescue from Egyptian bondage—due, in historical terms, to the (sometimes violent) collapse of the Egyptian Empire in Canaan—was a transformation of identity, which included a journey to the promised land, or, in more mundane terms, to the Canaanite highlands.

For the Israelites, it would have been natural to attribute this marvelous transformation to God's miraculous defeat of Pharaoh. As the Song of the Sea—the earliest text of the exodus story—relates, "The LORD is my strength and my defense; he has become my salvation" (Exod 15:2 NIV). The word for "defense" *(zimrâ)* has a second resonance as "song." The exodus story is, in this sense, the song of God's strength and salvation, celebrating his rescue of Israel from Egyptian bondage. The story is, as God explains in Exod 10:1–2, intended to be a cultural memory, transmitted by parents to children in each generation, creating and revitalizing Israel's religious and political identity. The story, even before it is finished, makes provision for its future commemoration.

The approach to the exodus as cultural memory provides a coherent explanation of the relationship between historical and archaeological data and the biblical texts. It also does justice to the theological power of biblical memory. The story of the exodus is an evocation of the past that created Israel. Through this story, in a sense, Israel narrated itself into existence, and it continues to do so in each generation. The exodus is a cultural memory of ethnogenesis, a miraculous story of origins, woven from memories of Egyptian oppression and liberation and laced with traditional motifs and drama.

I emphasize that this model of the exodus as cultural memory is not something that I can empirically prove. Proof is not a relevant criterion in historical inquiry, including mnemohistory. All we can do is construct a model of the past that best accounts for the existing evidence of the past. In our case, the evidence consists of texts and other material culture from ancient Egypt, Canaan, and Israel. But I emphasize that one should not isolate selected bits and correlate them with other bits, if one wants to construct a plausible model. All the evidence needs to be taken into account. I submit that the model sketched here accounts for all the evidence we have, from the mass of archaeological and textual evidence about the Egyptian Empire, to the details and composition of the biblical text, to the current state of Egyptology, Assyriology, and Levantine archaeology. It has a blend of explanatory scope and detail that recommends it.

But this model is incomplete, since we lack clarity on the compositional history of the book of Exodus and the early history of Israel. It is therefore subject to correction, revision, or rejection, according to better analyses or new textual or archaeological discoveries. We should not burden scholarship with the standard of inerrancy. We should remember that our understanding can always be improved and that historical scholarship is corrigible: it is a generations-long conversation that strives for the truth but is never complete.

I also acknowledge that this approach presents a challenge to contemporary theology. It contends that the biblical representation of the exodus is not wholly historical; it is in part imagined, and much of the actual history has been forgotten. But it also shows how cultural memories have, by their very nature, lessons and resonance for the present. As the Passover haggadah instructs, those who hear the story should regard themselves as if they were there at the exodus, experiencing the liberation from Egypt and the passage from slavery to freedom. Through this personal memory, mediated by parents and grandparents (Exod 10:2), they will come to know God and themselves. The complicated nature of the exodus poses a challenge to modern Jews and Christians, but as Moses and his generation knew, religion and faith aren't necessarily easy. We should take seriously the moral truths and partial magic of our constitutive past.

RESPONSE TO RONALD HENDEL
(THE FIFTEENTH-CENTURY EXODUS VIEW)

SCOTT STRIPLING

Professor Hendel deserves credit for challenging traditional exodus paradigms and thinking outside the box. Those who prefer sociological and anthropological approaches to historiography will find validation in his essay. As a student of mythology, I found it interesting. I have organized my critique into two parts: Hendel's positive contribution to the exodus discussion and the flaws in Hendel's case.

Positive Contribution

Hendel accurately portrays slavery in the New Kingdom period. He is correct that the descendants of Jacob were not the only Canaanite slaves in Egypt or the only slaves to experience emancipation. Abraham Malamat, cited by Hendel, posits that there were probably many small exodoi from Egypt. Common sense informs us that slaves attempt to escape from their masters, sometimes with success. In my view, Moses led one such escape after God humbled the Egyptians through a series of miraculous plagues. The Moses-led exodus was larger than any of the other departures and was the one referred to by the biblical writers.

Hendel cites two notable Eighteenth Dynasty examples of the enslavement of Canaanites. He writes that "Thutmose III . . . took 2,503 Canaanite captives after his victory at Megiddo, according to his list of booty. His successor, Amenhotep II, claims to have taken more than 100,000 captives after his second campaign in Canaan." Hendel cites Mario Liverani to establish the problem with the enormity of this number. I agree that this large number likely represents Egyptian hyperbole and propaganda, but a similar event did likely occur, albeit with a smaller total number of captives. Unknowingly, Hendel provides a probable synchronism to the historical exodus during the reign of Amenhotep II. I make the case for this identification in my chapter in this volume. The slave procurement campaign of Amenhotep II, his Second Asiatic Campaign, occurred in the ninth year of his reign. In my view, the loss of his labor force because of the exodus necessitated this expedition.

Hendel rightly points out an inconsistency in the hermeneutical approach of evangelicals who embrace biblical inerrancy yet advocate for an exodus date other than in the fifteenth century BC. Hendel writes, "Kenneth Kitchen argues for a date of the exodus in the middle of the 1200s and uses comparative evidence to explain why 1 Kgs 6:1 is incorrect. He argues, 'Mesopotamian monarchs sometimes give long-range dates (like . . . 1 Kgs 6:1, 480 years) which are invariably too long in absolute years.' The biblical chronology is wrong, but the faithful scholar can correct it."

I agree with Hendel that late-date advocates avoid the plain meaning of the text.

Students of ancient Near Eastern literature will appreciate Hendel's parallels between the biblical plagues and Mesopotamian, Egyptian, and Northwest Semitic texts. He notes that "seven of the exodus plagues have parallels in the curse section of Esarhaddon's Succession Treaty, which was composed and distributed . . . in 672 BCE." While this is interesting, it in no way implies, at least in my mind, that the Pentateuch was penned sometime after 672 and was in some way dependent on this ancient text. If any connection is to be made, it seems more likely that Esarhaddon belies an inherited cultural awareness of divine purposes being accomplished through plagues. Similarities between biblical literature and other ancient Near Eastern writings should not surprise the student of Scripture, since "Moses was educated in all the wisdom of the Egyptians" (Acts 7:22 NIV). Moses likely knew the ancient Near Eastern literature very well, as evidenced by his incorporation of Hammurabi's *lex talionis* in the Israelites' legal code (Exod 21:22–25).

Flaws in Hendel's Case

Hendel's analysis contains several flaws. First, in making analogies to the American Thanksgiving, he creates a straw man caricature, someone who believes that the Pilgrims practiced religious tolerance and freedom of speech. If this person exists, I have not met him or her. In Hendel's view, the Pilgrims' "antagonism to liberty and religious freedom has been airbrushed out of the conventional account." I come from the cultural right, but I do not fit this caricature, and neither do those in my circle of acquaintances, and I believe Hendel overreaches here. What would be the point in people denying that John Winthrop expelled Roger Williams from the Massachusetts Bay Colony? By choosing an inaccurate liberal talking point as an analogy for cultural memory, Hendel immediately inclines a portion of his readers to be less receptive to his larger message.

Second, Hendel errs in his assumption that those who embrace biblical inspiration take "liberties with the traditional doctrine of inerrancy." Evangelicals do this, he writes, "by replacing many of its [the Bible's] miracles with natural events." He devotes two thousand of his ten thousand words to make this point. He takes to task those evangelicals who seek to replace the miraculous plagues with naturally occurring events. Yet Hendel fails to inform readers that there is no anti-supernatural consensus among evangelicals, though he is correct that a number of scholars hold this view. I come from an evangelical faith tradition and have no problem with supernatural plagues or a supernatural parting of the *yam sûp*, for that matter.

Third, as part of Hendel's understanding of cultural memory, he advocates Jan Assmann's views on mnemohistory. Hendel and Assmann believe that kernels of truth of experiences from the past crystalize at some point as history, when they are needed to establish an identity or underpin a theology. Hendel is careful not to claim any empirical evidence for his views. He states that "individual events are not as significant as the broad sweep of events in the period leading up to the rise of ancient Israel." As a result, I find it difficult to draw on the literary or archaeological record to critique Hendel's views. After all, he does not claim to base his views on anything empirical: "I emphasize that this model of the exodus as cultural memory is not something that I can empirically prove." Hendel's transparency reflects well on him.

Fourth, in the mnemohistory section, Hendel lays a false predicate when he states that the Merenptah Stela is the earliest textual evidence of Israel. In the chapter I have written, I offer several earlier examples of inscriptions, including the Berlin Pedestal and the Soleb Hieroglyph. In light of these earlier inscriptions, Hendel is incorrect that the late thirteenth–twelfth century BC "is the era when we would expect a nascent Israelite identity to crystallize, and with it a story of its foundational past."

Fifth, Hendel offers extensive evidence of slavery in ancient Egypt, but he does not close the loop on connecting it to his larger case. Earlier, I noted that Hendel's references to ancient Near Eastern slavery were helpful in understanding the general cultural background of Israel's bondage and miraculous manumission. However, two thousand words on this non sequitur data was not needed. Hendel could have made the point succinctly, allowing space to explore other aspects of his theory. If other ancient Near Eastern cultures invented their histories, those parallels would have added weight to his arguments.

Sixth, Hendel claims that his cultural memory paradigm "is compatible with the archaeological and historical evidence that indicates that the biblical account is historically problematic." In our respective chapters, Professor Hoffmeier and I both present compelling cases for the historicity of the exodus. This watershed event is certainly more than a cultural memory. Hendel also mentions the impossibility of an exodus with millions of people, as if it were a problem for those who see a close synchronism between the archaeological and extrabiblical evidence and the biblical text. Hoffmeier and I both explain that the semantic range of the Hebrew word *ʾelep* likely includes "clan" or "military unit." Our reading, held by the vast majority of evangelical scholars, points to a number of approximately fifty thousand people, perhaps far less.

Seventh, while I cannot disprove Hendel's claim that a collapse of Egyptian control over Canaan gave rise to an exodus myth, he certainly did not prove his thesis. Repeatedly claiming that a paradigm is possible or reasonable does not make it so. In Hendel's own words, "Israel narrated itself into existence."

Two final statements for Hendel's case deserve mention. First, he informs readers that "proof is not a relevant criterion in historical inquiry." If proof is irrelevant, what then is the goal of our inquiry? At the very least should we not seek to determine where the weight of evidence lies? Plausibility is a worthy pursuit for historians. Second, Hendel writes, "The model sketched here accounts for all the evidence we have." In my estimation, however, evidence inexorably connects to proof. Finally, Hendel's last sentence lacks clarity: "We should take seriously the moral truths and partial magic of our constitutive past." A clear conclusion may have advanced his argument.

Conclusion

I acknowledge that cultural memory, as defined by Hendel, exists. I need look no farther than my home state of Texas and the mythology surrounding Davy Crockett. I grew up admiring Crockett's courage in the face of overwhelming odds and certain death at the Alamo in 1836. When Hollywood cast John Wayne as Crockett, the legend seemingly became history. Then, in 1955, the diary of a Mexican lieutenant colonel named José Enrique de la Peña was published in Spanish, and twenty years later the publisher released the English version.[42] De la Peña was present at the Alamo, but rather than confirming that Crockett fought to the death, his diary recorded that Crockett surrendered after the Mexicans breached the mission's venerable walls. Mexican soldiers delivered the frontiersman-turned-congressman-turned-freedom-fighter to Santa Anna, Mexico's cruel dictator, who promptly ordered Crockett's execution. In light of this written account, which version do we choose to believe? In my view, the written account is likely accurate. Surrender in the face of overwhelming odds does not make Crockett a coward, but it does wreak havoc with our need for mythical heroes.

But Crockett is not Moses, and Santa Anna is not Amenhotep II. To extend the metaphor, those who accept a historical exodus are analogous to historians who favor de la Peña's written account and discount the conflicting oral tradition. In dating the exodus, we have five different books by five different biblical writers that all point to the mid-fifteenth century BC. In addition, extrabiblical inscriptions and histories point to the same century, and archaeological remains establish a clear verisimilitude.

I appreciate Professor Hendel's willingness to engage in this debate, and I benefitted from the ideas and sources that he shared.

---

42. José Enrique de la Peña, *With Santa Anna in Texas: A Personal Narrative of the Revolution*, ed. and trans. Carmen Perry (College Station, TX: Texas A&M Univ. Press, 1997).

RESPONSE TO RONALD HENDEL
(THE THIRTEENTH-CENTURY EXODUS VIEW)

JAMES K. HOFFMEIER

Professor Ronald Hendel is well positioned to write "The Exodus as Cultural Memory" as his contribution to this volume. He has advocated this approach for two decades now.[43] I am grateful that he sees some form of historical memory in the exodus narratives, although how he decides what is historical poses a serious problem. However, before Hendel defines and develops his thesis and explains how cultural memory works, he swerves from that task by offering a diatribe against Christian scholars for their embrace of the doctrine of the inerrancy of Scripture. Then, in a bizarre twist, he denounces Kenneth Kitchen and me for not being faithful to what he believes is our inerrantist creed.

Because he raised this issue in his essay, I wish to point out that Hendel has a history of animus toward conservatives and believes traditional positions should not appear in scholarly publications.[44] At one point, he temporarily withdrew his membership from the Society of Biblical Literature in protest.[45] His aversion to conservative scholarship

43. See Hendel, "The Exodus in Biblical Memory," 601–22. A version of this article appeared as "The Exodus as Cultural Memory: Egyptian Bondage and the Song of the Sea," in Levy, Schneider, and Propp, *Israel's Exodus in Transdisciplinary Perspective*, 65–77.

44. Ronald Hendel, "Farewell to SBL: Faith and Reason in Biblical Studies," *BAR* 35, no. 4 (July/August 2010): 28, 74. In an op-ed ten years ago, Hendel objected to the Society of Biblical Literature allowing "fundamentalist groups" holding their meetings in conjunction with SBL, and opined that Bruce Waltke's conclusion that Prov 1–24:33 was Solomonic when reviewing Michael Fox's commentary on Proverbs was "rationally absurd."

45. While Hendel directs his harangue at SBL, his grievance really is directed at evangelical scholars because their more traditional approach to the Hebrew Bible is "rationally absurd"; therefore they should be excommunicated from the guild. The SBL chat room buzzed for several weeks as members went back and forth, with some scholars chiding Hendel while

bubbled over publicly at the exodus conference at the University of California, San Diego, May 31–June 3, 2013.[46] Geologist Stephen Moshier, whose vital work on the northeastern delta of Egypt has revealed the Bronze Age paleoenvironment of this region,[47] presented a paper,[48] and Hendel was upset by the suggestion that the route from (Pi)-Ramesses through north Sinai might have something to do with the exodus itinerary. He immediately denounced Dr. Moshier, asserting, "To go from text immediately to geology in the modern context of critical scholarship is *intellectually indefensible*."[49] Manfred Bietak, a giant in northeastern delta archaeology, demurred with Hendel, thanking Moshier for his "fascinating study" and stating, "It is absolutely *legitimate and cogent* to find out the physical backgrounds to what is possible and not possible" regarding the exodus. Hendel's and Bietak's diametrically opposite responses expose the academic divide between historians and archaeologists and modern "critical" biblical scholars. As a strong advocate of the liberal arts and a multiplex approach to study of the Hebrew Bible, I resonate with Gary A. Rendsburg's salutary affirmation that "the purpose of the humanities is to open doors of inquiry, not to

---

others dashed to his support. Between June 23, 2010, and August 15, 2010, ninety-five postings were made; see www.sbl-site.org/membership/farewell.aspx.

46. All the lectures and subsequent discussions are available on video (http://exodus.calit2.net/) and were published in Levy, Schneider, and Propp, *Israel's Exodus in Transdisciplinary Perspective* but without the questions and comments.

47. Moshier's geological work took place between 2000 and 2007. See James K. Hoffmeier and Stephen O. Moshier, "New Paleo-Environmental Evidence from North Sinai to Complement Manfred Bietak's Map of the Eastern Delta and Some Historical Implications," in *Timelines: Studies in Honour of Manfred Bietak*, ed. Ernst Czerny et al., OLA 149 (Leuven: Peeters, 2006), 2:168–76; Stephen O. Moshier and Ali El-Kalani, "Late Bronze Age Paleogeography along the Ancient Ways of Horus in Northwest Sinai, Egypt," *Geoarchaeology* 23 (2008): 450–73; James K. Hoffmeier and Stephen O. Moshier, "'The Ways of Horus': The Main Road from Egypt to Canaan," in *Desert Road Archaeology in the Eastern Sahara*, ed. Heiko Riemer and Frank Förster, Colloquium Africanum 5 (Cologne: Heinrich-Barth-Institut, 2013), 485–510; Stephen O. Moshier and James K. Hoffmeier, "The Geological Setting of Tell el-Borg with Implications for Ancient Geography of Northwest Sinai," in *Excavations in North Sinai: Tell el-Borg I*, ed. James K. Hoffmeier (Winona Lake, IN: Eisenbrauns, 2014), 62–83; Stephen Moshier and Bahaa Gayed, "Geological Investigation of the Ballah Depression, Northern Suez Canal Zone, Egypt," in *Excavations in North Sinai: Tell el-Borg II*, ed. James K. Hoffmeier (University Park, PA: Eisenbrauns, 2019), 5–20.

48. The paper was jointly published with me as "Which Way out of Egypt? Physical Geography Related to the Exodus Itinerary," in Levy, Schneider, and Propp, *Israel's Exodus in Transdisciplinary Perspective*, 101–8.

49. Emphasis is mine in Hendel's and Bietak's quote. One can still hear the entirety of Hendel's nearly four-minute critique in the lecture videos: http://exodus.calit2.net/.

close them."[50] In his criticisms of evangelical scholars, Hendel seems bent on closing doors to scholars who don't share his "critical" readings.

Nowhere in my essay is theology or a particular doctrine of Scripture mentioned. Since my first published refereed article in 1975, I have never used a theological argument to advance a historical idea. I have written on the limitations of both the modern, rationalistic approach of higher criticism and the "new" literary approaches of postmodern hermeneutics in Old Testament studies.[51] I prefer the phenomenological approach, which takes events and various phenomena in narratives seriously. Phenomenology "rejects the assumption that only what is rational is real."[52] I treat Hebrew and Egyptian texts in the same manner.[53]

Professor Hendel seems to believe that conservative scholars who affirm the inerrancy of the Bible must also be literalists. This is false. Kitchen and I are attacked for "swerving from inerrancy" and "a departure from the plain sense of the Bible" when we question literal readings such as the 480 years or the six hundred thousand Hebrew men leaving Egypt. Our sin is that he views these details among the "Bible's errors" that we seek to correct by "replacing them with historically plausible reconstructions." Hendel rejects our interpretation of the ten plagues for diminishing them to natural phenomena. Accordingly, "the Bible, in a sense, misrepresents or misunderstands the plagues, which the modern scholar can correct." I never seek to "correct" any text; rather I strive to understand it! Nevertheless, to prove his point, Hendel quotes my *Israel in Egypt*: the plagues were "natural occurrences known to Egypt," the consequence being, in his words, that "the biblical events are largely emptied of their supernatural character." My qualifying quotation from Nahum Sarna's wonderful Exodus commentary, however, is overlooked:

---

50. Gary A. Rendsburg used the memorable line in a lecture I organized at the University of Toronto for the Society of Mediterranean Studies.

51. I adopted this approach in my dissertation that was subsequently published as *"Sacred" in the Vocabulary of Ancient Egypt: The Term ḎSR, with Special Reference to Dynasties I–XX*, OBO 59 (Freiburg: Universitätsverlag, 1985). Later I applied the approach to biblical narratives; cf. James K. Hoffmeier, "Understanding Hebrew and Egyptian Military Texts: A Contextual Approach," in *Archival Documents from the Biblical World*, vol. 3 of *The Context of Scripture*, ed. William W. Hallo and K. Lawson Younger (Leiden: Brill, 2002), xxi–xxvii; idem, *Ancient Israel in Sinai: The Evidence for the Authenticity of the Wilderness Tradition* (Oxford: Oxford Univ. Press, 2005), 8–27.

52. Hoffmeier, *Ancient Israel in Sinai*, 33.

53. For an example of my approach to Egyptian texts that deal with the supernatural, see Hoffmeier, "Understanding Hebrew and Egyptian Military Texts," xxi–xxvii.

"They [the plagues] are instances of God's harnessing the forces of nature for the realization of His own historical purpose."

I further nuanced my position, arguing that Egyptians and Israelites understood that "the world in which they lived was not divided into dichotomous categories such as church and state or natural and miraculous. Rather, these concepts were dynamically interrelated; all the forces of nature were divinely controlled."[54] From the modern, scientific perspective, the first nine plagues are "natural" occurrences, but to the Hebrews and Egyptians, they were divine, miraculous actions. When Hendel declares, "In this model, supernatural events are replaced by natural ones," he misrepresents my position. The phenomenological approach is intended to evaluate an experience, event, or phenomenon from the perspective of the narrative's ancient context.[55]

After Hendel's initial apologetic for the "clear sense of the Bible," he champions "the exodus as cultural memory" because it "embraces the miraculous quality of the events." In reality he does not believe these events were supernatural or natural phenomena, nor is there a cause-effect between the plagues and the release of enslaved Hebrews. Hendel's plagues are literary, not literal. For him, they possibly derive from lists of plagues and curses known from ancient Near Eastern texts like Esarhaddon's Succession Treaty. Consequently, "biblical scholars have surmised, such traditional material was drawn into the exodus memory," although possibly some sort of regional plague may be remembered in the biblical story that is hinted at in some ancient Near Eastern literature.

Indeed, during the reign of Amenhotep III (1380–1373 BC), serious disruptions occurred, perhaps because of plague or what Arielle Kozloff called "serious disease events,"[56] which may be reflected in the texts Hendel cites. When the Philistines fought against Israel in 1 Sam 4, they recognized the power of Israel's deity "who struck the Egyptians with all kinds of plagues" (v. 8 NIV), and when plague did strike Philistia because of the ark of the covenant, they asked, "Why do you harden your hearts as the Egyptians and Pharaoh did? When Israel's god dealt

54. All quotes here are found in Hoffmeier, *Israel in Egypt*, 149.

55. Hoffmeier, *Ancient Israel in Sinai*, 27–33.

56. Arielle Kozloff, *Amenhotep III: Egypt's Radiant Pharaoh* (Cambridge: Cambridge Univ. Press, 2012), 112. For her discussion of this troubled period, see pp. 111–15.

harshly with them, did they not send the Israelites out so they could go on their way?" (1 Sam 6:6 NIV). The Philistine plague prompts them to recall specifically what occurred in Egypt to the Hebrews, not a vague, distant memory of pandemic that struck their region.

Hendel's cultural memory hermeneutic sees a merging of "aspects of history, traditional lore, and narrative imagination into a powerful cultural memory," "a mixture of history and fiction." But he offers no methodology for identifying what is history, fiction, and mnemohistory in a narrative. Perhaps he follows Jan Assmann's guidance: "It is only through continual historical reflection that the workings of memory become visible."[57] "Historical reflection" is excessively subjective, in my judgment. Objective criteria is lacking, and herein lies the problem with a cultural memory reading of the biblical narratives. The reader subjectively and arbitrarily determines what happened or did not happen and what qualifies as cultural memory.

While many scholars have jumped on the cultural memory bandwagon, insightful criticism has also been leveled.[58] William Dever rightly dubbed it as "vogue among some biblical scholars and historians."[59] However, he sees postmodernism's philosophy at work and opines that cultural memories "deal mostly with the transmission of the story, not any reality behind it. This seems to me yet another myth and myth-making, ancient and modern—another legacy of postmodernism."[60] Thus the lines blur between ancient history and the memory historian's new, creative mythical machinations. The Copenhagen scholar Jens Bruun Kofoed cautions that according to some scholars

57. Jan Assmann, *Moses the Egyptian: The Memory of Egypt in Western Monotheism* (Cambridge: Harvard Univ. Press, 1997), 21.

58. See Hans Barstad, "History and Memory: Some Reflections on the 'Memory Debate,'" in *The Historian and the Bible: Essays in Honour of Lester L. Grabbe*, ed. Philip R. Davies and Diana V. Edelman (London: T&T Clark, 2010), 1–10; Jens Bruun Kofoed, "The Old Testament as Cultural Memory," in *Do Historical Matters Matter to Faith? A Critical Appraisal of Modern and Postmodern Approaches to Scripture*, ed. James K. Hoffmeier and Dennis R. Magary (Wheaton, IL: Crossway, 2012), 303–23; idem, "Tell Your Children and Grandchildren! The Exodus as Cultural Memory," in *"Did I Not Bring Israel out of Egypt?" Biblical, Archaeological, and Egyptological Perspectives on the Exodus Narratives*, ed. James K. Hoffmeier, Alan R. Millard, and Gary A. Rendsburg, BBRSup 13 (Winona Lake, IN: Eisenbrauns, 2016), 177–96.

59. William G. Dever, "The Exodus and the Bible: What Was Known; What Was Remembered; What Was Forgotten?" in Levy, Schneider, and Propp, *Israel's Exodus in Transdisciplinary Perspective*, 399.

60. Dever, "The Exodus and the Bible," 399–400.

(especially of the Copenhagen school), the cultural memory approach to the book of Exodus presupposes a traditional source-critical analysis of the Pentateuch, and therefore it offers "a construct based on hypothetical and nonextant sources."[61] A questionable reconstruction of exodus memory events is built on the flimsy foundation of nineteenth-century source criticism.

Ronald Hendel believes that "for the exodus story to take root in early Israel it was necessary for it to pertain to the remembered past of settlers who did not immigrate from Egypt."[62] This dubious assumption notwithstanding, he seeks an explanation for how the Israelites who had been in Egypt could find common cause with Canaanites and other indigenous groups. Since all of Canaan in the Late Bronze Age was under the boot of Egypt, they were Pharaoh's slaves. When the Egyptian Empire collapsed (ca. 1150) and her garrisons returned home, so the argument goes, all of Canaan along with the Hebrews could celebrate liberation from Egypt. Time prohibits a full critique of this imaginative reconstruction of Egypt's empire (not colony!) and its impact on Canaan. But several points must be made.

True, thousands were taken to Egypt as POWs, and tribute flowed from the Levant to Egypt. But Pharaoh used local officials and kings to administer Egypt's affairs.[63] Fealty to Egypt by these elites lasted generations, and some emulation of Egyptian culture in Canaan persisted.[64] Hendel quotes Westbrook's observation that Egyptian vassal states "were all slaves of the emperor" to illustrate Canaan's shared experience with Hebrews. He fails, however, to include Westbrook's following explanation that "the term was used metaphorically."[65] The Canaanites were not literally slaves but subjects. Canaan had a love-hate

---

61. Kofoed, "Tell Your Children and Grandchildren," 190.

62. Hendel, "The Exodus in Biblical Memory," 605.

63. For a distinction between how Egypt administered its empire in Canaan versus its colony in Nubia, see James K. Hoffmeier, "Aspects of Egyptian Foreign Policy in the 18th Dynasty in Western Asia and Nubia" in *Egypt, Israel, and the Ancient Mediterranean World: Studies in Honor of Donald B. Redford*, ed. Gary Knoppers and Antoine Hirsch, Probleme der Ägyptologie 20 (Leiden: Brill, 2004), 121–41.

64. I intentionally use the word *some* over against Carolyn R. Higginbotham's view that there was a limited Egyptian military and administrative presence in the Levant; see her *Egyptianization and Elite Emulation in Ramesside Palestine: Governance and Accommodation on the Imperial Periphery*, CHANE 2 (Leiden: Brill, 2000).

65. Westbrook, "International Law in the Amarna Age," 29.

relationship with Egypt. Some Canaanite elites enjoyed being educated in Egypt and serving as Pharaoh's agents. Abdi-Heba, king of Jerusalem, is one such individual (cf. EA 286, 287, 288). Some foreign princes, like Aper-el, were trained in Egypt and became viziers (a prime minister) in Egypt under Amenhotep III and Akhenaten in the fourteenth century.[66] Surely, Levantine polities welcomed the end of Egyptian control, but no declaration of independence has survived from that region. All Canaanites were not slaves in the same way the Hebrews were in Egypt, as portrayed in the Bible.

Nubia, on the other hand, was colonized by Egypt from ca. 2000–1700 BC and again from ca. 1500–1050 BC. Egypt's harsh exploitation and military oppression of Kush far exceeded the experience of western Asia and lasted much longer. Yet when freed from Egyptian control, for the next fourteen hundred years Kushite royalty built pyramids and wrote monumental inscriptions in Egyptian hieroglyphics, and no Egyptian liberation saga exists. Instead Nubia replicated Egyptian culture and saw themselves as legitimate Egyptian rulers in the Twenty-Fifth Dynasty.[67]

In the end, we are left only with Israel's exodus-freedom story. Others joined this new people group, including some Midianite/Kenites and Canaanites. Their decision to join was based on what they understood YHWH had done. The Midianite priest and father-in-law of Moses, Jethro, "heard of everything God had done . . . and how the Lord had brought Israel out of Egypt" (Exod 18:1 NIV), and Rahab, a Canaanite of Jericho, confessed, "We have heard how the Lord dried up the water of the Red Sea for you when you came out of Egypt" (Josh 2:10 NIV). There is no hint of Canaan's emancipation from Egypt's domination here. Evidence that Canaanites identified with the Hebrew sojourn-exodus experience or that the Hebrews could relate to the Canaanite oppression under imperial Egypt is illusory. The theory of a shared common memory of Egyptian enslavement, based on my "historical reflection," is fanciful fiction.

---

66. Alain Zivie, "Pharaoh's Man, 'Abdiel: The Vizier with a Semitic Name," *BAR* 44, no. 4 (July/August 2018): 22–31, 64–66.

67. László Török, *The Kingdom of Kush: Handbook of Napatan-Meroitic Civilization* (Leiden: Brill, 1997); Stuart T. Smith, *Wretched Kush: Ethnic Identities and Boundaries in Egypt's Nubian Empire* (New York: Routledge, 2003).

RESPONSE TO RONALD HENDEL
(THE THIRTEENTH-CENTURY HYKSOS/LEVITE-LED EXODUS VIEW)

PETER FEINMAN

Alone among the five contributors, Ronald Hendel does not suggest a date for the exodus. Instead he approaches the event as a "cultural memory." Like Rendsburg, he uses the Pilgrims as an example, and Hendel notes the way in which the Pilgrims have become part of the American cultural memory. Certain undesirable features of their way of life in general and their actions in Massachusetts in particular have been airbrushed from the traditional account. Recently some aspects of that behavior have received more attention. Hendel chooses not to identify the Wampanoags by name. His reference to them as Native Americans uses an inclusive term which could refer to hundreds of Native American peoples throughout the United States. This reminds me of the Egyptian use of the term "Shasu" for the bedouin tribes rather than identifying a tribe by its individual name.

Be that as it may, Hendel states that the "memory of Israel's oppression and escape from Egyptian bondage exemplifies ideals that were central to ancient Israelite identity," as the Pilgrims are to America. After all, Exod 20:2 defines the Israelite deity according to this action of deliverance. Hendel even compares the two exodus traditions, the one from Egypt and the other from the Old World. He might have added that this parallel was why colonial Americans thought of themselves as God's New Israel. The exodus is part of the cultural memory of both black and white Americans.

One might assume that Hendel would conclude that just as the Pilgrim voyage to America was real, regardless of how it is remembered, so too the Israelite departure from Egypt is a specific event in history. However, he does not make that conclusion here. Instead Hendel turns to the biblical requirement to remember and recount the exodus story for future generations. He states, "The command to remember the exodus resounds in the Bible."

Hendel then shifts to pointing out "the differences and advantages of [his] approach to others in this volume." He raises the issue of biblical inerrancy, arguing that adherence to such a doctrine "limits the kinds of inquiries that evangelical and orthodox scholars can pursue." Those very limitations prompted a rescue effort by evangelicals. In doing so, they took liberties with this approach by reinterpreting biblical events to correct the biblical description. By contrast, Hendel claims that the Bible errs "but faithful scholars can restore the true picture." He even calls such efforts a form of cultural memory whereby miracles are replaced with natural events. In his conclusion Hendel returns to this theme. He recognizes that he would like to know more about the compositional history of the book of Exodus and early Israelite history and acknowledges that the cultural memory approach "presents a challenge to contemporary theology."

I did not directly address the doctrinal position elucidated by Hendel. It does not apply to my contribution, which at the time of Hendel's writing he had not read. In my responses to the other contributors, I questioned their reliance on the biblical texts for genealogies as evidence of what people actually said, using the *Iliad* as an example. Even if all the leading characters of the *Iliad* were real, that does not mean Homer had their actions or motives right. In this regard I am sympathetic to the warning Hendel gives about the restrictions of evangelical scholars (because of their beliefs).

In support of this admonition, Hendel offers as his first example 1 Kgs 6:1. I did not mention this verse in my contribution, and my sense is that some of the contributors launched a preemptive strike in anticipation of what Stripling would write. Hendel does not offer a critique of the 1446 BC dating based on this verse as much as he criticizes evangelicals more generally for relying on it. Ironically, here is an example of over-reliance on the biblical evidence. As Hendel states, "Identifying the Bible's errors and replacing them with historically plausible reconstructions is a curious strategy for evangelical scholars.

It clearly departs from the traditional doctrine of inerrancy." This statement is less a contribution to Hendel's own understanding of the exodus than a response to the positions held by others.

His next example of "stretching inerrancy" involves the plagues. He is opposed to the rationalizing of miracles into natural events to create a historically plausible account. He cites James Hoffmeier as an evangelical scholar who engages in this rationalizing approach. However, in his contribution to this book, Hoffmeier does not do this. Based on numerous papers I have heard Hoffmeier deliver in academic settings, I am aware that he can present academic material without disclosing or intimating an evangelical perspective, and that is the approach he has taken in this volume. Hendel seems to have anticipated that Hoffmeier would take an evangelical approach and decided not to wait for his response to the chapter to undermine it.

Hendel is correct to observe that the plagues were standard operating procedure in the storytelling of the ancient Near East. They were an effective way to deliver a message about the attitude of the gods toward the people, and especially toward the king. I would have preferred for Hendel to have spent more time on the plagues in the ancient Near East and saved his evangelical criticisms for his responses to contributors. He writes, "The purpose of the plagues is to make a great story, which the Israelites will tell their children and grandchildren." Is that all? I would have liked to have seen him make an effort to contextualize the specific plagues in the biblical narrative. Why these plagues? Why this sequence? Why this number? What would these plagues mean to an audience in Canaan without the Nile River environment? Did they all become part of the cultural memory at once? By whose authority? These questions are of greater interest to me than his criticisms of evangelicals.

Hendel then turns "to the historical events and circumstances that arguably lie in the historical background of the exodus." He is right to note the existence of the Egyptian Empire in Canaan and dates its cessation subsequent to the reign of Ramesses III, as I did in my response to Rendsburg. He is right to note the archaeology and Merenptah Stela as situating the emergence of Israel in the thirteenth–twelfth centuries. He then writes, "This is the era when we would expect a nascent Israelite identity to crystallize, and with it a story of its foundational past." This is exactly right, and remembering the exodus from the time of Ramesses II is consistent with this view. Think of the Song of the Sea, the name Israel, and the definition of the name of the deity as examples of such memories.

Based on Egyptian imperialism, Hendel examines Egyptian slavery in two locations: Egypt and Canaan. He examines the slavery in the Eighteenth and Nineteenth Dynasties under various pharaohs and then takes the next step. Hendel doesn't limit himself to lists of captives claimed by Egypt; he extends that impact into Canaan itself. In addition to the captives, there were the annual tributes Canaanite cities had to pay to the crown. Combined, these actions ripped apart the Canaanite social fabric, and families throughout the land were affected. Everyone in Canaan was a slave to Pharaoh under imperial ideology.

Hendel does an excellent job in expanding the slavery horizon to include people beyond Egypt. He includes Canaanites in Canaan who never went to Egypt, although family members and neighbors may have been enslaved in Egypt. Hendel posits that "a shared memory of Egyptian slavery was probably a bonding agent in the formation of a new people in the Canaanite highlands." Here Hendel refrains from suggesting that slavery formed a bonding agent of a new people in Egyptian captivity. He should explain why he thinks this happened in the highlands but not in Egypt.

Hendel draws on the work of Egyptologist Ellen Morris to describe what happened in the land of Canaan with the collapse of the Egyptian Empire. Specifically, he focuses on the destruction of Egyptian fortresses and administrative bases in Canaan at the end of the Nineteenth Dynasty. Morris mentions a number of sites in the time period 1213–1190 BC (mostly the reign of Merenptah). Morris notes Israel among the foes Merenptah faced in the rebellions, as listed on the Merenptah Stela. Hendel also cites biblical archaeologist Aaron Burke, who refers to "patterns of resistance to Egyptian domination" at this time.

Hendel has honed in on what I call the Canaanite spring. In my chapter I surmised that following the failure of Ramesses II at Qadesh, Moses expected and hoped for a Canaanite spring, for the reasons and along the lines Hendel mentions here. But it didn't happen. Ramesses cracked down in Canaan, beginning with his campaign in year 8. The Canaanite spring was delayed until the time of Merenptah, and in the interim Israel wandered in the wilderness until the coast was clear during the second half of the reign of Ramesses II and began settling in the highlands. While much of the attention is focused on his campaigns against the Libyans and Nubians, Merenptah did campaign in Canaan. As with his father before him, he knew of the potential for rebellion in Canaan, and he did not want Israel to be a catalyst, a spark that ignited other rebellions based on their success in leaving Egypt.

Hendel is perfectly willing to accept the likelihood of "many small exodoi" from Egypt. He is willing to accept "a story of miraculous escape from Egypt [as] a unifying catalyst for a new cultural identity." He will even accept that such "a story may have been formulated by slaves who had escaped from Egypt . . . or may have featured them as protagonists." He elaborates on these views to suggest a symbolic "rite of passage." "The exodus story transformed these historical events, facilitated by the shared memory of Egyptian bondage." All that is missing from this scenario is an explanation for Moses. Why should Canaanites in Canaan who vastly outnumbered the small exodoi accept Israel as the catalyst and choose to become part of Israel? Why go through all these iterations instead of simply positing that a Canaanite hero, like a Joshua, simply liberated the land from Egyptian rule? Why invent the exodus or make such a minor event so pivotal to their identity?

Here is where my own contribution and my response to Rendsburg fill in the gaps to this historical reconstruction. The recognition of a Hyksos-led exodus from Egypt explains the prominence of the Israelite opposition to Pharaoh. It recognizes that for most of the reign of Ramesses II, the Canaanite kings (like the king of Jericho) remained good vassals. One should consider the possibility that the Canaanite people would rebel against Egyptian imperialism and the vassal kings and that Canaanite people would ally with Israel against a common foe. The awareness of the Israelite exodus also was part of the Canaanite cultural memory, and the recognition that Sisera was Ramesses III explains why diverse elements of Canaanites and Transjordanians accepted Israelite leadership against Egypt.

Slavery is not simply a legal term. Israelites in the corvée of Pharaoh Solomon saw themselves as slaves (see my Rendsburg response) without legally being slaves, just as white Americans viewed themselves as slaves of King George III. The cultural memory of the historical exodus contributed to political actions and writing in the tenth century BC.

Hendel overlooks that not only Israel and the United States have cultural memories. Egypt remembered the Hyksos slaying of Seqenenre and the exodus. Canaanites remembered Egyptian slavery and the exodus. Hendel is wrong not to recognize that the historical kernel at the basis of the Israelite cultural memory was a real, historical exodus. A real exodus from Egypt occurred in the time of Ramesses II, and the memory of that event impacted Egyptian-Canaanite history for centuries to come. Strangely, Hendel concludes that "as Moses and his generation knew, religion and faith aren't necessarily easy." Yet nothing in his contribution suggests that Moses actually existed. But he did, and he led the exodus from Egypt.

RESPONSE TO RONALD HENDEL
(THE TWELFTH-CENTURY EXODUS VIEW)

GARY A. RENDSBURG

Ronald Hendel is less interested in the historical nature of the exodus per se and instead reminds us that in truth all we possess is the memory thereof as recorded by the later Israelites. This approach constitutes a sobering reminder for those of us who seek to reconstruct historical events described in the Bible, especially when a distance of several centuries separates the events themselves and their "canonical" narrative.

Which is to say, this is less of a problem for most of the events described in the book of Kings, whose canonical version is plainly based on annalistic material written more or less contemporarily with the events described.[68] Thus one finds various elements—including detailed ones—of the reigns of Omri, Ahab, Jehu, Menahem, Pekah, Hoshea, et al. in the northern kingdom of Israel, and of the reigns of Ahaz, Hezekiah, Manasseh, Jehoiachin, et al. in the southern kingdom of Judah, confirmed by Moabite, Aramean, Assyrian, and Babylonian sources.

By contrast, the issue of a memory is a crucial one when dealing with earlier biblical material, both for the books themselves (e.g., Exodus) and for the stories narrated (e.g., the exodus). The distance of centuries between historical event and recorded narrative creates a sizable gap. How, then, should we approach this matter?

Since we have no direct confirmation of any of the events mentioned in the greater exodus narrative in the Bible (eisodus, exodus, wilderness),

68. See the fundamental article and the summary chart in Baruch Halpern, "Erasing History: The Minimalist Assault on Ancient Israel," *BRev* 11, no. 6 (November/December 1995): 26–35, 47.

the best approach is to seek and analyze comparanda, especially from the wealth of Egyptian documentation. While I have not cited the material to be analyzed in my contribution to the present volume, I have done so in prior publications.[69] Hendel himself cites one of the key Egyptian texts, so apparently he would agree with this overall approach.

We differ, however, over one crucial item. Before I expand on that point, I want to first issue a demurral regarding Hendel's labeling of a particular scholar or group of scholars as "evangelical." Does such a label matter? Should it matter? A particular scholar's personal religious beliefs should not enter the conversation. We all have one goal: to reconstruct as best we can the ancient past, including whatever we can discover to elucidate the world that produced the Bible.

Since Hendel raised the issue, and even though I am no expert on this matter, I believe Hendel errs by conflating biblical inerrancy and evangelical beliefs. In doing so, he unfortunately confuses the evangelical approach with a fundamentalist one. Evangelical scholars believe in the essential historicity of the biblical narrative, but they do not always accept a literal reading of Scripture. They engage in critical research, and they understand the importance of historical and archaeological inquiry for the field of biblical studies. By blurring the boundaries between the evangelical and fundamentalist approaches,[70] Hendel misrepresents the former. To repeat, I do not understand why it is necessary to enter into this discussion, nor why it is necessary to label a particular scholar's personal religious stance.

With that aside, I turn to the crucial item indicated before. Whereas I see the Israelites as distinct from the Canaanites, with origins among the Shasu bedouin, Hendel views the majority of the Israelites as "previously Canaanites." The biblical account of the slavery, accordingly, is not a slavery in Egypt per se; rather it serves as an echo of the political

---

69. Gary A. Rendsburg, "The Early History of Israel," in *Crossing Boundaries and Linking Horizons: Studies in Honor of Michael C. Astour on His 80th Birthday*, ed. Gordon D. Young, Mark W. Chavalas, and Richard E. Averbeck (Bethesda, MD: CDL, 1997), 433–53; idem, "Israelite Origins," in *"An Excellent Fortress for His Armies, a Refuge for the People": Egyptological, Archaeological, and Biblical Studies in Honor of James K. Hoffmeier*, ed. Richard E. Averbeck and K. Lawson Younger (University Park, PA: Eisenbrauns, 2020), 327–39.

70. Though I admit that many nonscholars (among the laity in general) who identify as evangelicals do accede to the fundamentalist approach. As indicated, though, my emphasis here (and Hendel's too, it appears) is on evangelical scholars.

situation in Late Bronze Age Canaan. During this time period, the Egyptian Empire controlled Canaan, with major garrison sites (Gaza, Aphek, Tel Mor, Tell el-'Ajjul, Beit Shean) dotting the landscape,[71] while some Canaanites were transported to work as corvée laborers in Egypt itself. In Hendel's reconstruction the Canaanite population came to see itself as slaves of the Egyptians. Later, when early Israel emerged out of the Canaanite matrix, they recalled this slavery to Egypt, though they also transferred the scene solely to Egypt itself. As far as I can tell, Hendel does not explain why or how this transfer took place. Why would the Israelite texts place the slavery solely within Egypt, if their historical memory related to events which primarily took place in the land of Canaan?

By contrast, I view the Israelites as originating in the general region of the Southland (equaling the great swath of land that stretches across the Sinai, modern-day southern Israel, and modern-day southern Jordan).[72] As such, the Israelites did not participate in the Egyptian "enslavement" of the population in the land of Canaan during the Late Bronze Age. Rather one should accord a greater value to the biblical account, especially given the resonance thereof afforded by three key Egyptian documents—Papyrus Anastasi VI, Papyrus Leiden 348, and Papyrus Anastasi V.

Papyrus Anastasi VI (see esp. 4:11–5:5) is dated to the reign of Merenptah and refers to the admission of the Shasu of Edom into Egypt, where they would be settled in the Tjeku/Per-Atum region "to keep them alive and to keep their flocks alive." The similarity of this passage to the biblical account of the eisodus is striking: Edom and Israel are "twinned" in the Bible (via the twinness of Esau and Jacob), so that the experiences of the two groups would be very similar; Per-Atum = Pithom (Exod 1:11); and the Israelites also arrive in Egypt with their flocks (Gen 47:4).

Papyrus Leiden 348, a model letter dated to the time of Ramesses II, reads (recto 6:6), "Issue grain to the men of the army and to the *'Apiru* who are drawing stone(?) for the great pylon of the [house?] of Ramesses." I do not believe that all 'Apiru/Habiru are the Hebrews

71. The standard work remains James M. Weinstein, "The Egyptian Empire in Palestine: A Reassessment," *BASOR* 241 (1981): 1–28.

72. See Rendsburg, "Israelite Origins," esp. pp. 327–28, 332–33, 338–39.

(a subject best left for another occasion), but in the present instance the association between the two terms is rather striking, especially since the Israelites were engaged in construction at the city of Rameses, according to Exod 1:11.

As for the exodus itself, Hendel cites the well-known parallel afforded by Papyrus Anastasi V, also dated to the reign of Merenptah. The key passage (19:6–20:2) describes two slaves who escaped from Egypt and whose tracks were followed by members of the Egyptian army, all of which sounds very close to the biblical account recorded in Exod 14. Neither Hendel nor I would connect this text to the exodus per se, but we both realize there are close parallels. I assent to his nod to Abraham Malamat, who proposed "many small exodoi from Egypt during the imperial era and after."

Oddly, Hendel does not note the most striking parallel between Papyrus Anastasi V and the biblical account—the mention of the toponym Migdol in both texts.[73] In his citation of the Egyptian report, he presents an ellipsis (. . .) at this key point in the document and then neglects to mention the presence of the place-name in Exod 14:2. Once again, this does not mean that the Egyptian text is a firsthand account of the biblical story, but the latter gains some modicum of historicity when read in light of the former. As I have suggested elsewhere, the presence of Migdol in both texts suggests that the place served as a way station of sorts for slaves escaping Egypt by the ancient equivalent of the Underground Railroad.[74]

The three Egyptian documents surveyed here imply that there is more historicity to the biblical account than Hendel would admit. True, he does not altogether deny the possibility that the biblical exodus tradition "may have been formulated by slaves who had escaped from Egypt (the exodoi of small groups addressed previously), or may have featured them as protagonists," but the main focus of his chapter is "to emphasize that this story could pertain to *all* Canaanites who were former subjects of the empire and who had joined the new tribal polity of Israel."

To state the point clearly: the one Egyptian text refers to the Shasu of Edom, while the other Egyptian text refers to the Habiru (the third

---

73. For the former, see James E. Hoch, *Semitic Words in Egyptian Texts of the New Kingdom and Third Intermediate Period* (Princeton: Princeton Univ. Press, 1994), 169–70.

74. Rendsburg, "The Early History of Israel," 444.

one speaks only of "slaves," without further qualification). As I indicated earlier, the former points to the great Southland, while the latter suggests people on the social margins. The Amarna letters make a clear distinction between the Canaanite petty kings who saw themselves as slaves of the pharaoh (e.g., Biridiya, king of Megiddo, whose letter Hendel cites), and the Habiru, who appear to constitute a group of brigands and marauders, with whom the Canaanite city-states must contend.[75] The Egyptian texts which most closely parallel the biblical account, few in number as they may be, do not consider the Canaanites per se as the ones migrating to and/or laboring in Egypt, but rather others (Shasu and Habiru).

Mnemohistory is a valuable tool in biblical studies. Hendel's summary statement about cultural memory is exceedingly helpful: "[The exodus account] is not plain history, nor is it pure fiction. It is a mixture of reminiscences of historical events and circumstances, traditional motifs, and narrative imagination. It recalls and revises the past, forgetting some aspects while foregrounding others, with the aim to make the past usable in the present, to anchor ancient Israel's identity and ideals."

I concur wholeheartedly, but the "past" underlying the biblical account is not an Israel which emerged out of Canaan and which in turn saw themselves as slaves to Egypt in Canaan. Rather there is more historicity to the biblical account than Hendel would admit, but which I, for one, am happy to promote.

Hendel begins his chapter with the story of the *Mayflower*, an analogy which I also employ in my essay, but this parallel works if and only if the *Mayflower* journey actually occurred and with the proper geography—the sailing forth from Plymouth, the crossing of the Atlantic Ocean, and the landing in Massachusetts. Shifting the story to the Netherlands, even though some Puritans were resident in Leiden for about a decade, would not suit the narrative and would not serve the American national cause, with its predominant British roots.

I conclude with reference to another epic tradition, *Beowulf.* The story is based on historical events which can be dated to the sixth century CE, the poem itself was written in the eighth century, and our

75. For general orientation, see William L. Moran, ed. and trans., *The Amarna Letters* (Baltimore: Johns Hopkins Univ. Press, 1992).

earliest surviving manuscript (in fact the only early manuscript) dates to ca. 1000. Is the story real? Is it based on a reality? My former colleague Robert Farrell wrote,

> *Beowulf* is a work of heroic history, i.e. a poem in which facts and chronology are subservient to the poet's interest in heroic deeds and their value in representing the ethics of an heroic civilization. A poet writing in this mode does not disregard absolute historical fact, history, that is, as we know it. He rather sees it as less important than other considerations. . . . His account will sometimes mesh reasonably well with history, as in the episode of Hygelac's raid on the Frisian shore. But more often, his work will be a freely-woven structure in which the characters and actions of the past will be part of an ethically satisfying narrative.[76]

And so it is with the Torah. The exodus narrative "will sometimes mesh reasonably well with history" (Shasu entering Egypt and settling in Per-Atum, slaves building the city of Rameses, slaves escaping Egypt via Migdol), but in general these "historical fact[s], history, that is, as we know it," are subservient to the greater goal of the writer, which in Israel's case is not only an "ethically satisfying narrative" but also a theologically nourishing one.

---

76. R. T. Farrell, "Beowulf, Swedes and Geats," *Saga-Book of the Viking Society for Northern Research* 18 (1970–1973): 220–96, esp. p. 229. If I may be permitted a personal aside, which might interest the reader, I recall fondly how Bob Farrell would regale us, his Cornell University colleagues, with vignettes from his years learning at the feet of the master, J. R. R. Tolkien. For more on the man, see Catherine E. Karkov, "In Memoriam: Robert T. Farrell (November 16, 1938–July 31, 2003)," *Old English Newsletter* 37, no. 1 (Fall 2003): 6, available online at www.oenewsletter.org/OEN/print.php/memorials/farrell/Array.

REJOINDER

RONALD HENDEL

I thank my fellow contributors for their thoughtful comments. In my understanding scholarship is a generations-long conversation about the evidence and our ability to comprehend it, from the big picture to the finely grained details. To this end, conversation and criticism—including self-criticism—are essential means. I was invited to this conversation, hosted by evangelical scholars and published in an evangelical series, with the knowledge that my views are outside the boundaries of evangelical scholarship. If I were to publish my work as a professor at an evangelical college or seminary, I would be fired. These are not just theoretical boundaries but very real ones. This is why I addressed the difference that a doctrine of inerrancy makes for understanding the exodus. Jim Hoffmeier and Gary A. Rendsburg criticize this decision, but I think it important to highlight the internalized boundaries in our discussions. As Mark Noll writes, "To know that a scholar holds an evangelical view of biblical inspiration is useful, just as it is helpful to realize that someone thinks genuine scholarship depends upon 'the historical-critical method.'"[77] But, of course, recognizing these boundaries is just a beginning. The quality of one's analysis of the evidence and the cogency of one's arguments are the meat and potatoes of scholarship. I hope I balanced adequately my attention to boundaries and my analytical and historical arguments.

The topic of cultural memory comes up several times in these responses. Scott Stripling thinks I misrepresent the American cultural

77. Mark A. Noll, *Between Faith and Criticism: Evangelicals, Scholarship, and the Bible in America*, 2nd ed. (Grand Rapids: Baker, 1991), 182.

memory of the Pilgrim Fathers. Perhaps I oversimplified. But when I think back to my schooling and that of my children, the idealized picture of the Pilgrims still seems to be normative. I recall telling my five-year-old son when he came home from school wearing a cardboard Pilgrim hat that the Pilgrims would have put a little Jewish child like him in jail, or worse, exiled him to Rhode Island. My son's response was emphatic. "Dad," he said, "you're wrong, because that's not what my teacher said." His teacher was the authoritative transmitter of American memory, not his too often jocular dad. This taught me some important things about cultural memory. First, cultural memory necessarily forgets inconvenient facts, such as—as Rendsburg points out—that the Pilgrims had been living mostly in the Netherlands, not England. Second, the authoritative interpreters in any community transmit cultural memory. The views of scholars and historians—and sarcastic dads—are secondary and easily dismissed.

I suspect that some of these features are also present in the exodus account. The idea that most early Israelites were local Canaanites has been forgotten in the Bible, except perhaps by odd figures like the prophet Ezekiel, who criticizes his contemporaries by recalling, "By origin and birth you are from the land of the Canaanites: Your father was an Amorite, and your mother was a Hittite" (Ezek 16:3). Like the forgetting of Dutch citizenship for the Pilgrims, the biblical exodus omits that many early Israelites were Canaanites—villagers, herders, and nomads—who joined the settlement of the Israelite highlands in the wake of the collapse of Egyptian rule and forged a new identity. Similarly, the transmission of this memory by authoritative interpreters of the past enabled it to grow and change, enhanced by literary motifs, theological ideas, and sometimes intergroup disputes. The versions of the exodus memory differ greatly from the book of Exodus to the Prophets, as we can see in Ezek 20 and elsewhere.

As a final note, directed at Hoffmeier's remarks, I would say that personal attacks (ad hominem) are inappropriate in an academic forum. By participating in this volume, I am actively working to keep doors open, not close them. His caricature of my positions (including "animus toward conservatives") and his dismissal of modern critical scholarship do not advance this project. He rejects my work for relying on "the flimsy foundation of nineteenth-century source criticism." But source criticism, despite having advanced significantly in the nineteenth century, is not dead because of it. As I recall, the study of electromagnetism also advanced significantly in the nineteenth century and, as far as I'm aware, is still an important area of scientific achievement. Which is to say, my iPhone works pretty well, as do other consequences of modern scholarship.

CONCLUSION

MARK D. JANZEN

Writing a conclusion to a book like this is a somewhat curious exercise. Many books end with their clinching argument or a summary of their most important arguments. Naturally, I can do neither here. "Conclusion" is therefore something of a misnomer. I prefer to think of this book as *beginning* a broader dialogue regarding the exodus among specialists and general readers alike and *continuing* a dialogue experts have participated in for decades.

It is quite clear that discussing the Hebrew exodus from Egypt requires a nuanced perspective incorporating a wide range of historical, archaeological, and linguistic evidence. This data frequently incorporates new information as archaeologists continue their excavations and as scholars analyze biblical texts through new lenses. Whatever conclusions we draw must always come with the caveat that further discoveries and innovative approaches have the potential to force reevaluations. The intent of this book was never to answer all the questions but rather to educate readers on the host of issues from multiple perspectives.

The Hebrew exodus from Egypt can evoke a wide range of emotions, even for scholars who are generally trained to approach topics dispassionately. In a book that encourages debate about biblical narratives, personal beliefs will inescapably be subject to scrutiny. Each of our contributors are leaders in their respective fields, and they've spent decades researching and drawing their conclusions. This book touches on deeply personal convictions and matters of faith involving positions from which people will not easily be moved.

As such it comes as no surprise that in a few places our authors felt that they were subjected to an ad hominem attack. In cases in which our contributors felt this way, I thought that the argument(s) or counterpoint(s) addressed the scholar's claims and did not veer into *merely* attacking him. At the same time, I did not want to silence anyone's concerns, so they remain in the book's final form. Still, I believe analyzing a scholar's previous work is not an ad hominem attack, nor is questioning whether one's presuppositions about something like biblical inerrancy impacts one's research and analysis. Perhaps the most important lesson here is that the divide between belief and knowledge is not always as clear as we scholars might like.

Ultimately, I wanted to provide detailed examination of the exodus and provide a launching point for curious readers to find out more about the exodus. In part this was motivated by a desire to prepare readers to recognize misinformation or exaggerated claims in other sources. To that end I believe the book succeeded.

But that does not mean I think we have provided all the answers. Quite frankly, the debate must continue. There remains no agreement on a host of important issues. I wish ours was the book to settle all of those debates, but such a thing is not possible with currently available evidence. I trust readers will understand that as the editor, I do not wish to give my views on these matters in this space, but to my mind here are four of the key, lingering issues that readers might like to pursue further.

1. *The reference to 480 years in 1 Kgs 6:1.* Stripling believes 480 should be taken as a literal number but adds that the temple construction would really have begun in the 479th year after the exodus. For him, this verse means the exodus took place in the fifteenth century. On the other hand, Hoffmeier, Feinman, and Rendsburg believe 480 to be symbolic (12 × 40). Hoffmeier notes that this fits with the ancient practice of *Distanzangaben*, whereby ancient people used symbolic, ideologically significant numbers when dedicating temples.
2. *The significance of the reference in Exod 1:11 to (Pi-)Ramesses.* This important delta capital was in use for less than 150 years (ca. 1270–1130).[1] Hoffmeier and Feinman thus use this verse (and

1. For more, see Mark D. Janzen, "(Pi-)Rameses—The Delta Capital of Ramesside Egypt," in *Lexham Geographic Commentary on the Pentateuch*, ed. Barry Beitzel (Bellingham, WA: Lexham, 2020 [forthcoming]).

other data) to posit a thirteenth-century exodus, while Rendsburg places the exodus during the twelfth century, at the tail end of the city's existence. Each of them regards this reference as one of the most important chronological clues in the biblical narratives (or even the most important!). Hendel, following Schipper, questions the authenticity of the reference, while Stripling thinks it might be a later editorial gloss. Clearly, there is no agreement.

3. *The curious case of biblical genealogies.* Without reviewing each view on each genealogy, it suffices to say that there is considerable disagreement about whether genealogies can be trusted. Are they too ideological and propagandistic to be reliable? Are they subject to telescoping and artificial lengthening or selective shortening? One's answers to these questions impact the math necessary to determine the exodus's date.
4. *Does the Berlin Pedestal mention Israel?* Stripling believes it does, but recent studies by Egyptologists, cited by Hoffmeier, dispute that reading. They point out linguistic difficulties with the spelling. Stripling countered that the alternatives proposed are not known place-names. Once more, there is considerable debate, and this source should be cited only with considerable care.

Such debatable issues do not make sound argumentation impossible; they demonstrate its importance.

I would be remiss if I did not address the proverbial elephant in the room. No doubt many of you have asked yourself at various points in your journey through this book, "Who do I trust?" This is understandable; we have seen different interpretations which prioritized different data and even at times reached different conclusions regarding the same evidence or artifact (looking at you, Berlin Pedestal). One expert says the exodus dates to one century, others say two different centuries, another says we cannot determine it. Sadly, there is no easy way to sort this out. If there were, this book either would not exist or would simply be *One View on the Exodus*. The best answer I can give is to never stop learning, draw your own conclusions, and think deeply and critically about everything you read.

When I discuss the exodus with students or interested laypeople, they eventually wonder if they can understand the issues at hand without graduate degrees. To this I say yes, you can! Read the narrative for yourself, over and over again. Read the other sources cited in the previous pages of this book. Read translations of the primary sources for yourself. Most major excavations now have excellent websites attached to them, so bookmark them and stay informed of the latest discoveries. Reading this book was an excellent first, second, or twentieth step; now I encourage you to simply continue learning regardless of where you are at on this journey.

Overall, it was a great privilege to oversee this project, and I'm sincerely grateful to my fellow contributors and our editors at Zondervan. Each contributor was a joy to work with, even in the face of every scholar's favorite limitations: strict word counts and hard deadlines. They truly made editing this book an easy process, considering all that it entailed.

Finally, I wish to thank our readers. I trust you have found the book to be educational, insightful, accessible, and entertaining. I hope it advances healthy conversations in our synagogues, churches, schools, and of course coffee shops. One of humanity's greatest narratives deserves nothing less.

AUTHOR INDEX

KEY SITES INDEX

SCRIPTURE INDEX